WESTERN WOMEN IN COLONIAL AFRICA

Contributions in Comparative Colonial Studies
Series Editor, Robin W. Winks

Empires in Collision: Anglo-Burmese Relations in the Mid-
Nineteenth Century
Oliver B. Pollak

Social Engineering in the Philippines: The Aims, Execution, and Impact
of American Colonial Policy, 1900-1913
Glenn Anthony May

The Politics of Dependency: Urban Reform in Istanbul
Stephen T. Rosenthal

Rhodes, the Tswana, and the British: Colonialism, Collaboration, and
Conflict in the Bechuanaland Protectorate, 1885-1889
Paul Maylam

Between Black and White: Race, Politics, and the Free
Coloreds in Jamaica, 1792-1865
Gad J. Heuman

British Rule in Malaya: The Malayan Civil Service
and Its Predecessors, 1867-1942
Robert Heussler

Economic Control and Colonial Development:
Crown Colony Financial Management in the Age of
Joseph Chamberlain
Richard M. Kesner

Constraint of Empire: The United States
and Caribbean Interventions
Whitney T. Perkins

Toward a Programme of Imperial Life: The British
Empire at the Turn of the Century
John H. Field

European Colonial Rule, 1880-1940: The Impact of the West on India,
Southeast Asia, and Africa
Rudolf von Albertini, with Albert Wirz
Translated by John G. Williamson

An Empire for the Masses: The French Popular
Image of Africa, 1870-1900
William H. Schneider

WESTERN WOMEN IN COLONIAL AFRICA

Caroline Oliver

CONTRIBUTIONS IN COMPARATIVE COLONIAL STUDIES, NUMBER 12

GREENWOOD PRESS
WESTPORT, CONNECTICUT • LONDON, ENGLAND

HQ
1787
.O4
1982

920.7
O48w

Library of Congress Cataloging in Publication Data

Oliver, Caroline.
  Western women in colonial Africa.

  (Contributions in comparative colonial studies,
ISSN 0163-3813 ; no. 12)
  Bibliography: p.
  Includes index.
  1. Women—Africa—Biography. 2. Explorers, Women—
Biography. 3. Missionaries, Women—Biography.
4. Travelers—Africa—Biography. I. Title. II. Series.
HQ1787.O4   960'.088042 [B]   81-24194
ISBN 0-313-23388-8 (lib. bdg.)   AACR2

Library of Congress Catalog Card Number: 81-24194
ISBN: 0-313-23388-8
ISSN: 0163-3813

First published in 1982

Greenwood Press
A division of Congressional Information Service, Inc.
88 Post Road West, Westport, Connecticut 06881

Printed in the United States of America

10 9 8 7 6 5 4 3 2 1

CONTENTS

Series Foreword	vii
Introduction	ix
1. Florence Baker: Explorer	3
2. Alexandrine Tinne: Traveller	50
3. Mary Kingsley: Explorer and Scientist	76
4. Mary Slessor: Missionary and Magistrate	95
5. Mother Kevin: Missionary and Foundress	145
Conclusion	189
Select Bibliography	197
Index	199

SERIES FOREWORD

Just on a decade ago, a group of undergraduate women in my course on the history of the British Empire accused me of ignoring the role of women in the development of the Empire. I promised them a lecture on the subject, and I failed to keep that promise, for despite a thorough search of the standard works on imperialism, I discovered the truth of what they already knew: that nothing coherent had been written to draw together British women as empire builders. There was, of course, a substantial and largely popular literature on the *memsahibs* of India. There were many passing references, frequently derogatory, to how the wives of colonial planters, agency house men, and District Officers fostered racialist attitudes, especially in Africa and Southeast Asia. There were a few colorful accounts of intrepid women explorers—Mary Kingsley figured prominently, as did Lady Hester Stanhope— and there was some statistical data on child bearing, disease, and even prostitution in the Empire, with emphasis on the West Indies and India. Yet none of this material appeared to have a clear point of view.

In the last decade the situation has changed, though imperial studies have been markedly slow to follow the productive leads provided by women's studies within the confines of the national historiographies of Britain, France, or the United States. Elizabeth Saxe has completed a remarkable and complex dissertation, as yet unpublished, on women merchants and traders in the East India Company, demonstrating the major role they played in the development of an economy heretofore viewed as virtually a male preserve. Here and there chapters appear on women in Hong Kong, or on the tea plantations of Ceylon, or even in scientific research and tropical disease. We now recognize that while the great romantic novelists of empire were men—Kipling, Henty, Haggard, Buchan—there were also women writers who reinforced imperial attitudes: Ouida, Christie, Ethel M. Dell. Still, the broader subject eludes us, perhaps because imperial historians have tended to focus unduly on administrative, constitutional, and military issues, so that women have been relegated to the interstices of social history, to examinations of "the missionary factor" in imperial history, and to colorful anecdotal filler. There have been distinguished women historians of empire—Dame Margery Perham, Helen Taft Manning, Mary Townsend come immediately to mind, and there are many others—but they have tended to write on the "mainline" subjects.

For many reasons, then, I am pleased to be able to include a volume on Western women in Africa in this series of volumes on comparative colonial and imperial studies, though above all the reasons, I am delighted at last to be able to keep that promise, nearly a decade old, to those students who knew better than I why the subject had been neglected. These charming, short biographies open up a subject in need of much exploration, and one hopes that Caroline Oliver's personal book, informed by her own special knowledge of Africa at first hand, will lead others to pursue the subject. We need many such books addressed to the questions Mrs. Oliver raises, however gently, in her concluding statement; and first, we need many more essays such as these on the role of women in the history of the Western empires.

Robin W. Winks

INTRODUCTION

I first saw Africa in the autumn of 1949, from a plane coming down at what was then Stanleyville in the Belgian Congo. The vast equatorial forest was beneath us, broken here by a mighty river turning a mighty bend. This was the Congo, which, having hitherto flowed generally northwards, turns very positively westwards towards the South Atlantic, 1,000 miles away. My husband, then a young lecturer at the University of London School of Oriental and African Studies, had come to do a pioneering survey of the possible sources for African history. It was hoped that his results would lay the foundations of African history as a new academic subject. Our car, an elderly Ford, had come up the river in a twelve-day journey by steamer from what was then Leopoldville. Within a week, we set off eastwards through the forest towards Uganda.

At first the road was wide and the trees kept a respectful distance. It was made, as were so many African roads, of red murram, or dirt. In time it narrowed, and the towering walls of forest, sometimes perhaps 150 to 200 feet high, pressed in on us. It also became steeply and perpetually hilly, though for the most part, only the gradient, and perhaps a little rocky outcrop coming through the murram, showed this. The forest walls obscured the contours. Twice our all-too-abrupt descent ended at a wide, swift-flowing forest river, which was crossed by ferries. At the bottom of every hill there was a turbulent stream, with a bridge consisting of two separate planks. After a fierce tropical rainstorm, when the red mud was almost liquid, we tended to approach these bridges more or less crabwise. Then, at the last moment, like a show jumper arriving at the jump, some instinct, or maybe a deft human touch, made the old car get the right wheels onto the right planks, and we crossed in safety, if always with relief. There was generally one dramatic thunderstorm a day, lasting perhaps an hour. Once it became so dark, and the rain was so solid, that visiblity was insufficient, and we drew up until the storm was over.

There was scarcely any traffic: perhaps two or three cars in the day and sometimes a lorry, lurching and swaying, with a gay human cargo whose multicoloured ragged shirts streamed in the wind and whose array of hats would have done credit to an Irish fair. Now and then there was a foot traveller, with his wife a few yards in the rear, carrying the family trunk on her head. Little parties of Pygmies going about their affairs showed that they were quite unconcerned with us; two white people in a car were just an irrelevance. In almost rhythmic waves there were crescendos of the chirping of crickets that rose above the noise of the car and died away. At night, in a hotel where the guest chalets were scattered among the trees, the noises were undefinable. It was only clear that the forest was not sleeping.

This, the Ituri Forest, is not the most beautiful part of the great African forest that I have seen. Creeping undergrowth 20 to 25 feet high obscures what would be lovely forest glades, and the road itself was insignificant. Also, there was little of the splendid colour that Mary Kingsley describes in the Ogowe forests. The occasional splash of a scarlet poinsettia, or a flame of the forest tree near a human habitation, almost accentuated the sombreness of the continuous green. Then, quite suddenly, the end of the long tunnel was in sight. We came to the top of a hill and looked down on a more open valley. It was still densely forested, but we could see across it to the opposite hill. Half way up, quite abruptly, almost in a hard line, the forest ended. Beyond were grassy hills like the English downlands, and on the horizon there was an individual little conical mountain.

Our road had followed the route that the explorer Henry Morton Stanley took in 1888, when he set out with a vast column to relieve Emin Pasha, a Provincial Governor in the southern

Sudan, who had been marooned there after General Charles Gordon's death. Stanley had underestimated the distance from the Congo to Lake Albert; presumably, he had not allowed for the hilly nature of the terrain. Hundreds of his men had died on the journey, some from disease, many more from starvation. He and his tattered band of survivors must have emerged from the forest near where we did, and he called the little conical mountain Mount Pisgah. In "purple prose" he describes his men breaking into a spontaneous cheer at the sight of the distant open country, and then turning round and cursing the forest for the murder of their comrades and for their own sufferings. For us, it had been a great and memorable visual experience. For me, certainly, it had also been a memorable human experience; for, quite by chance, during those four days in the forest, I had met a handful of outstandingly courageous white women.

Our first stop after leaving Stanleyville had been at a big mission station in a wide clearing. The wife of the head of the mission had contacts with my husband's college. A very talented linguist, she was engaged in writing down the local language for the first time. When driving about Africa, if you call at one mission, you are liable to find that you have become missionary postmen. From that first stop, we carried a billet-doux from a young man to his girl friend at a mission about a hundred miles farther on. From there we delivered some medicine that another mission up the road was known to need.

We were always offered hospitable refreshment. Once, when we were being welcomed into a cool parlour for lunch, I noticed a young boy recumbent on some sort of bed on the verandah. Later, through the window, I saw an African servant pick him up in his arms to carry him off somewhere. Some other missionaries told me that he had been born unexpectedly one night when his father, a doctor, had been away in the forest tending a badly wounded Pygmy woman. There had been complications, and the mother had had no expert help. The result was a hopelessly deformed and moronic child. The parents alternated their leaves to the United States, so that one of them always remained with him.

Another time I was sitting over a cup of tea with two missionary women. They talked of their first journey to the Ituri Forest from the East African coast, which was long after the days when the pioneering aristocrats of the missionary world could proudly boast of having "walked from the coast." Their journey had been by train and subsequently by lorry over rough tracks. One of them had carried her ailing baby boy in her arms for much of the way, but he had died before they reached their destination.

Then, on the third night of our own journey, we had turned at dusk into the clearing of a big mission called Lolwa. As we walked up the path to what seemed to be the principal house, we heard an American woman's voice saying, "I hear folks talking English. I hope they are staying the night." That is just what we were hoping. We had expected to reach a hotel some distance ahead before dark, but we had found a giant tree, blown down in a recent storm, right across our road. It had taken three hours of what seemed to us excellent African forestry for a way to be cleared. We gladly accepted the offer of a lodging and joined Mr. and Mrs. Spees and some small children for their supper. Afterwards we gathered in the parlour for the evening Bible reading. I noticed a photo of a rather older child, a laughing golden-haired girl, on the harmonium. When I asked if she was away at boarding school, Mrs. Spees said "No. That is the one the Lord has taken from us." Mrs. Spees's elderly parents came in from their own little house nearby. They had begun their Bible reading a long time ago, at Stornaway in the Hebrides, and had emigrated to California before coming out to the Ituri Forest as missionaries. They had brought up their family there, and their son, Mrs. Spees's brother, had been invalided home, crippled with arthritis. As we settled down to an intimate, gossipy chat about the evening's Bible passage, we could hear African children's voices practising "Stilly Night" for Christmas in a schoolroom across the forest clearing.

Next morning, Mr. Spees asked us if we would like to see the lepers. Being new to Africa, it took us by surprise, and I am not sure whether it would have been more cowardly to say yes or no, but I will always be grateful that we went. About a mile away from the mission, the lepers from over a considerable area of the forest had been collected into a village. In this way they had been rescued from the desolate isolation the disease entails and had been given something of a community life. Poor little huts made of mud, with grass roofs, straggled up a rough village street. They had two rooms, because, although leprosy is contagious, it is not infectious, and if the children sleep in a separate room, they can escape it. A few emaciated old people, presumably hopeless cripples, crouched on the ground by their houses, not seeming to see very much. Others, less afflicted, came towards us, patently pleased to see our host. The missionaries had helped them to clear little garden plots, and some of them wanted to talk of their horticultural problems. We had no common language and could not communicate with them, but their smiles were friendly. The whole occasion seemed unexpectedly pleasant.

Back at the mission, I asked Mrs. Spees about the risks of catching leprosy. Many of the lepers came over to the mission dispensary to have their sores dressed, and a Swedish missionary doctor had laid down strict rules about the necessary precautions. But rules had to be broken occasionally. She described the day when she and her husband had last returned from their American furlough. The whole population of Lolwa was lined up to welcome them. Belgian hand-shaking had caught on, and Mrs. Spees said that her arms had begun to ache as they worked their way along. And then, at the end of the line, they saw the lepers waiting expectantly. "There was nothing for it," she said. "We just had to shake hands with the whole lot."

It was thus that my attention was drawn to the lives of white women in Africa, and I built on my profound impressions of the Ituri Forest in the library of the nascent University of Makerere in Uganda. I started to read of a number of European women who had distinguished themselves greatly in Africa in the century between 1850 and 1950. Their stories are well known, but mostly, I think, only to specialists on Africa. I thought they deserved to be known to a wider public, and that the wider public, in turn, would be interested in them. I do not think I am remotely a feminist, but I am always pleased by feminine achievement. And so I had the idea of writing short biographies of some of these women. The selection was largely dictated by adequate documentation and , to a certain extent, by the part of Africa in which they had worked or travelled.

I thought I would tell their stories better if I could myself visualise something of their African backgrounds. I have spent a night beside the Cross River, that beautiful, sombre forest gorge near where Mary Kingsley and Mary Slessor met and talked and laughed together in the small hours. I have driven extensively over the red dusty roads of Uganda, up and down which Mother Kevin and her devoted troop of builders raced in their lorry on their way to build churches, hospitals, and schools. I have crossed the Nile not far above Gondokoro, the highest point that Alexandrine Tinne reached. And I have climbed Patiko, the naturally fortified hill on which Samuel and Florence Baker lived for some months in tremendous state and comparative peace.

The personalities are naturally very diverse. There is a world of difference between the wealthy Dutch heiress who explored the Bahr el Ghazal accompanied by her closest female relations and their ladies' maids, her grand piano, and her pet dogs, and the little Dundee mill hand, Mary Slessor, who reached her solitary forest home barefoot and carrying on her back, or leading by the hand, her little family of rescued orphan babies. But there was one thing they all shared in great abundance: courage. Perhaps in some slight degree, their stories will serve as a memorial to countless other courageous women who must remain unsung.

In the spring of 1950, we circumnavigated Lake Tanganyika in the S. S. *Liemba*. This little steamer was built by the Germans for use by the Crown Prince of Germany on his state visit to Tanganyika in 1914. The visit never took place because of the European war. The *Liemba* was then plying between Kigoma, two-thirds of the way up the eastern shore, and the southern tip of the lake, calling at many of the lake-shore villages. The round voyage took about three weeks. Tanganyika has been described as a strip of water completely surrounded by White Fathers, and there were several of them on board. We tied up off Karema and, along with some friends, were carried ashore piggy-back from a rowing-boat. We climbed a wide village street for perhaps a mile, until we came to the large white convent building of the White Sisters.

Karema had originally been one of the research stations proposed by King Leopold II of Belgium at his conference in Brussels in 1876, which was summoned to discuss the exploration of Central Africa. At this conference, the International African Association (IAA) was founded. At the time, Cardinal Lavigerie was planning the strategy for the missionary penetration of East

Africa by his White Fathers. He was in close touch with King Leopold, and it was natural that he should place his stations next to those of the IAA. These stations were garrisoned, by Zouaves, or Vatican-recruited troops, against the marauding bands of Arab slave traders. They were also structurally fortified. After Stanley's dramatic descent of the Congo River, King Leopold, ambitious to have his own African dominion, changed his strategy and decided to approach Central Africa from the Congo mouth. The White Fathers remained in the original IAA stations.

While the rest of the party were chatting with the Reverend Mother and some of her nuns at the front of the convent, I slipped round to the back to photograph the fortifications. I was fiddling with my camera when I noticed an aged nun approaching. In her white robes she seemed almost square, and she glided as nuns do, but very slowly, her eyes peering down at the missal in her hands. When she finally saw me, she stopped dead, clearly astounded. It is probable that she had not seen a lay white woman for a very long time. Karema's sole overland communication was a rough footpath which was quite impassable in the rainy season, and the *Liemba* only called once a month. It was, therefore, unusually isolated from the great world. The old nun took me by the arm and led me towards a bench by the high, white convent wall, and as we sat down, I tried to explain my presence. She had put her missal down, and she turned to lay her hands on both of mine. "Je suis la Soeur Géneviève" ("I am Sister Géneviève"), she said. "Violà cinquante-sept ans que je suis ici." ("I have been here 57 years.") I knew that this was likely to be true. At that time, the White Fathers went home for a visit after about 14 years, but the White Sisters never visited home. I thought of the long, hard trail she would have travelled on foot in 1893; the last lap perhaps by canoe or sailing dhow on the lake. Tears were falling slowly and her head nodded as she repeated herself. "Cinquante-sept ans" ("Fifty-seven years"). And then, "Peut-être que j'ai pu faire quelque chose pour le bon Dieu—peut-être—peut-être." ("Perhaps I have been able to do something for the good God—perhaps—perhaps.") It is to Sister Géneviève and her 57 years of devoted service by Lake Tanganyika that I would like to dedicate my essays.

WESTERN WOMEN IN COLONIAL AFRICA

1

FLORENCE BAKER:
Explorer

In the winter of 1858—1859, the Maharajah Duleep Singh and a rich, middle-aged Englishman, Samuel Baker, went cruising together down the Danube River. They hired a 70-foot-long boat and a crew of oarsmen in Budapest. The craft was luxuriously equipped and plentifully supplied with gastronomic fare, including champagne, and the Maharajah had English servants with him. The object of the voyage was mainly shooting, a sport to which the Englishman was inordinately addicted, and he was incidentally setting a fashion for English sportsmen by pursuing it in Hungary. Baker had shot game in many parts of the world, especially in Ceylon, where he owned great tea estates, and his ambitions at the time were thought to be chiefly centred on shooting game in a great many more regions. He was still recovering from the death of a much-loved wife four years earlier, and had left his four young daughters in England in his sister's care.

The progress down the Danube was eventually halted by ice at the small town of Widdin in Moldavia, then under Turkish rule. There, by strange and happy chance, he met a lovely, young Hungarian girl, Florence von Sass, in circumstances never fully explained. One family legend said that he bought her in a Turkish slave market, and even if such a romantic episode were conducive to embroidery, there was certainly an element of truth in the story. She had, as a small child, witnessed the assassination of her father and brothers during the revolution of 1848, and she and a devoted governess had escaped from Hungary. The governess does not seem to have been in Widdin at the time, but Baker is thought to have traced her and learned Florence's story. It was certainly something of a rescue operation that he carried out, but he also fell in love with the 17-year-old girl, and she with him.

River transport was exchanged for riding horses and a carriage, and chaperoned by the Maharajah, they went to Bucharest. Presumably, it was there that some sort of marriage ceremony took place, but since she was a Catholic, there were difficulties, and Baker resolved to remarry her by the Anglican rite whenever they should return to England. The Maharajah, deprived of his travelling companion, went off to Italy, and Samuel and his bride took up residence in the Dubrushka, where he had engaged himself to help in the construction, by an English firm, of a railway from the Danube to the Black Sea.

Baker's contentment did not last long. Making railways, even in the Balkans in the mid-nineteenth century, was too tame for Samuel Baker. He wanted to move on; in fact, something far more significant than the pursuit and destruction of animals had been stirring his imagination for some years. This was the enticing possibility of exploring unknown Africa. He had made an unsuccessful attempt to be included in the expedition that David Livingstone had led up the Zambesi River in 1854. But there still remained the infinitely glamorous mystery of the Nile sources. Baker knew that John Hanning Speke and James Grant were then engaged in the search for these sources, and that it was hoped that they would in time descend the Nile from the great lake that Speke had discovered on a former expedition. Baker decided to travel up the Nile, possibly to meet them, possibly to assist them, or possibly to take up their task if they had failed or died. So, with his young bride, he went from the Black Sea to Cairo.

Livingstone's Zambesi expedition had been in some ways disastrous, and Baker thought that the failure had been due partly to the size of the party. If he were to go in search of the Nile sources, he had long determined to have his own expedition and at his own expense. But there was the complication of Florence.

Had I been alone it would have been no hard lot to die upon the untrodden path before me, but there was one who, although my greatest comfort, was also my greatest care; one whose life yet dawned at so early an age that womanhood was still in the future. I shuddered at the prospect for her should she be left alone in savage lands at my death; and gladly would I have left her in the comforts of home instead of exposing her to the miseries of Africa. It was in vain that I implored her to remain, and that I painted the difficulties and perils still blacker than I thought they would really be: she was resolved with woman's constancy and devotion, to share all dangers and to follow me through each rough footstep of the wild life before me.

So Florence Baker, not yet 21 years old, set out with her Sam on one of the great journeys of exploration. They left Cairo in a sailing dahabiyah on April 15, 1861. A strong north wind swept them rapidly upstream, and together they watched the "mysterious waters with a firm resolve to track them to their distant fountains."

Samuel Baker had ambition, both personal and, in a splendid, Victorian way, patriotic. He wanted to be famous, and he wanted it to be "Old England" that found the Nile sources. He had many good qualities for an explorer: courage, formidable determination, and tremendous competence and inventiveness in practical matters. He was also a little naive and, for such a widely travelled man, a little insular. Florence was to prove an intrepid traveller: brave, quick-thinking, and serene in adversity and crisis. Samuel, with rather patronising understatement, said that she "was not a screamer." But she was in no way a masculine, sport-loving woman, and she was interested in the adventure only because, as Samuel claims, she was devoted to him. She was essentially feminine and efficiently domestic, and her gentle wisdom was to prove invaluable. With more than 20 years separating their ages, she was in many ways the more adult of the two.

In spite of the accommodating north wind that swept them upstream so rapidly towards what turned out to be a historic meeting with Speke and Grant, Samuel had a diversion in mind. If he were to move into the heart of Africa, it would be with a caravan officered by Arabic speakers. He was rightly apprehensive of interpreters, and had planned to spend a year exploring the Ethiopian tributaries of the Nile, shooting, fishing, and learning Arabic. By the middle of June, they had reached the junction of the Nile and the Atbara rivers, where they disembarked and travelled up the Atbara Valley. The southeastern tributaries

descend much more rapidly from high mountains than does the
main Nile stream, which oozes through lakes and swamps. With
the rising ground, the climate was comparatively congenial, and
the valleys often beautiful, and in the course of a year, there were
many enjoyable camps.

Florence, who was destined to become the formidable chatelaine of English manor houses, organised her bush ménages with
excellence. Her staff must have been raw, to say the least, but
they were evidently very devoted to her. There was an abundance of game, and she was able to keep a good table. Samuel
would fish the mountain streams, while Florence, seated in a
flowery bower, watched and stitched away at the cotton panta-
loons she was making for him or, suprisingly in the 1860s, for
herself. The Bakers were unlike most of the nineteenth-century
explorers, because they dressed in sensible comfort for hot countries. Instead of the thick tweeds of Livingstone, Speke, and
Stanley, the black petticoats of Mary Kingsley, or the crinolines
of the Tinnes, they wore loose cotton tunics and trousers stuffed
into boots and gaiters. Samuel made the latter himself out of
giraffe or antelope skins, which were both pliable and resistant to
stony paths and thorny bush.

Presumably, there was a reasonably competent tutor of Arabic
in the party with whom both studied, and Samuel satisfied himself that he acquired a sufficiency to deal with his dragoman, or
Wakil (headman). He recruited personnel for his caravan as he
went along. Two young Germans, whom they met accidentally,
joined his party, and when one of them was killed by a lion, Sam
inherited his servant Richarn, who proved in time a valuable
asset. A lady named Barrake, apparently no great beauty, who
was recruited in some capacity, was so overcome when she
discovered that she was not to be Sam's slave that she enveloped
him in her powerful arms and smothered him with castor-oily
kisses. She had decided she was to be a spare wife. Sam's comment that "it looked improper and the perfumery was too rich" is
typical of his particular brand of humor. How Florence reacted is
not on record, but by all accounts, she would have been capable of
laughing uproariously, though equally capable on occasion of not
being at all amused.

After exploring several of the Atbara tributaries, the Bakers
crossed into the Blue Nile river system. They reached Khartoum

by way of the Blue Nile Valley in the middle of June 1862, just a year after they had left the main Nile to ascend the Atbara. They stayed there for six months, comfortably lodged in Consul Petherick's house, the Consul being away with his wife on business. A population of 30,000 people of many different races, with neither drains nor cesspools, made Khartoum immediately unattractive. It was also especially loathsome as the center of the White Nile trade, which was by then, to a very large extent, the slave trade. The mechanics of slave trading were horrid, and it was destined to impinge a great deal on the lives of the Bakers. Syrians, Turks, Egyptians, Circassians, Greeks, and other Europeans in Khartoum were all either directly or indirectly involved in the business, and the process of organising an expedition to travel up the Nile cannot have been congenial.

But Samuel, by his own confession, thrived on difficulties. He supervised the making of the saddles and saddlepacks for the transport animals. He supervised the dyeing of the trim uniforms he had made for his servants and escort, concocting the dye himself from the bark of the mimosa tree. The sailing dahabiyah was made comfortable under his direction, and the two sailing barges, or nuggars, were arranged for baggage and livestock. Attending to the smallest details himself, he had everything ready for departure on December 18, 1862. Musa Pasha, the Governor, himself deep in the slave trade, sent his agents to extract exorbitant dues as a condition of permission to sail, and there was even an attempt at sabotage. But Samuel, blissfully confident of the superiority of his race, in the efficacy of his firman (passport) from the Khedive of Egypt, and, in the last extreme, of the competence of his own fists, ignored the opposition and sailed south towards Gondokoro. The British flag flew bravely from all three boats.

Shortly after leaving Khartoum, rifle volleys and waves were exchanged with the Tinne ladies from Holland, who were returning from Gondokoro in the only steamer then on the Upper Nile. Privately, Samuel made some very acrimonious remarks about the unsuitability of their whereabouts. With Florence beside him, he was himself in a glass house, but no doubt thought that his efficient chaperonage made all the difference. Besides, Florence was there out of devotion to himself, which was much more suitable, and not as an explorer in her own right.

Florence was occupied at the time in nursing young Johann Schmidt, the survivor of the two Germans they had met up the Atbara. A carpenter by trade, he had been invaluable in the reorganisation of the boats. He had, however, been ill most of the time in Khartoum, presumably with malaria or blackwater fever. The Bakers had begged him to remain behind, but he had argued that sailing on the river would be beneficial. He probably knew he was dying and wanted to remain in the sympathetic company of Samuel and, more especially, Florence. By Christmas Day it was obvious that he was not going to live, though it was not till December 31 that he died, Florence caring for him with great tenderness until the end. They buried him by moonlight on the banks of the river. Sam paddled himself ashore in his "spongeing bath," and made the tall cross for the grave out of the trunk of a tamarind tree with his own hands.

Johann's death was a depressing prelude to the long, slow voyage to Gondokoro. The great river is for many miles all but lost in greater marshes, and at fluctuating times of year, its own slow stream becomes clogged with vegetation and is scarcely distinguishable from marsh. The passage through this "Sudd" is never enjoyable. Samuel was always active in caring for his boats and animals, and in taking notes on the river peoples and the fauna and flora. Florence was busy with her domestic concerns, and she had acquired a devoted little disciple in a 12-year-old boy called Saat. When he was only six, he had been captured by slave traders while tending his father's goats. He had escaped and found his way to the Austrian Missionary Fathers at Cairo, and had eventually gone with them to Khartoum. While the Bakers were there, he had been thrown out of the mission along with a number of other boys who had been caught stealing. Looking up from her tea one afternoon, Florence saw him kneeling in the dust beside her. She thought he was begging, but he refused food and implored her to engage him as a servant. On enquiring at the mission, it was learned that his expulsion had been a mistake and that his reputation for honesty was singularly good. From then on, he sat figuratively, and whenever possible, literally, at Florence's feet. Even Samuel, who was often tediously critical of savage morals, waxed enthusiastic about the excellence of his character. Saat made friends with Richarn, the only other non-

Arab, who was sadly missing the fleshpots of Khartoum and spending most of his time sprawled drunkenly on the baggage like a "sick crow." But Richarn came to share with Saat his utter devotion to the Bakers, and this was a very precious asset in their situation.

On January 31 at long last the view changed: a distant mountain was sighted, the marshes gave way to dry pasturage, and there were well-defined banks. On February 2 they reached Gondokoro, perched 20 feet high and dry above the river. Apart from the refreshing view of mountains, the sight of green trees, and the welcome pasturage for the animals, the place was not prepossessing. The ruins of the Austrian Mission were visible among citrus orchards, but otherwise, it was a miserable encampment, used for perhaps two months in the year by the slave and ivory traders' agents and their carousing and murdering followers.

These men, quite incapable of understanding Baker's objectives, thought he was either a rival or a spy, and plotted in every way to prevent his further progress. The first tangible evidence of this was when his own men, who he was beginning to hope were learning some discipline, announced their intention of going on a cattle raid to get more meat. They had clearly been influenced. Baker assembled them at drum-call for an admonitory address, which served to escalate their mutinous feelings. Their ringleader, Easur, became so insolent that Sam ordered Saati, his Wakil, to give him 25 lashes. Easur, confident of the support of his fellows, then rushed in fury to attack Sam, who knocked him down in the crowd several times over. He called to Saati to bring a rope to tie him up, but the mutineers rushed to save him, and the situation was very dangerous.

It was at this moment that Florence, who was lying ill with fever in her cabin on the boat, came to the rescue. She forced her way into the middle of the crowd, collecting a few wavering mutineers in support on the way. The sudden diversion momentarily let down the heat, and Sam was quick to act. He shouted to the drummer boy to beat the drum and called sharply to the men to fall in, which, from force of habit, most of them did. He then ordered Easur to be brought forward for punishment, but Florence once more took a hand. She implored Sam to pardon him if he, in his turn, asked for pardon. The men seemed to think this was a just and suitable compromise and insisted on Easur's doing his part. He kissed Sam's hand, and the affair was over. An ox was provided for a feast, contentment reigned, and even Easur, despite some disarrangement of his features due to Samuel's fists, expressed undying devotion. But Sam now knew what sort of reliability to expect from this bodyguard, whose function was to protect them in the bush.

Large quantities of grain were stored in local granaries for the return journey, and some of it was designated for Speke and Grant should they arrive. The Bakers then settled down to await the arrival of a trading caravan belonging to a Maltese trader called Debono who did a very big business. It was coming from the south, and Samuel hoped to enlist the returning porters for his own overland transport. Suddenly, on February 15, 1863, the distant rattle of musketry announced the approach of Debono's caravan, and some of Sam's men ran to the boat in great excitement to say that two white men were arriving with the caravan.

Speke and Grant, a year overdue, were emerging at last from the heart of Africa. They had walked the whole way from the Zanzibar coast and had witnessed the birth of the Nile on the northern side of Victoria Nyanza. It was more than two years since they had seen a white face, and now, as they walked down the riverbank, they saw Samuel Baker running towards them, waving his cap in the air and shouting, "hurrah for old England." After a rapturous welcome, he escorted them in proud excitement to his boat, while his men gave the traditional reception of volleys of musket fire. It was a meeting as dramatic in its way as a famous one by Lake Tanganyika eight years later, but it was completely spontaneous: whereas the austere formality of the later one was carefully rehearsed by Stanley the night before he actually met Livingstone.

A few days after the appearance of Speke and Grant, Mr. and Mrs. Petherick arrived. He had been subsidised by funds raised by the Royal Geographical Society to meet Speke coming down the Nile and to provide him with what he needed for the continuation of his journey. Petherick had forwarded adequate supplies to Gondokoro to await the travellers, but he and his wife, Anne, had been trading in the west and had been delayed for many months by illness and by excessive floods. Though he was officially a British Consul, his commercial activities were a necessity because of the meagreness of the consular salary at that time. His late arrival at Gondokoro meant that Samuel Baker had stolen his role in being the first to aid the travellers. Rightly or wrongly, Speke was critical of Petherick's failure to meet him, and Anne Petherick, by way of defence, wrote a moving account of the appalling difficulties which had caused it.

There were, therefore, two gallant white women at Gondokoro in 1873, but in descriptions of the "party of four" that assembled in the Baker's boat, they might not have existed. Actually, Sam asked Speke not to mention Florence's presence. He had not informed his family of her existence, and he seems to have mistrusted the validity of the Catholic marriage ceremony, which was all he had been able to procure in Bucharest. So Florence may well have been present at the fascinating discussions that took place on the boat between Speke and Grant and her husband about the origins of the Nile.

Sam was generous in his admiration for the great feat of exploration, but inevitably, there was some personal disappointment for him. He had at his command a very costly expedition, in good shape as he thought, to travel into the dark continent in search of the age-old mystery, but the mystery was apparently solved. There was "not one leaf of the laurel" left for him. But there was, in fact, such a leaf, and Speke and Grant were both generously anxious that he should go south and try to close a gap in their own exploration. They had heard of another great lake that was evidently an important part of the river system. They had crossed the Nile at Karuma at a point where it was not flowing northwards as it did out of Victoria Nyanza, but westwards. Local informants had told them that some distance to the west it entered this other lake and flowed out again forthwith, to the north, and they very much regretted that circumstances had prevented them from going there. This was Samuel Baker's chance, and he decided, come what might, to take it. Speke and Grant handed over the precious map they had made and gave Sam all the instructions and information that was likely to be useful. Then, on February 26, they departed downstream in one of Baker's hired boats, en route for their triumphant reception in England.

The powerful and ancient kingdom of Bunyoro was the key to the great lake that Baker was to look for. It was apparently bounded on the north by the stretch of westward-flowing Nile that Speke, for sentimental reasons, had named Somerset Nile. Its western frontier was the unexplored lake which was known locally as the Luta Nzige, or water that stopped the locusts. The ruler was the Omukama, or King, Kamrasi, and an approach to the lake could only be made with his permission. As the crow flies, the distance from Gondokoro to the Somerset Nile is under 200 miles. It could have been reached in a couple of months of easy marching. In fact, thanks principally to the sabotage operations of the slave traders, it was not until the end of January 1864 that the Bakers reached the river frontier at Karuma, where Speke had crossed over. In spite of the superbly planned expedition force, apparently in perfect readiness to march, it was only two months after Speke's departure that they started, almost in desperation, with hardly any men at all.

Debono's Wakil, Muhammed, had promised them porters, but he departed south without telling them, leaving a threatening message about his being followed, and having completely undermined Baker's own men. The two non-Muslims, Richarn and Saat, kept Florence informed of the mutinous intentions of the escort, who had been jeered at for working for "Christian dogs." Samuel threatened his Wakil with adverse reports to Khartoum, which could result in his being hanged, and he succeeded in rallying about 17 of the men. The baggage was too much for the pack animals, the escort was now too slender, so Samuel tried to negotiate with another trader, a Circassian called Khurshid, who was the agent of the great firm of Aqqad in Khartoum. He asked him to fetch more soldiers from Khartoum and , in the meantime, to lend him some men so that he could spend the intervening time elephant shooting. Khurshid was honest enough to report back that his men were not willing to serve Baker.

As one frustrating episode followed another, the Bakers became more and more determined to pursue their plans. They must have discussed the possibility of giving up, for Samuel states clearly that Florence never once advised withdrawal. With every trader's hand against them, and working up hostility among the local peoples on the route, the chances of survival, let alone success, must have seemed slight. Nonetheless, on the evening of March 26, with only a small escort, and with the baggage animals overloaded because of an absence of porters, Samuel and Florence led a very inadequate caravan out of Gondokoro. They were both mounted on horses, and the Union Jack was carried immediately behind them. They marched eastwards initially rather than southwards, as it was the only direction in which the men could be persuaded to go.

Samuel hoped that, once on the march, his men would prove more manageable. Richarn and Saat warned him that a mutiny was planned when the vicinity of a certain trading station was reached, but Sam trusted to his blackmailing hold over the Wakil to control them. A trading party of Khurshid's, commanded by one called Ibrahim, was ahead, and knowing that they were likely to provoke the hostility of the local people either deliberately or indirectly by cattle raiding, Samuel tried to outflank them and get ahead. He thought he had succeeded; but when he and Florence were waiting in a narrow valley for their own caravan to catch them up, the Turks overtook them. They passed by with flaunting insolence. Last of all came Ibrahim on a donkey, and he did not even glance in their direction. Samuel's masculine or English pride was outraged and he was speechless. At this moment of crisis, either feminine or Hungarian common sense prevailed. Florence had evidently assessed the chances of their continuing on their road while in opposition to the traders as negligible. She called out to Ibrahim to come over to them, which he did. Her eloquent exposition of the excellence of English people, and the powers of England to reach out and punish if they came to harm, combined with the promise of handsome presents from Sam, secured them a very valuable ally. Ibrahim's immediate boss, Khurshid, had a base and slave depot seven days' march east of Gondokoro. There, more of the Bakers' men deserted to another trading party, with whom they could raid for cattle at will.

Sam prevented a complete exodus, once more largely by the use of his fists. He virtually manhandled the survivors into loading camels. He cursed the deserters roundly, and when they were all murdered later in an encounter with an African village, the affair gained him a much-respected reputation for sorcery. His success as a medical practitioner also gained him great renown. He made good use of the predictable tartar emetic as a remedy, which both traders and Africans thought magical. He had particular success with Ibrahim as a patient and, in that way, got the upper hand with him. The alliance paid off more and more. Later, the coincidence of his demonstrating his two-finger butcher's boy whistle and the arrival of much-needed rain gained a useful alliance with the powerful chief of Obbo, to which they travelled southwestwards from Latuka in company with Ibrahim's band. Florence, too, made an impression on Katchiba of Obbo, and Sam, despite his incessant jeering at Turkish and African barbarity, left her in his care for some days while he went hunting.

The many delays meant that they were unable to cross the Aswa River Valley before the rains made it impassable, and many months were spent moving back and forth between Latuka and Obbo in increasing misery and discomfort. Local porters were recruited from time to time, but camels were cumbersome in the stony mountain passes and a nuisance away from their accustomed desert milieu. They ate the wrong things and sickened and died, and many hundredweights of porterage were lost. The horses survived longer, and Samuel had some splendid mounted shooting, sometimes accompanied by Florence to hold his horse, act as loader, or carry his spare rifle. But in time the horses died, leaving only donkeys, and they, too, were doomed. Every care had been taken, every soft antelope saddlepack personally supervised, but it was always realised that the animals would die as they advanced into the equatorial regions.

The Bakers themselves had remittant attacks of malaria and gastric fever, and Samuel constructed a canopied palanquin for Florence to ride in. Sick or well, rain or fine, they had to travel when Ibrahim's band did, and there were some grim marches. Three oxen, named Beef, Steak and Suet, were trained for riding, but palanquins had to be used when the fever was bad. Once, when crossing a muddy river, the porters decided that Florence on her angarep, or camp bed, was too heavy to carry over, and Sam hoisted her onto his own back and attempted the crossing alone. He stumbled and fell in the deep mud. They were both pulled out, but with little time to spare. With admirable fortitude they pushed on, and at the end of January 1864, they saw the Somerset Nile. Ibrahim had by good luck acquired a woman slave, Bacita, who had come from Bunyoro and who spoke a little Arabic. She was able to interpret for them in the negotiations about crossing the river to the south.

The kingdom of Bunyoro, once known as Kitara, claims to be the oldest of the four ancient kingdoms of Uganda. The claim is disputed by Buganda, and reliable legend maintains that they were in fact founded by twin brothers, probably around the late fifteenth century. At the time of the Bakers' visit, during the reign of the Omukama Kamrasi, Bunyoro had given way in importance to Buganda. Speke certainly compared it unfavorably to Buganda, but the Bakers, after months of wandering among the stateless, scantily clad Upper Nile peoples, were at first impressed by the organised kingdom, by the decency and elegance of the bark-cloth garments, and by the artistic sophistication of the black-glazed pottery. On the other hand, they were not impressed by the manner of their reception. They were probably unaware of it at the time, but the rival trader Debono or his agent had returned from escorting Speke to Gondokoro and had crossed into the country, claiming to be his emissary. Having had no success, Debono had joined forces with Kamrasi's rival and enemy, Rionga, with the idea of adding Bunyoro to his trading empire. Kamrasi was naturally apprehensive of all strangers. There was a long, undignified wait on the south bank of the Nile while messengers were sent to the court at Mruli for instructions. Sam reckoned they had an even chance between a welcoming invitation to proceed and extermination. He had, therefore, made plans for a rapid withdrawal across the river to where the main part of both the Bakers' and Ibrahim's party had been left, by order of the local people. Ibrahim, now very much under Samuel's domination, had undertaken to make his band obey the Baker rules as to cattle raiding and other abuses while in Bunyoro. This had to be rigorously enforced at a time when serious food shortage added to the miseries of delay.

Finally, an encouraging message came. Kamrasi was convinced that Samuel Baker and his wife were of the same species as Speke and Grant, and the caravan was allowed to proceed south on January 31. Porters were provided from village to village, the local inhabitants were instructed to supply the King's guests with shelter and all the food they needed, and, but for illness, the ten-day journey would have been easy. But Florence was seriously ill with gastric fever, and the onward pace was relentless. Then, Samuel collapsed with malaria, and, having run out of quinine, he was in a very bad way and had to halt for a whole day. At last, on February 10, they were ferried over the Kafu River to what they thought was the Omukama's palace. It turned out to be a sort of island in an unhealthy marsh, where some miserable, reeking huts were destined for their lodging. Speke and Grant had also been accommodated there, because Kamrasi preferred his visitors to be safely confined. It was, in fact, adjacent to the swampy Lake Kyoga, through which the Nile flows after leaving Victoria Nyanza, but none of the travellers was then aware of its existence.

The Bakers' sojourn at the Omukama Kamrasi's court was a prodigious feat of courage for two very sick people. It was also a formidable exercise in self-control for Samuel, who had been seething with outraged dignity at recurrent intervals ever since he had crossed the Somerset Nile. They had been made to leave a part of their luggage at the penultimate camp before they reached the capital, which meant that, fever-ridden as they were, they had to sleep on the sodden ground in their hut. At first, they were both too weak to stand up, and the prospect of the necessary confrontation with the Omukama cannot have been pleasant. But Sam was at his indomitable best when things were difficult. Preceded by endless canoe loads of chiefs and soldiers, Kamrasi crossed the river, and a throne made of copper and leopard skins was erected for him. Samuel was carried into the King's presence in the arms of his porters and placed recumbent on a mat by the throne. It was not perhaps the best position from which to carry out the interview, but his social self-confidence was well up to the situation, and he did "old England" honour. Florence was still too ill for even a recumbent presentation at court, and she lay prostrate and alone in her miserable hut, wracked with anxiety about the progress of the interview.

The King was tall and well dressed in flowing robes. He was surrounded by the dignitaries of the kingdom. His first request was for Baker's help in hostilities against his brother Rionga, who held rival court on a group of islands in the Nile. When Samuel expressed his inability to involve himself in local politics, he did not press the point. Presents were then exchanged. Kamrasi had arrived with 17 head of cattle and quantities of beer. Samuel ordered his men to unroll a Persian carpet and to display some handsome finery and some firearms. He was then carried back to his hut exhausted, where he and Florence lay side by side, each too ill to comfort the other.

The interviews continued for many days. The Bakers' fever came and went, and there was continual frustrations. Kamrasi told them that the lake was a six-month journey. In fact, his men were going there regularly in quest of salt and returning within a few weeks. But mutual confidence of a sort developed slowly, and on February 21, the visitors were allowed to leave their unhealthy swamp and cross the river to drier quarters. By then, most of their requests had been promised, though delivery was agonisingly slow, and they were hoping to reach Gondokoro again before the annual exodus of boats down river. Ibrahim was provided with ivory and was allowed to depart with his followers en route for their usual preserves. His contract with the Bakers had ended. Before going, he obliged by selling the invaluable interpretress Bacita for a few guns. Like most African monarchs, Kamrasi was rapacious in his demands for presents, and would have taken absolute necessities like watches had not Samuel given some sort of guarantee that he would find a way of sending him bigger and better things from Europe. Kamrasi was satisfied with this promise. Guides were provided to the lake, as well as a bizarre-looking military escort, and porters were to be available from village to village. The Bakers' party now consisted of their 12 remaining men, Richarn and the boy Saat, and four women, including Bacita, and also a kindly and devoted character called Karka.

At the beginning of March, they were ready to start, when Kamrasi produced one more request: he wanted Florence. Samuel described the scene that ensued as a coup de théâtre. He whipped out his revolver and virtually held it to Kamrasi's chest. He would certainly have used it, and the whole vast throng at the court could not have prevented the death of their King. With pointed gun, he explained the awful nature of the insult. It was probably very puzzling to Kamrasi, who may have thought he was paying a compliment. Florence, now recovered from fever, rose in her anger, and "with a countenance almost as amiable as Medusa," addressed Kamrasi witheringly in Arabic, which he did not speak. Bacita, taking the insult to her mistress to herself, fearlessly translated the speech, displaying considerable histrionic talent as she did so. Kamrasi, whether embarrassed by his faux pas, or relieved not to have to add this white virago to his company of wives, was only too pleased to speed the departure. Samuel helped Florence onto her riding ox and mounted his own, and they left the capital. The last touch of knockabout farce to the whole episode was only revealed to them later. The man they had dealt with throughout as Kamrasi was, in fact, his brother Mugambo, standing in for him for security reasons. The real Omukama had been watching the departure concealed behind a tree.

Marching generally westwards, they crossed and recrossed the marshy Kafu River. As a result of Kamrasi's proposal, Florence for once admitted to nervousness. She had long been determined to die rather than abandon the search for the lake, but the possibility of being Kamrasi's wife was quite different. She was depressed and weakened by fever and she found the military escort menacing. Sam watched her carefully, and when crossing the Kafu by way of a tightly packed carpet of surface weeds, he was quick to notice her sinking through them and down into the deep water like a log. She was purple in the face and could not speak. They dragged her through the river to the bank, and Samuel diagnosed sunstroke. He had her carried to the night camp on an angarep and managed to insert some water through her clenched teeth. He watched by her all night, and only her desperately slowed breathing and an occasional suffocating rattle showed that she was still alive. The military escort danced and yelled far into the night and jarred so much on Sam's nerves that he sacked them next morning. He had to threaten to shoot them piecemeal in order to get rid of them. For two more days and nights Florence remained insensible, and Sam rode or marched beside her litter all day and sat by her bedside most of the night. He had to press on all the time. There was little food in the country, and if they were to get out at all now, the most likely route was by way of the lake and down the Nile. His own fevered state made his ordeal so much the worse. Then, on the third day, he went to the door of their overnight hut for a breath of the cool morning air, and he heard her say "thank God!" He turned to her in great excitement and saw that the staring eyes were seeing at last but they were mad. She had brain fever, which lasted for seven days.

Sam skates over the period of derangement, which was probably even more of an ordeal than the unconscious period. He thought Florence was dying, and one of his greatest anxieties was that he might not be with her when it happened. After a few days, he so despaired that one of his many chores when setting up camp each evening was to cast an eye around for a possible burial place. The hyenas were watching, and the burial would have to be quick. On the seventh day, he thought the end was near, and his men were told to sharpen their axes in preparation for digging the grave. His own physical resilience was extraordinary, but he could not always fight off exhaustion, and that night he fell into a deep sleep for many hours. He awoke in a panic, thinking that he had deserted her at the last, and found her sleeping peacefully and normally. She was shattered and terribly weak, but in her right mind and able to go on in a litter. She must have been fundamentally a strong woman, and in her infinitely practical husband, she had a good doctor and a good nurse combined. Improvement continued slowly as they gained higher and drier country. Food became more plentiful, and they stayed for two nights in a village where the supply for chickens and eggs were good for convalescent cooking. On March 13, Sam learned from his guides that the misty blue range of high mountains that he had been watching for some days was not between him and the lake as he had thought, but rose steeply from its western shore. He was told that he would reach his goal the next day.

Sam could scarcely contain himself, and the next morning, March 14, 1864, the little caravan marched before daybreak. He raced ahead of the others, and a clear, sparkling day had dawned when he saw the great lake from a point 1,500 feet above the surface. The place is still featured on the maps as "Baker's view." A dream of many years had come true, and he made an important contribution to the age-old mystery of the Nile sources. He had drilled his men in advance, so that he could line them up to give three rousing old English cheers on the great occasion. But when the moment came, he was so overcome that he sank on his knees and thanked God instead. Then, to please his recently bereaved Queen, he gave the name Albert to the lake. Thus, for a time at least, the two greatest reservoirs of the Nile were called Victoria Nyanza and Albert Nyanza after the Sovereign and Consort of some little islands in the North Sea.

It was only human that Sam should have spurred his ox and rushed up the hill from which the lake could be seen, ahead of Florence on her litter. But, though still weak, she was able to stand beside him and share in the happiness of success. In his rather purple passage describing the sensation of looking down on the waters, he is gallant enough to use the pronoun "we" at least some of the time. His wife was a great woman, and he was not ungenerous about it. The long, tortuous descent to the water level was impracticable for the oxen, and Sam strode ahead, gripping a short staff, with Florence tottering behind, supporting herself on his emaciated but sturdy shoulder. She had to stop to rest every few minutes. At the foot of the escarpment, there was a mile of green pasture to traverse before they reached the white-pebbled beach. There, in a sort of ritualistic ecstasy, Sam rushed into the water and "drank deeply of the sources of the Nile."

Local reports, translated by Bacita, gave Sam the mistaken idea that this Lake Albert stretched a long way to the south, well beyond the Equator. In fact, he was then not far from its southern end. There were high mountains across the lake on the western shore, but he saw none to the south. The snow-capped peaks of the Ruwenzori Range were potentially in his line of vision to the south, and at no great distance; but they bestride the Equator, and are almost continuously wrapped in heavy cloud and are usually quite invisible. Sam wanted his own special lake to be as large as possible, and he may have accepted Bacita's interpretations too readily. In fact, with its affluent, the Semliki, and the thousands of mountain streams that feed it, Lake Albert receives a very high proportion of the Nile waters in one way or another, and it is all-important in the river system. In the context of the controversy over the Nile source at the time, it was a pity that he placed its southern extremity as far away as he did.

At a banquet on the beach to celebrate Florence's recovery and their arrival at their goal, Sam tried to explain to his men the nature of their achievement. They had been very impressed by the sight of the lake, the existence of which they had long doubted, but they cannot have had very much idea of the significance of their discovery. He reminded them that, but for the bad behavior of their colleagues, they would have arrived a year earlier. And then, remembering Henry V's address on the night before the battle of Agincourt, he added that the honour was all the greater for the smallness of the party.

Travellers are always especially subject to malaria, as they do not stay long enough to develop immunity from the local mosquitoes. Camping on the level ground by the lake, the whole Baker party came down with it, and Florence, in her weakened state, was very ill. Sam recovered quickly as usual and engaged himself with preparations for a cruise. He had sent the riding oxen north with the guides who were instructed to meet him at Magungu at the northern end of the lake. Then, he engaged two canoes with the requisite boatmen.

Sometimes his account of his infinitely various activities makes him seem like a caricature of the perfect Boy Scout. His baggage always contained the requirements of the moment, and he had provided the proper tools for adapting canoes for greater comfort and greater speed. He inserted curved supports for a thatch-and-cowhide canopy to protect Florence from sun and rain, and he fixed a mast with a sail made from one of his beloved Scottish plaids. The sail, in addition to the paddles, gave them speed and also made them independent of the vagaries of paddling labour. For 14 days they voyaged north, camping at night on sandy beaches. Once, a midday thunderstorm whipped up the lake dangerously when they were a few miles off shore. They shipped a lot of water and might have sunk, but suitable vessels were, of course, available, and Sam organised rhythmic bailing operations. They reached a safe beach, as did the other canoe, a

mile behind them, without Sam's captainship, though no doubt
carefully instructed by him. Towards the north, the lake narrowed, and the high cliffs on the eastern shore dwindled gradually down to near marshland. Eventually, they reached the wide
estuary of what they were assured was Speke's Somerset Nile,
and kept their rendezvous with the guides and the riding oxen at
the village of Magungu.

From a hill near Magungu, Sam was able to see where the Nile
made its exit from the lake in the extreme north. He was told that
it was navigable for canoes to within a week's march of Gondokoro. Had they gone that way, they could probably have caught
the boats leaving for Khartoum at the end of April. With the state
of Florence's health and, indeed, of his own, it is surprising that
they did not try the river route. But Sam wanted to be thorough.
In this supposed estuary of the Nile coming from Lake Victoria,
there was no apparent current, and it had been a fast-running
river that they had crossed away to the east on their journey
south to Kamrasi's. In any case, this stretch of the river was
completely unknown, and he felt he had an obligation to Speke to
explore it. So, feeble and battered as they were, they turned aside
from the direct way homewards and sailed up Speke's Somerset
Nile. Brave or foolhardy, thorough or exhibitionist, it was a
decision that nearly cost them their lives, and they were both
quite prepared for it to do so.

The riding oxen were again sent overland, and the Bakers
travelled by canoe. This time, it was Sam who was seriously ill.
Florence had to help him down to the water, and on the first
night, he was carried ashore unconscious, and it was she who had
to do the night watching. But resilient as usual, he was soon
observing a distant westward-flowing current, measured easily
by the floating vegetation known as Nile cabbage. They were on
a beautiful stretch of the river then unknown but visited today
by thousands of tourists, where each succeeding patch of riverside pasturage is grazed by a different herd of elephants, buffa-
loes, or hippos, and where dozing crocodiles jostle close together
on the banks. In time, they heard the roar of falling water, which
was no surprise, because Speke had calculated that the Nile must
fall over a thousand feet between the Karuma Falls, where he
crossed it northbound, and Lake Albert. When the current

became really strong, the boatmen had to be persuaded to continue, and they rounded a bend and saw the Nile's greatest waterfall. Here, the powerful river coming from Lake Victoria forces itself through a narrow gap 19 feet wide and humanly jumpable by Olympic standards, and drops perpendicularly for over 120 feet. Sam named it the Murchison Falls, after Sir Roderick Murchison, then president of the Royal Geographical Society. It has since been renamed Kabarega Falls, after Kamrasi's son and successor as Omukama of Bunyoro.

The falls were the end of the canoe journey, and the riding oxen were there to meet them. But they arrived in wretched condition and could not be ridden. The Bakers were both sick, and to have to walk was discouraging. But they marched on up the riverbank in expectation of meeting the porters and supplies promised by Kamrasi for the first lap of their return journey. Travelling south, they had very much liked a trading station in Acholi country, close to Mount Shoa, and that was their first destination. It was a centre for Ibrahim's caravans, and they thought his further escort would be useful on the march to Gondokoro. Neither porters nor supplies appeared, and the country along this rapidly flowing stretch of river had been devastated in recent wars against rebellious chiefs.

For two months, they lived in near starving conditions. Their diet was rancid porridge made from some mouldy meal found in a deserted hut and some spinach-like vegetable. The demise of Saat's little riding ox provided a welcome change of diet for the men. Sam's greatest wish at the time was for an English steak and Alsopp's pale ale, but he could not bring himself to eat deceased cow. They both became weak and emaciated, and they thought that death must surely be the outcome. Without mentioning anything so dramatic as a suicide pact, they quietly determined that neither would survive the other. They had won their prize, and careful arrangements had been made so that the documentary evidence of the journey would be delivered to Khartoum. Then, they heard that Kamrasi was in the neighbourhood and had been there for some time. Despondency changed to angry indignation, at which Sam excelled. He sent the haughtiest of messages, maintaining that Kamrasi was an insignificant little upstart compared to someone of Sam's importance and magnificence. The snobbish line worked well, or else Kamrasi thought he had gone far enough. His object in starving out Baker was to blackmail him into helping in the war against Rionga. Now food arrived, and sufficient porters appeared to transport the baggage to the Omukama's abode.

On arriving at the village of Kisuna, near the current royal camp, the great surprise was to find ten members of Ibrahim's band there. One-time enemies though they were, the two parties had marched for long together, and there was a rapturous welcome, the usual salute of guns, and a great deal of osculation between the men of the two parties. Unknown to Baker, Ibrahim's men had been retained by arrangement, as an addition to the Bunyoro army. The Bakers had been reported as dead, and they, Florence especially, were received with admiring enthusiasm. "By Allah, no woman in the world has a heart so tough as to dare to face what she has been through. Thank Allah. Be grateful to Allah." Mugambo, whom they had know as Kamrasi, came to call at once, and was greatly amused at the change in their appearance. He said he would scarcely have recognised them and roared with laughter, which was not soothing. Sam abused him roundly for not supplying food but got no sympathy, because he was told he could have it at any time that he agreed to fight for "my brother Kamrasi." His laughter and these words made Sam conclude that he was drunk, and it took him some time to realise that he had been completely duped on his first visit to the court. He relieved his feelings by a vitriolic outburst at Kamrasi's cowardice in not appearing himself.

Among the presents delivered to them later that day was a milking cow, and, for the first time in many months, they revelled in quantities of milk. Always practical, they began making and storing small cheeses. For a time, Sam remained on his high horse and felt too insulted to visit Kamrasi. But Florence and expediency prevailed, and he knew he must give in. This time he got himself up in full Highland dress, having a kilt and plaid of Atholl tartan and a sporran and Glengarry in his baggage for just such an occasion. Sitting on his camp bed, he was carried into the presence and placed on a stool. The costume was an instant success. Kamrasi, of course, asked for it for himself, but Sam does not say whether, in fact, the MacBaker tartan became the Mac-

Kamrasi. He never gave him a certain small Fletcher rifle, which he begged for with obsessive regularity the whole time the Bakers were in his country.

Sam and Florence stayed for some months at Kisuna. They disliked the dull elephant-grass country, but food was plentiful, and relations with Kamrasi were peaceful, if not especially cordial. Sam refused to join forces in a war of aggression, but he promised to help if Kamrasi was attacked. The milk, butter, and cheese diet was invaluable as a restorative, and they both gained weight. Sam suffered a short daily bout of fever, which was mitigated to some extent by a vapour bath that he devised for himself. He boiled castor oil plants and water in a big pot, which he placed under a stool. He then sat on the stool with a blanket all round to keep in the steam, and he was convinced that the sweat that ensued was beneficial. Altogether, life was not especially agreeable but at least comfortable.

Then, news reached the several camps that Kamrasi's enemies were advancing, strengthened by a force supplied by the slave trader Debono. Sam forthwith hoisted the dear old Union Jack on his hut and organised a deputation to the invaders. It returned with some of Debono's men, who had come to verify the presence of the Bakers, who had been reported dead. With supreme self-confidence, Sam pointed to the British flag and claimed Bunyoro for himself as its discoverer. He explained that he had given the ivory concession to Ibrahim on certain conditions of behaviour. If Debono attacked, he would be violating the sacred flag of England and would probably end up on a gallows in Khartoum. The technique was completely successful, and Kamrasi was convinced that the good old British flag had mystical qualities, as perhaps in those good old days it had. He hankered after it nearly as much as he did the little rifle.

Early in September, war threatened again, this time from Buganda. According to Sam, there was universal panic, and he had to take charge. He organised a withdrawal of all parties to better-prepared positions in the vicinity of the Karuma Falls. The country there was more open, and there were hills from which a lookout could be kept. He also sent four messages to Shoa in Acholi, where Ibrahim was reported to have arrived from Gondokoro. They were to inform him that Sam had large quantities of ivory for him. This had been given by Kamrasi, and Sam was resolute in not accepting ivory himself. Second, they were to ask Ibrahim to send as large a force as he could spare to help in the coming encounter with the Baganda. The Bakers themselves marched to Karuma by night. They had nothing fit to ride, and Florence staggered there miserably on foot. The whole exercise was probably as much in the interest of their eventual getaway to Shoa en route for Gondokoro as in the Bunyoro-Buganda wars.

Ibrahim arrived at Karuma with a very considerable force and with a packet of mail for Samuel that he had brought from Gondokoro. There was, of course, none for Florence, who had no Hungarian relations and who had not as yet met the ready-made family she was to acquire in England. The war raged around them with much accompanying horror, but with well-armed assistance from Ibrahim's company, the Baganda were defeated and withdrew. Kamrasi was delighted with Ibrahim and gave him almost overwhelming quantities of extra ivory. It took them some time to arrange for the porterage of it all, and the Bakers had to wait patiently until the end of November. Samuel was, of course, as busy as usual. Around Karuma there were many acres of sweet potatoes, and he was longing for alcohol. He devised a still by boiling potatoes in a vast pot, in the neck of which he inverted a smaller pot. From a hole at the top of the latter, a reed pipe led to a kettle which was weighted down in a basin of cold water. This was the condenser. Sam managed to produce a great many gallons of "potato whiskey" in this way, and deprived of such luxuries for so long, it proved a stimulating treat. In fact, Sam was convinced that hot toddy cured his persistently recurring malaria completely in time. There were many willing pupils for the art of distilling, and the reformation of the now valuable Richarn was retarded by his enthusiasm for still-minding. Mugambo took a bottle to Kamrasi, who got drunk so gloriously quickly that he asked Sam to set up a still for him. Many years later, people in Bunyoro were deprecating the introduction of spirits by Samuel Baker, but no doubt the Bunyoro would have learnt the distiller's art sooner or later.

At last a party of nearly a thousand was assembled, made up of 700 porters, 75 armed escorts, and women and children. The

lengthy business of ferrying them all across the Nile was commenced on November 17. Bacita, who had proved to be worth her
considerable weight in gold as the sole interpreter to the expedition, had operated as a first-class intelligence officer during the
war, listening for news from all directions as diligently as a *"Times*
reporter." Now she disappeared and they heard of her no more.
Her husband had been among Kamrasi's enemies, and she was
evidently afraid of being abandoned near Kamrasi's camp. The
latter came to say goodbye, and expressed regret at their departure. He made one last attempt to acquire the little Fletcher rifle,
but he had to be content with the promise of future largesse.

With a sojourn of a couple of months at Shoa, in the Acholi
country which they found comparatively congenial, the Bakers
reached Gondokoro the following March. Their reception was
disappointing. They had long been written off as dead, and there
was no mail for them, and no arrangements had been made for
them. Plague was raging in Khartoum and also among the crews
of boats coming up the river. A dahabiyah was available, and Sam
had it scrubbed with sand and fumigated. Nonetheless, plague
broke out on the journey, and though Sam and Florence escaped,
Florence's devoted Saat caught it. She sat by his bedside, adminis-
tering sips of sugar and water for hours, and Richarn, his insep-
arable companion, nursed him tenderly. But it was hopeless, and,
aged only 15, he died before they reached Khartoum. Inevitably,
the Bakers thought of that other young man, Johann Schmidt,
who had died at almost the same place when they were outward
bound.

At Khartoum, Sam took steps to ensure that some of the
traders who had endeavoured to sabotage his expedition were
punished. They had probably been acting on licence of some sort,
but he had seen them do very unpleasant things and felt strongly
that they should suffer. The Egyptian Government was, in fact,
beginning to take some tentative steps towards the suppression
of slaving, and gunboats were on the river for the purpose.
Riddled with plague, the place was less attractive than ever. The
population had been very much depleted, and there were great
difficulties over arranging transport to Berber. It was not till
January 1 that they sailed. From Berber, they crossed the desert

to Suakin on the Red Sea, a route thought preferable in August to that northward route across the desert to Korosko, which cuts out the great westerly bend of the Nile.

The party was now small. Besides themselves, there was a servant recruited in Khartoum and Richarn and his new wife. She was a six-foot-tall charmer from the Dinka tribe whom he had married in Khartoum. During a scrap with some Arabs over a share of the shade at a small desert oasis, she came up behind Richarn's assailant and struck him on the head. One does not doubt Sam's basic veracity, but the whole episode reads as though caricatured from the "Boy's Own Paper." Sam himself parried swords with his umbrella, until he got his own sword mobilised. Then, with his back to a tree, he kept three antagonists at bay at the same time. He disarmed them one by one, Florence rounded up their weapons, and the foe was put to flight. It was the only hostile incident on the journey.

At Suakin they sailed in an Egyptian troopship to Suez and to good old English comforts at last. In the bar was the cold Alsopp's ale for which Sam had expressed what he thought was a dying wish near the Somerset Nile. In the bar, too, were Englishmen on their way to India, who were no doubt proud and delighted to meet Baker of the Nile. There were also English ladies wearing the recently introduced chignon, which astonished Sam and entranced Richarn. Florence, who was about to enter the English beau monde for the first time, would soon be wearing this hair style.

In Cairo they learned that the Victoria Gold Medal of the Royal Geographical Society had been awarded to Sam, at a time when it was not known whether he was alive or dead. Cairo was also the scene of the final parting with Richarn, who, completely reformed of his drinking, had served them devotedly, and of whom they were now very fond. They arranged good jobs for him and his wife with the manager of Shepheard's Hotel, and Richarn was at the Cairo railway station to bid them an emotional farewell. "I left my old servant with a heart too full to say goodbye; a warm squeeze of the rough but black hand, and the whistle of the train sounded,—we were off!" The noise of the rushing train was such a civilised noise that it was hard to remember the reality of the last few years. The search for the Nile sources could have been a dream. But sitting opposite Sam was the lovely young girl, still only 24, whom he had brought from Hungary four years before, and she was the living witness of the fact that it had been anything but a dream. "A face still young, but bronzed like an Arab with years of exposure to a burning sun; haggard and worn with toil and sickness, and shaded with cares, now happily past, the devoted companion of my pilgrimage to whom I owed success and life—my wife."

No. 1 Savile Row, now the premises of a famous military tailor, was the original headquarters of the Royal Geographical Society. It was there that all the great travellers of the mid-nineteenth century reported on their return, and there that David Livingstone's body was taken when it was romantically returned to England in 1873. The great reception arranged for Samuel Baker on a foggy night in November 1865 seems to have been held in the nearby Burlington House, which was presumably better able to accommodate the large throng that went to do him honour. Speke's recent death, in a shooting accident in Wiltshire, the day before he was due to debate the Nile sources with Richard Burton at Bath, heightened the interest in the occasion.

Sir Roderick Murchison, in his introductory speech, referred to Baker's assistance to Speke and Grant, and to the fact that he had explored the Nile sources, briefed by them and with their historic map in his possession. This map was duly produced by Baker during his own address. Murchison concluded his remarks by saying that he was authorised to make what must have been the sensational announcement that Mrs. Baker had accompanied her husband throughout his perilous travels. He added that Baker had assured him that much of his success had been due to her, and that she "by her conduct had shown what a courageous wife can do in duty to her husband." The word "duty" today is obnoxious. It is true that Florence Baker was not herself ambitious for adventure, and that she preferred above all an orderly domestic existence. But it was not stern duty, but quite simply love for her husband, that took her along unexplored paths with him. Samuel Baker himself, whose Victorianism makes one smile, albeit with affection, put it much more generously. At the end of his own address, and after the formal expressions of gratitude to Speke and Grant and the Royal Geographical

Society, he added: "And there is one whom I must thank, and whom I am truly glad to thank in your presence, one who though young and tender has the heart of a lion, and without whose devotion and courage I would not be alive to address you tonight. Mr. President, my Lords, Ladies and Gentlemen, allow me to present my wife." Then, leaving the platform quickly, he brought her on, her arm in his as she would have wished it, and dressed now as an elegant young woman of fashion. Florence Baker had stepped onto the stage in that most masculine of all masculine worlds and was acclaimed in her own right.

The Bakers had taken a London house, and Florence was getting to know her four step-daughters aged from 9 to 18 years. The eldest, Edith, was so nearly her contemporary as to make her a greatly appreciated companion in her early days in England, and she learned much of her English from her. In addition to the London house, Hedenham Hall in Norfolk was acquired as a country residence. There, the Bakers were neighbors of the Prince and Princess of Wales at Sandringham, and they also met them at country-house parties. Shortly after their return to England, Sam had remarried Florence at St. James's Piccadilly. It is unlikely that this was legally necessary, but it is understandable that he should have wanted a ceremony by his own Anglican rite.

But mischief was made in some quarters about the supposed second marriage, and it reached the Queen. It did not interfere with Sam's knighthood, awarded in 1866, but Florence was not presented at court because of it. In 1868, the Queen wrote to the Prince of Wales, then staying at Dunrobin Castle with the Duke and Duchess of Sutherland, to warn him of the unsuitability of the Bakers as fellow guests for himself and the Princess. The Prince, well used to such admonitions from his mother, replied that there was no truth in the rumour that "Lady Baker had been on intimate terms with her husband before she was married." He added, "She is one of the quietest and most ladylike persons one could see, and perfectly devoted and wrapped up in her husband."

The Queen's disapproval made no difference to the Prince's association with the Bakers, and, strangely, it resulted in their taking the long and dangerous road to Bunyoro again together. The Suez Canal was to be opened in the autumn of 1869 by the

Empress Eugenie. It was considered undiplomatic for the Prince to be present at that particular event, but a royal visit of some kind to the Khedive was thought desirable. This took place in 1868. The Prince and Princess took a large party with them which included Samuel Baker. He was the Arab interpreter and dragoman for the voyage up the Nile to Luxor, and he supervised the arrangements in the boats.

At the conclusion of the state visit, the Khedive Ismail gave a fancy-dress ball in Cairo. Sam was there, and during the evening, the Prince of Wales had a private conversation with him. The Khedive had asked the Prince's advice about the command of a military expedition he intended to send up the Nile, with the object of suppressing the slave trade. Baker was not a soldier, but his knowledge of the Upper Nile was exceptional, if not unique, and the Prince had recommended him for the job. The Khedive was liberal by Khedivial standards, and he wanted to stand well in the world. At that moment when Cairo was splendidly en fête, he probably thought that the exercise was easy to execute. In fact, the abolition of the slave trade in Egypt and the Sudan was extremely difficult at that time without very revolutionary measures. Every government official based in Khartoum was either directly or indirectly implicated in it, and government revenues depended on it. But a start had to be made, and Baker's optimism, based on confidence in his own ability, in his own race, and, of course, in the justice of his mission, was infinite. He probably never thought of refusing and knew that his Florence would want to accompany him. The salary was to be enormous, and all facilities were to be provided. He was to command a considerable fighting force, and his power was to be absolute.

The formal brief made it quite clear that the Khedive had imperialistic ambitions. Baker was to suppress the slave trade and was also to extend the Khedivial dominions south of Gondokoro. He accepted this charge without question. Indeed, the immensity of the task was very gratifying. He would have argued that only by the effective extension of Egyptian rule could the slave trade be exterminated. As far as extension to Gondokoro went, this was no doubt true, if the administration could be divorced from the trade itself. But the lake kingdoms farther south were not then seriously affected by slavery and, therefore, not really relevant to his mission. To Baker, however, they were peopled by contemptible savages, cowardly and wholly unaware of European standards of hospitality. But they could be improved, and he thought that Egyptian rule, whatever that might have meant at such an unmanageable distance from Cairo, was desirable. And so, with an Egyptian army recruited largely from the jails, and subsequently augmented from the redundant retinues of slave traders, he set off once more for equatorial Africa.

Sam reached Egypt in May 1869, and Florence and his nephew, Julian Baker, joined him during the summer. Julian, on special secondment from the Navy, was to act as aide de camp. Other European members of the party were a doctor who went mad en route and an English valet and ladies' maid, neither of whom stayed the course. There was also a party of English engineers to tend the many steamers required and to supervise the transport of the sections of the steamer that they were to construct above the rapids to the south of Gondokoro. The steamer was intended for the circumnavigation of the Albert Nyanza. There were tiresome delays in despatching the various convoys upriver to Khartoum, due largely to the concentration by officialdom on the celebrations for the opening of the Suez Canal. The Bakers took no part in these, but from Alexandria they watched the great procession of boats, headed by the Empress in her yacht, steaming towards Suez. They met the Empress privately several times, and she took a liking to Florence. They finally got away on December 6 and went very rapidly via Suez and Suakin to rally with the expedition at Khartoum.

By this time Florence spoke English well, though she retained a slightly guttural accent all her life. She kept a journal in English, and also wrote long letters to her step-children. The 1972 publication of parts of the journal and some of her letters[1] gives, for the first time, some impression of her as a traveller, other than that given by her husband. Her English is very good, if a little stilted, and there is sometimes a faulty construction of a sentence, which has charm in its own right. She was by then the Lady Baker, wife of Sir Samuel Baker, now by Khedivial decree Major-General Baker Pasha, of Hedenham Hall in Norfolk, and her expressions are subtly upper class.

Her letters give the children news of their dear Papa and accounts of the excellence of his activities. The poor slaves are "so happy" when he frees them and has their irons removed. The weather is unfailingly reported on. If a European is ill, he is always "not quite the thing." The little bag that dear Lady So and So gave her is so useful. The Lady Bountiful rescues and cossets many a tiny orphan slave, and old Karka, a veteran of the first expedition, acts as Nanny to them and baths them rigorously. And in her turn, Florence is always asking for news of the darling girls at their boarding schools, especially of darling Edith, the eldest, now married, and her darling babes, whom Edith is instructed to kiss on Florence's behalf.

As usual, Khartoum was unpleasant, and there were many frustrations. Not all of the several convoys that had left Cairo had arrived. It had proved impossible to haul 15 sloops up the cataracts, and they had returned downstream. The cavalry, when inspected, proved so unprepossessing that Samuel decided to dispense with it and sacked it then and there. The appearance of the rest of the troops was far from reassuring, but he hoped that they might be drilled into some sort of discipline. In time, he formed a crack unit from among them which became known as the Forty Thieves and which was valuable, but the rest were a doubtful liability.

Baker sensed the fierce hostility to his mission, for the liberal ideas of Cairo were quite foreign to Khartoum. The Governor, Djaffer Pasha, was an old acquaintance whom he liked, but it was not until a subsequent brief return to Khartoum that he realised the full extent of the government's involvement in the trade he was commissioned to suppress. Aqqad and Company, with whose agents he had associated south of Gondokoro in the early sixties, had a trade concession that covered over 90,000 square miles. His old enemy, Debono, had sold up, but many of the other companies employed over 2,000 men, and the Governors of stations on the river, like Fashoda, were trading at firsthand. The slave part of their businesses was probably not so large as Baker maintained, but it was nonetheless substantial. The horrors of it were all too apparent.

The departure from Khartoum took place on February 8, 1870. There were nine steamers and 155 sailing craft. Florence watched with great amusement as her husband and nephew were embraced by the local officials. The musketry saluted and the bands played, and on board the Baker's private dahabiyah, there was a feeling of gaiety in leaving the abominable city behind. Every delay and frustration imaginable was ahead of them. Craft were frequently shipwrecked through mishandling or collision with hippos or sheer decrepitude. The precious sections of the steamer for Lake Albert were involved in several mishaps but were rescued. Then, the Sudd, the great barrier of river vegetation in the vicinity of the Bahr el Ghazal junction that impedes the river traffic to a greater or lesser extent each year, was at its worst. The route up the Bahr el Giraffe branch was attempted and persisted in with enormous determination. But, after two months spent hacking a passage through semifloating islands, the attempt was abandoned at Florence's insistence. They were back on the main Nile by April 18, and the low level of the river meant that no further progress south could be made for many months. Baker's contract only ran until April 1873, and the delay was serious. He decided to establish a station near the Sobat junction, where the whole expedition could wait.

Travelling now in the Khedive's service, his geographical designations were no longer English, and he called it Tewfikiah, after the Khedive's son. Florence presided over Tewfikiah as she did over Hedenham Hall. She and Samuel lived on board their dahabiyah, and their drawing room was under a shady mimosa tree, where splendid oriental carpets were thrown over seating arrangements and spread upon the ground. Tents were set up in orderly rows; vast supplies of food were organised; medicaments were dispensed; and matrimonial troubles were advised on. When a large party of freed women slaves were given the option of returning to their homes or taking husbands from among the troops, they one and all chose husbands, and Florence made them look respectable with dresses from the camp stores. Occasionally, the Bakers went off together for a picnic, and if neither Samuel nor Julian shot anything for the picnic lunch table, there were always luxurious tins from Fortnum and Mason in London. The pursuit of game went on all the time, and Samuel became interested in ostrich shooting. Ingenious as ever, he devised a fake ostrich: a wooden head with broken glass for eyes, stuck on a pole encased in a grey canvas gun bag. His intention was to go stalking with this in his left hand. Unfortunately, the impersonation never took place for lack of ostriches to stalk. The spectacle of Sam Baker imitating their curious, ultra-rapid skating motion would have been worth seeing.

With 1,600 men and their dependants, the expedition sailed again from Tewfikiah early in December. The voyage to Gondokoro might have been accomplished in 40 days. In fact, with more Sudd trouble and other mishaps, they only reached it four and a half months later, on April 15, 1871. Two of the four years for which Baker had contracted had gone by, with only a few incidental slave rescue operations to show. Gondokoro had gone further downhill since 1863, and Sam's first task was to establish an orderly government station there, which he named Ismailia. Such a station certainly offered as good a strategic base as possible from which to operate against the Nile slave trade. Consolidation there might have been very effective, and there seems to have been a letter from the Khedive, which was never delivered, telling him not to try to go south of Gondokoro. It may have been intercepted by those with vested interests. The same letter extended his mission for an extra year, which, presumably, he, though not Florence, would have welcomed.

Ismailia, where he remained for nine months, proved difficult to administer. The local traders were in aggressive opposition, but that had been expected. But the local Africans, the Bari, were uncooperative about the food supplies for perhaps 2,000 souls, and hungry people are hard to discipline. Sam was outraged at the ingratitude of the Bari in not supplying cattle to the people they should have looked upon as their saviours. He failed to appreciate that the ownership of cattle was a part of the structure of their society, and there was no item of barter that they could legitimately accept in compensation. Sam was forced to allow his starving men to go on cattle raids, and the Bari became increasingly hostile and allied themselves with the traders, who were quick to exploit the situation. He then marched 12 miles south to where he had heard there was a better supply of food. While he was away, over a thousand of his men returned to Khartoum in 38 of his boats. Aqqad and Company's agent, Abou Saoud, almost certainly had a hand in this.

Ismailia was nonetheless built, and administration of a kind was established. The depletion of the garrison was probably more serious with reference to the next move. He had been unable to bring camels, and he now had insufficient porters to transport his precious steamer round the last cataracts en route for Lake Albert. He reacted as he always did to this kind of frustration. He ditched the steamer and the engineers, and on January 22, 1872, he went south with Florence and Julian, a small but reasonably well-trained force of about 250, including the Forty Thieves, and small herds of cattle and sheep.

The first objective was Patiko, the natural, rocky hill fortress near Mount Shoa in Acholi country, where they had stayed for some time during their return journey from Bunyoro in 1863. In appearance, it is not unlike a mediaeval castle, with green lawns between huge granite boulders. It commands attractive country in all directions and even a distant glimpse of a silver thread of river, which is the Nile on its way from Lake Albert to Gondokoro. Aqqad's agent, Abou Saoud, was in camp nearby, but he moved off quickly, and the Acholi were very welcoming. The bugles were sounded as the three Bakers, mounted on well-groomed horses, reached the rocky eminence. Two hundred soldiers, in scarlet tunics with snow-white trousers, led by a band, followed them. The dependants and the herds of livestock brought up the rear.

Florence had trained an efficient household staff, well disciplined and completely honest, so a measure of formal domestic state was immediately available. A Shilluk cook had been Arab-trained, and six house servants were dressed uniformly in navy blue suits with red facings, worn with a red fez. For waiting at table, they had white uniforms with red facings. But by Florence's rigid rules, these had to be removed for the washing up after a meal. There was also a ceremonial dress of scarlet and a strong brown cotton suit for travelling and rough work. Florence had no doubt supervised the making of all these uniforms, and she had made Sam's cotton suits herself. Her own costume was now, on occasion, more conventionally feminine than formerly, her skirts even hinting at the prevailing crinoline fashion. She wrote home from Patiko for sundry items of dress, such as six pairs of gloves and French stays, which might not have been thought very necessary there. But she was now the wife of a proconsul, and the niceties of dress were no doubt considered important.

Like Ismailia, Patiko made good sense as a base. But Sam, racing against his allotted time, wanted to fly flags in more spectacular places. He also wanted to see his lake again. After only two weeks at Patiko, he left for Bunyoro. A very much reduced force and a greatly extended line of communication did nothing to deter him. From what he had seen of the Banyoro on his first visit, he envisaged no difficulty in co-opting them into the Ottoman or Khedivial Empire. After all, he believed he was doing it for their own good. He never realised the extent to which Bunyoro was a highly centralised kingdom, with an organisation very different from that of the disparate Nile peoples such as the Bari and the Acholi. Sam had held the Omukama Kamrasi in contempt, and never realised that he had, in fact, shown considerable shrewdness in studying and assessing what Baker was up to when he came as an explorer. Now there was Kamrasi's son, Kabarega, a young puppy of 21, apparently an even more contemptible monarch. And now Baker was not just looking at a lake, but was intending to annexe the country to Egypt. The young monarch was apparently expected to behave well.

Both Sam and Florence refer repeatedly to "the young cub Kabarega." In fact, Bunyoro had, after many generations, acquired a great soldier-king. Had he not chanced to live at the time when England became interested in these African lake kingdoms, he might have restored it to the importance of the ancient Kitara and put the traditional rival Buganda in its place. Had Baker not given him good reason for apprehension, and so seriously denigrated him in Egypt and England, he might have come to terms with the British, as did the Baganda. Instead of this, he was sent eventually to tragic but comfortable exile in the Seychelles. In April 1872, when the Bakers arrived, his court was at Masindi. Quite uninvited, they made their camp within a few hundred yards of the palace. The first formal call on the Omukama was carried out with full military escort led by the regimental band. Sam says that he explained his mission from the beginning: the country was to be taken under the "protection of Egypt; it was to be saved from the rapidly encroaching slave trade; and civilised commodities were to flow in as legitimate barter. It was, of course, to lose its sovereignty, and unsuspected by Baker, Kabarega appreciated this. The fact that he was to be retained as Governor, presumably for as long as he behaved himself, is unlikely to have impressed him. But Baker was satisfied that everything was going well: his "work had now fairly commenced, and Kabarega and his Chiefs were assured of a grand reform."

The building of Government House was set in train immediately. The one private apartment was decorated with scarlet blankets hung on the walls and 21 prints of life-sized, gorgeously dressed white women, with tinsel stuck on for jewellery. A similar print of the Princess of Wales seems to have been in better taste and was, in fact, the most admired. There was also a photo of Queen Victoria, two long mirrors, and some sporting prints. Florence later used to talk about "my pretty little house at Masindi," and nothing of the kind had been seen in those parts before. It certainly impressed Kabarega, especially the mirrors and the picture of the Princess. The tables were spread with cheap novelties, as examples of the great benefits that trade was to bring to the country when two-penny mirrors would be exchanged for ivory tusks. Kabarega asked for, and by native custom was probably entitled to, everything he saw. Samuel called it begging and concluded that the fellow could not be a gentleman. Kabarega, on the other hand, complained that everything he asked for, including a little revolver, appeared to be unobtainable, because it was the property of "El Sitt," the lady. On May 14, 1872, the Ottoman flag was hoisted on Government House, and at a ceremony to which he invited Kabarega, Sir Samuel Baker took formal possession of Bunyoro in the name of the Khedive of Egypt. The band, augmented by local musicians, played; and Sam's soldiers, plus an irregular force recruited from the slave bands, formed a battle square. Kabarega was invited to inspect this from the inside and to have a lesson in military tactics. He was inattentive, as he apparently found the situation uncomfortable, and perhaps that was the object of the exercise.

While in residence at Masindi, Samuel had some communication with Kabaka Mutesa of Buganda. He never met him, but he later praised him as much as he denigrated Kabarega, and he found him especially helpful in a matter very close to his heart. In 1862, Sam had "found" Speke and Grant at Gondokoro. Now he very much wanted to "find" Livingstone, whose long absence in the interior of Africa was arousing much speculation and concern. He wrote a flattering letter to Mutesa, telling him that he had won worldwide renown by his kindness and hospitality to Speke, and asking him to make enquiries as to Livingstone's whereabouts. He had left supplies at Gondokoro on the chance that Livingstone might arrive there. According to Florence, this would have been "a great and wonderful event." It would have been even greater and more wonderful to find him in the bush.

Later, when the Bakers were homeward bound, Sam received a letter from Mutesa with the information that Livingstone was reported to be in the vicinity of Lake Tanganyika. Sam wrote to Livingstone via Mutesa, telling him that he was by then certain that the Lakes Albert and Tanganyika were one and the same. In fact, about 300 miles, great mountain ranges, and several other lakes lie between them. His informants may have been describing the Rift Valley, in which both lakes lie but which has a high-level watershed of its own, but Sam does not seem to have had Speke's gift for geographical interpretation. Unknown, of course, to Sam, Stanley had already pulled off the dramatic "finding" of Livingstone, and he and Livingstone together had explored the northern end of the Tanganyika and had seen that the flow of waters in the north was into, and not out of, the lake. It was a disappointment for Sam not to pull off another dramatic encounter, and in her own way, Florence too was disappointed when she wrote, "We are very sorry as we cannot hear any news of poor Dr. Livingstone, how delightful it would be if we could only find him,"[2] as though she was speaking of a chance social encounter in Hyde Park.

One wonders to what extent Samuel was aware that the situation was far fom comfortable—indeed, that Kabarega was actually hostile. There is a strange innocence about his subsequent behaviour. He planned further exploration of Lake Albert and also an expedition to Mutesa of Buganda. He started a school of sorts, and a small boy called Cherri Merri, the son of the Prime

Minister, who had attached himself to Florence, provided a ready-made nucleus. Trade had commenced very profitably. He reckoned that the bartering of two-penny mirrors and knives for elephant tusks yielded a profit of 2,000 percent. He thought his colonial governorship was doing well.

Then one night, there was none of the usual nocturnal singing, dancing, and yelling, and the abnormal silence was disturbing. At 9 P.M. it was broken dramatically by a stupendous roll of drums, which was succeeded by a more deathly silence. All of a sudden, thousands of voices yelled, and thousands of fifes, drums, and whistles sounded, though not a soul could be seen. Samuel, still contemptuous of Bunyoro military potential, decided it was a demonstration of power, but of more power than in fact existed. He had himself once, when reduced to an inadequate escort, ordered it to play the stage army round and round the tent in which he was interviewing a potential enemy, for the same sort of reason. But with cool courage, he decided to treat the episode as a compliment and, by way of returning it, ordered his own band to play. Kabarega did not appear, but Samuel thought he was probably drunk, which was not unusual at that time of night. Also, he had become suspiciously elusive.

Presumably as a counterdemonstration, Sam and Julian held a military parade in the centre of Masindi, on the open ground in front of the palace, where Kabarega was wont to watch his "buffoons" giving their entertainments. The local population melted away as if by magic, and the great war drum sounded. Its hollow notes continued as thousands of warriors with shields and spears poured in from every quarter, yelling their war cries. Sam ordered his men into a battle square with fixed bayonets but told them not to shoot. He and Julian bravely left the battle square together and walked among the crowd. Finally, Sam led his soldiers through a narrow lane between the local warriors back to Government House. Little Cherri Merri stepped forward and, holding Sam's hand, marched all the way with him, an unwitting hostage. On arriving, he found that Florence, "my good little officer...my wife upon whose cool judgment I could always depend," had the situation well in hand. All hands were armed and competently placed for defence, and Sam's guns and the requisite ammunition were laid out for him.

The fact now had to be faced that Kabarega could call up a formidable army at a moment's notice. It was necessary to build a fort. Fences were based on heavy piles driven into the ground, and efficient earthworks were erected in a matter of days, and Sam installed his men within the foritifications. With their superior firearms, they could have held out indefinitely, had it not been for the shortage of food. A strange correspondence went on with Kabarega, who denied the responsibility for mobilising his army but who never appeared. He sent them a present of seven pots of pombe, or beer, which proved to be poisoned. Numbers of the men were laid low, but Sam dosed them all with tartar emetic, mustard, and brine, and none died. The three Bakers, either by luck or judgment, had not themselves drunk any.

This seemed to be real war, but Sam went on trying, and next day he walked calmly up and down the avenue leading to Government House, chatting to Florence and smoking his pipe. It was June 8, his birthday. Gradually, they became aware that many pairs of eyes were watching them from the bushes. Then shots were fired, and the sergeant walking behind Sam was killed by a bullet presumably meant for Sam. In some extraordinary way, like the highest-paid members of the cast of an adventure film, the Bakers always just escaped death. Sam and Florence ran for the fort, and the bugle was sounded to muster the defence. A volley of fire into the bushes routed the watchers, and fire missiles were thrown at Kabarega's palace and at the grass huts around it. Masindi, built mainly of dried grass, was soon in flames. Kabarega had already removed himself, and so, after an hour and a quarter, the battle of Masindi was apparently won.

With a telescope, the Bakers watched Karbarega's court reassemble on a hill 700 yards away. Incredible as it may seem, some sort of communications were resumed, in which the Omukama again denied all responsibility for the attack. All he wanted was peace. That was what Sam wanted, too, and he continued to think he could get it. Presents were once more exchanged, and Sam sent Kabarega what he described as a "cache-pot," which Florence, in a letter to the children, called a "flower-pot." They watched him holding it aloft in delighted triumph to show the court. Kabarega's son, Tito Winyi IV, who received many European visitors with gentle courtesy, used to point to a piece of crockery kept in his drawing room that Lady Baker had given his father. It seems likely that it was the same object.

Further attempts were made to reestablish friendly contact with the natives, but the result was more attacks. Finally, on June 10, when Florence was in her bath in the private apartment, the strength of the attack left no doubt that it was officially inspired. Florence, whose nerve had been cracking throughout the cat-and-mouse activities, especially after each near-miss suffered by Sam, persuaded him to give up hoping for Kabarega's friendship and to try to get away. Both Kamrasi and Kabarega had solicited Sam's help in attacking the rival claimant, Rionga, on his island in the Nile, 78 miles away. Sam decided to make a dash to Rionga. Still playing a sort of charade with himself, he thought he would depose the impossible Kabarega and put Rionga on the throne in his place.

The seven-day march to the Nile was a nightmare both in prospect and in the event. Apart from the expectation of attack, they knew that no food would be supplied to them in a country made hostile by Kabarega's decree. At the last moment, Florence revealed that she had stored away a quantity of flour in six iron chests especially for such an emergency. Their situation would have been desperate without this. With her usual competence, Florence packed such of their effects as could be carried by themselves and their men, as there were no fit transport animals. Samuel, incensed by what he felt was Kabarega's imcomprehens-ible behaviour, determined to scorch the earth behind him. Florence's "pretty little house" with most of its contents, including the out-sized pictures of ladies, were burned; then, in well-organised single file, they set off. Only one member of the company had ever travelled the path before, and that but once.

From Sam, rather than from Florence's eventual letters home, it is clear that they all, but especially Florence, suffered miserably during the ensuing days. She struggled for over 12 miles a day on blistered and septic feet, over rough bush or through deep swamp waters, carrying her own load and her own little revolver, with which she intended to shoot herself if Sam and Julian were killed. Many of the comforts they started with had to be shed as they went, and soon they were sleeping on the hard ground. On the last lap, Florence was literally dragged along by Sam. There was ambush after ambush when the men faced left and right in small batches and used their superior firepower effectively. Nonetheless, one wonders whether Kabarega really meant to kill the Bakers, or was just chivvying them out of his country. Once, a thrown spear passed only inches above Florence's head when she was crouched on one knee taking her place in the firing line. Her letters to the children after it was all over must have made strange reading in English schoolrooms, but the flavour is that of a description of a difficult cross-country railway journey, which Papa had organised very effectively. "Everybody would have been killed without Papa, but he managed everything so well that there was never much time lost in acting...."[3]

When the party reached the Nile, a stockade was built on suitable ground, and the construction of the canoes and rafts was begun for the crossing of the river. A message was sent to Rionga, and when contact was established with him, Samuel submitted, albeit reluctantly, to the ceremony of blood brotherhood in which each participant sucks a drop of the other's blood in a token of eternal friendship. Julian Baker and the Colonel in Chief went through similar ceremonies with Rionga's dignitaries. The affair of Kabarega's deposition and replacement by Rionga is treated unconvincingly by Sam, but he left some soldiers with Rionga to strengthen his attack on Kabarega. Then Sam left for Patiko, 79 miles away. His party, besides Florence and Julian, consisted of the Forty Thieves and porters supplied by Rionga. What seems, in retrospect, a completely senseless, slightly ridiculous but certainly courageous episode was over.

On August 1, the party was within ten miles of Patiko, and very early in the morning, it left on the last lap. A halt was called a mile or two short of the fort, and the Forty Thieves donned their scarlet tunics and white trousers. By then a horse was fit enough for Sam to mount and inspect his tiny regiment and to carry Florence for the last few miles. There was a rapturous welcome from old friends, but there was a hostile troop of traders in a camp almost adjacent to the fort. They attacked immediately without warning. Florence rushed out of her hut with Sam's rifle and cartridge belt, and the bugle was sounded for a bayonet charge. Florence, describing it for Agnes Baker at her boarding schools, says: "Papa did not give them much time—he rushed out of the zareeba, and immediately charged with the bayonets, and he fired as fast as he possibly could with his nice little rifle, which frightened everybody...." The traders' party panicked and ran, and Sam says that he and Julian pursued them for over four miles. They captured 306 cattle, over 100 slaves, 43 prisoners, 7 flags, and the traders' camp. One has to suspect the Sam was not understating the details. A ten-mile march and a four-mile bayonet charge was hungry work, and they had not as yet breakfasted. By the time they returned, Florence had a mutton curry all ready for them, and she had had one of the captured cattle milked, so they had lovely café au lait to drink. She had also stationed sentries on the huge rocks in the centre of the fort.

The stay at Patiko lasted nearly six months this time. Florence described the place as "quite the paradise of Africa." They seem to have got on better with the Acholi than with any other African people, and these were peaceful and happy months. The rocky eminence, designed by nature as a fort, looks out afar over fine country. Having lost his English doctor early in the journey and an Egyptian doctor later, Samuel was physician, surgeon, and dental surgeon when required. For some days he was busy attending to and operating on the wounded. He then set in train the strengthening of the fortifications, which he was anxious to accomplish before the holiday of Ramadan undermined his labour force.

Florence settled down in great contentment to her domestic duties, and one gets an excellent picture of the daily round from her diary. The repair of the family wardrobes has first priority. She makes herself two suits of "Bengal stripes," and Samuel gets two made of a brown material which she dyes herself and a grey flannel for the "shooting season." There is a rapid harvest from the seeds planted soon after their arrival, and they are eating cucumbers by the end of September. Florence pickles them but is dissatisfied with her home-brewed vinegar, which won't come out quite right. Karka is bottling butter, presumably for the next march. Florence packs nice shooting lunches for Sam and Julian, never forgetting the pepper and salt for the hard-boiled eggs. She deals constantly with matrimonial troubles among the servants. "Little Mahommet had a quarrel with both his wives today, and they came to say they are not going back to him, but I made it up with them all." Her servants are not allowed followers. The local ladies, clad lightly in fringes and beads, dance for them. A slave trader prisoner escapes, but he is killed, and his head brought back as proof. Florence thinks of the darling girls on Christmas Day while she drinks a not very good liqueur made from merissa ale and burned sugar. Alternately, she longs to be on the way home, or wishes she could stay at Patiko forever—that is, if only her hair were not falling out so alarmingly. At long last, after over two years, some English mail arrives, and there is lots of news. "That dear young creature the Duchess of St. Albans is dead....What a blow for him, poor man." And the Bakers' darling second daughter, Constance, has grown up and has been brought "out," and Florence regrets she was not at home to do the "bringing."

When Samuel left Rionga's, he said he intended to return when the weather was better to proceed with the deposition of Kabarega. It is possible that he needed to tell himself this while suffering the indignity of being virtually hunted out of Bunyoro. In fact, he never went back, and it is doubtful if Florence would have let him. At last, in spite of the delights of Patiko, she had had enough of both black and brown races, and she longed for England. On March 20, 1873, mounted on mules and carrying umbrellas, they left Patiko for Ismailia. They were homeward bound at last. The fort that they had made survived them and was later used by General Gordon. The natural feature is, of course, there today, and traces of the fortifications and the artificial caves are still visible.

A letter from Samuel Baker at Gondokoro to his sister claims that his mission had accomplished three things: it had abolished the slave trade; the countries between Gondokoro and the Equator had been annexed to Egypt; and, at his direction, a passage had been cleared through the Sudd for steamers. There was an element of truth in the last claim; in the first two, there was hardly any. He was very much on the defensive about his foray into Bunyoro with a hopelessly inadequate force. And on the strength of an unconfirmed rumour about wars in Bunyoro, he comforted himself with the erroneous conviction that he had actually brought about the deposition of Kabarega. In the field of discovery he had accomplished nothing. A personal wish to explore his Lake Albert further was almost certainly a contributory factor in his going to Bunyoro, but he had been thwarted in his attempt to get a steamer there, and had not been able to reach it overland before he was expelled. He persisted in his idea that Lakes Albert and Tanganyika were one and the same; a fact that had been already virtually disproved.

On the credit side, his two forts at Ismailia and Patiko later proved useful bases to his successor General Gordon, and he probably made a very small step towards the suppression of the slave trade. Samuel was to learn just how small a step it was as he sailed down the Nile, where it was patently still prospering. And he must have regretted that he had not concentrated his operations nearer to base and achieved more. He claimed that he had worked "with heart and soul" for the suppression of the trade. In an amateurish way, this may have been true, but it was a pity that his head had not been similarly engaged.

But Sam was brave, and by the standards of his day, he was also kind. There were tearful farewells to be said all the way. Some ladies whom he had liberated had to be removed forceably from around his neck by the Forty Thieves,and the farewell with the Thieves themselves at Gondokoro was no less affecting. Old Karka, who had followed them faithfully on both expeditions, was found a comfortable billet in Khartoum. They had planned to take her back to England, but she was not thought entirely suitable for English domestic life. They did take the small Ethiopian boy, Amarn, who Florence had rescued from a brutal master by hiding him under her full skirts, and he became a well-known member of their English household. In Cairo, the Khedive decorated both Sam and Julian, but he is thought to have been far from pleased with the expedition. Sam, for his part, was incensed at the Khedive's failure to punish Abou Saoud, on whom he laid all the blame for his misadventures. In England, they were welcomed as returning crusaders by the greatest in the land. They had been lost for so long and frequently reported dead, and their appearance once more on the platform at the Royal Geographical Society was an emotional occasion.

On both expeditions Florence had proved herself a real traveller. Always the great lady, her ability to organise domestic order in the wilds must have been an invaluable comfort. But competent though she was, her greatest quality was probably her diplomatic wisdom. Tales of El Sitt, the lady, are still told on the Upper Nile. In Acholi she was called the "Daughter of the Moon," and in Bunyoro "Morning Star." And it was in Bunyoro that Gordon's Provincial Governor, Emin Pasha, heard her spoken of with especial admiration. A sentence in Emin's imperfect English describes perhaps most clearly the greatest gift she had as Sam's companion. The Banyoro told him that she had been "the kind inter-mediatrice between her husband and our duty." A kind mediatrix, perhaps, between Victorian pomposity and very puzzled people.

The Bakers continued to be worldwide travellers, but never again on untrodden paths. They lived for most of the year at Sandford Orleigh House, near Newton Abbot in Devonshire, and Florence had a great reputation as a formidable chatelaine. Many grandchildren or great-nephews or great-nieces came to them for annual summer visits, which were looked forward to eagerly. Their first excitement was always a glimpse of Grandpapa Baker waving a white tablecloth from a point in his garden, from where he could see the train running up the Teign Valley. Then, after the drive in smart carriages from Newton Abbot station, there was a rapturous welcome on the doorstep from him and "Granny" Florence. The house was full with the heads of creatures that Sam had shot. The children's favourite was the head of the grinning crocodile, with a bead necklace in its jaws that had been found in its interior. There was always a luxurious table and bowls of Devonshire cream and strawberries in season for tea. The young ones were despatched to bed promptly at 6 P.M., but not before Florence had extracted some *langues de chat* from her secretary drawer. Guests of whatever age and social importance had to retire to their bedrooms at 10, so as not to keep the servants up. No doubt Florence's rules about followers were more easily enforced in Devonshire than at Patiko. But she was generous, and she could be amusing, even in Arabic, if the joke was esoteric. Samuel Baker was thought of as a great man, but it was Florence who ruled his household and probably his life.

General Gordon did two tours of service for the Khedive in the suppression of the slave trade, and he opened up many more

government stations. The trade was not suppressed in his life-
time, but it was much more thoroughly policed under his administration. Then, the progress was abruptly halted. In 1883, one of
the recurrent claimants for the title of Mahdi, or descendant of
the prophet, had arisen in the Sudan. The militant following that
he generated was sweeping everything before it, and Khartoum
and Gordon's advanced garrisons were threatened. By this time,
England was heavily involved in Egypt and had a responsibility
for these garrisons. Gordon was asked to go back to withdraw
them. He was, at the time, interesting himself in King Leopold's
Congo, and was under a promise to the King to go there as
Governor-General. He had kept in touch with Sam during his
Sudan years, and though well aware of Sam's mistakes, he
respected his knowledge. Sam, for his part, had been angry with
Gordon for his, probably sensible, employment of Abou Saoud in
his service, but he had forgiven him and had delighted in his
letters from the places he knew so well. He had resisted all
Gordon's attempts to lure him back so as to sail to the south end
of Lake Albert when the steamer eventually got there.

Now, in 1883, Gordon wrote to him from Brussels and asked
him to go to the Sudan as Governor-General in his place. Samuel
refused, but probably with reluctance, because he asked Gordon
to come to Sandford Orleigh. Gordon came at once, and Sam met
him at Newton Abbot station and took him straight away for a
long drive. Gordon's dynamic personality was irresistible, and
soon Sam was dreaming again of the glamour of colonial governorship and adventures in distant places. After the first hour of
driving, they were planning strategy together and discussing
personnel, and Sam was wild with enthusiasm and very excited.
Then they returned to Sandford Orleigh for tea. Florence knew
at once what had happened, but she waited for Sam to bring up
the subject. When he did, she said very quietly that it was impossible for her to go and that she would not let Sam go alone. And
that was that. Gordon left immediately for Khartoum.

Had Florence been prepared to face the discomforts and
dangers of the Sudan again, it might have been the bodies of Sam
and Florence that lay sprawled on the famous blood-stained
staircase at the residence in Khartoum in January 1884. But, of
course, Sam might have played it differently from Gordon. One

would not have really put it past him to have dressed up the local ostriches in scarlet uniforms with white trousers to impersonate General Wolseley's relief force and so frighten off the Mahdi. More seriously, had the relief forces got there as soon as Gordon, there was time, of which Gordon did not avail himself, to have extricated themselves and some at least of the garrisons before the Mahdi reached Khartoum. With Florence to counsel him, it is really quite likely that he would have done so. Gordon was a greater man, but he did not have Florence.

Sam died in December 1893, hating the idea that he had to desert his "Flooey," even in her safe, luxurious home surrounded by many kind relatives and friends. "Granny" Florence lived on at Sandford Orleigh until her own death 23 years later. She continued to provide a much-appreciated centre for the wide family circle until the end—always rather formidable, always very efficient, and always inspiring the greatest affection among the many young people who gathered round her.

NOTES

1. Anne Baker, *Morning Star* (London: William Kimber, 1972).
2. Ibid., p. 146.
3. Ibid., p. 160.

2

ALEXANDRINE TINNE:
Traveller

At a crossroads near Juba in the southern Sudan, an obelisk commemorates many of the travellers who, during the nineteenth century, endeavoured to solve the mystery of the origins of the White Nile. Among the names are those of two women: Florence Baker and Alexandrine Tinne. The name of Miss Tinne's mother, Henrietta Tinne, might very properly be there, too. For if the daughter was the driving force in their Nile travels, her devoted mother who accompanied her was an intrepid and competent traveller who, in fact, gave her life for her daughter's exploring aspirations.

Mrs. Tinne was a rich Dutch widow, and Alexandrine, or Alexine, was herself a great heiress. Though technically English, she thought of herself as Dutch. Her father, Philip Tinne, was Dutch by birth, but the vicissitudes of the Napoleonic wars had led him to sugar farming in the West Indies and thence to British nationality and a substantial Liverpool-based business. He was a widower with grown-up sons when, in 1830, he married Henrietta, or Harriet, van Capellen at The Hague. She belonged to an aristocratic Dutch naval family, with a close connection to the Dutch royal house. One of her sisters was lady-in-waiting to the Queen, and another to the Russian-born Queen dowager. The Tinne family, which had moved about Europe as a result of recurrent Protestant persecutions, claimed descent from a crusader who had distinguished himself on the third crusade by clambering to a foothold on the stone walls of the Saracen fortress at Rosetta. The name Tinne is actually derived from a German word for stone parapet.

Philip and Harriet made their home in a fine town house at The Hague. For people of their kind, the Dutch capital was doubtless more congenial and gayer than Liverpool. There, in 1835, Alexandrine Petronella Francina Tinne was born. She was the long-awaited and much-wanted daughter of Philip's old age and of Harriet's middle age. In 1845, while wintering with his family in southern Europe, Philip Tinne died in Rome. Alexine was only 9 and her mother 47.

Alexine's critics, of whom there are many, should remember that she was taken on adventurous travels from a very early age, first, by both parents, and then, by her mother. The nomadic passion that led in the end to disaster was inculcated by the mother and then shared by mother and daughter with great mutual enjoyment. Both were formidable personalities, and they were devoted to each other. Alexine's education was excellent. European languages were a necessity in the Tinne's social world, and she eventually acquired considerable knowledge of Arabic and some other non-European languages. She became an accomplished pianist, and painted just well enough to give herself pleasure when travelling. On the scientific side, she proved an efficient botanist in virgin fields and, what was rare at the time, an amateur photographer. The Tinne carriage at The Hague was fitted out so that it could be used as a darkroom. The stimulating life of other European capitals was in itself an education, and Alexine grew up to be a very adequate young lady. She was not a great beauty but, from photographs, the face is attractive and humorous. A marble bust of her when she was quite young shows refined features and a gentle expression. Only the small mouth betrays formidable strength of will.

The railway lines were only just reaching out over Europe when the Tinnes travelled together in the 1850s. If there was a gap in the railway network as they crossed the Continent, a whole diligence was engaged for the party. In Scandinavia, they did mountain journeys of many days' duration, in convoys of one-seater pony carriages, accompanied by a grumbling but devoted Dutch maid, Flora, several menservants, and a lot of dogs. In the Pyrenees, they rode horses over the mountain passes.

As they travelled, the mother received several tentative offers for the hand of her charming daughter, but no one was encouraged until a dashing, young military attaché arrived at The Hague from Saxony. He was Joseph Königsmark, a member of a well-known German family. It was indeed said to have been on account of an earlier dashing young Königsmark that the Elector of Hanover, who became George I of England, imprisoned his young wife Dorothea. Alexine became great friends with the young soldier, and it was generally thought that such a marriage into a good German Protestant family was ideally suitable for her. In 1855 she went to Dresden to attend a ball given by the Königsmarks. It is not known what went wrong, but something happened on the night of the ball to make Alexine wish never to see her soldier again. A couple of years later he was still pursuing her on her travels, even as far away as Turkey. All her mother was ever able to persuade her to do again was to bear his company occasionally at a hotel dinner table—and this only after overwhelming solicitation and adroit manoeuvering on his part. When they finally said goodbye to him, both mother and daughter were sincerely sorry for him.

It was because of whatever had upset her at the Königsmarks' ball that Harriet decided to take Alexine on the grand tour. They were moving towards Vienna when news of a cholera epidemic diverted them in Venice. There they discovered that there were passenger ships, steamers with auxiliary sails, plying between Trieste and Alexandria. The temptation to visit Egypt was too much for them. Maybe Alexine remembered her redoubtable ancestor of Rosetta fame, and thought it would be romantic to visit the scene of his exploits. In any case, the Middle East has always attracted European travellers. Shepheard's Hotel in Cairo in 1856 was tremendously fashionable. It was then in the old city, and in appearance it resembled an oriental fortress, which no doubt added to its charms, if not to its comforts. When the Tinnes arrived, there were 300 Europeans at dinner in the vast dining room. Many of these would have been in transit to or from India, a category of travellers for whom the hotel principally existed; but many were wealthy and distinguished tourists, and their company was doubtless congenial.

With their Dutch retinue, the Tinnes remained for nearly two years in the Middle East. The winters were spent in Egypt and the summers in Palestine. Even by the standards of the wealthy tourists of the time, they were exceptionally enterprising and courageous. Twice they sailed up the Nile by dahabiyah, which was quite an undertaking. Harriet did all the hiring negotiations herself and insisted on being in command of the vessel. The crew added to her own party made a formidable number of persons to feed, and livestock and vegetables had to be carried for the commissariat.

The long river passages were enlivened by social life. There were callers, and English milords, with dahabiyahs as fast and as expensive as theirs, raced with them and escorted them on visits to the great temples. Alexine always had to go one better than all the rest. At Luxor, when returning from their first voyage to the first cataract at Aswan, she had a strong wish to see the Red Sea. Her mother very much disliked camel riding, but she submitted to many exhausting days of trotting on a donkey across the desert to satisfy her. On the second voyage, they rode round the first cataract, their mountainous baggage loaded onto camels, and reembarked in less luxurious craft for Wadi Halfa. There, much to their annoyance, the second cataract halted them. In the summers they settled in well-appointed quarters in the hills behind Beirut, and made long expeditions in the Biblical lands to Jerusalem, the Dead Sea, Damascus, and the Cedars of Lebanon. And they not only kept up with, but magnificently overtook, the travelling Joneses when, at vast expense, they visited Palmyra in Northern Arabia on the trade route to Mecca. Their Bedouin guides, though urging them to hurry away in the interests of their safety, assured them that they had stayed longer than any other Europeans. The money was deemed well spent.

In September 1857, they at last turned their footsteps homeward. They travelled slowly through Turkey, the Aegean Sea, Greece, Austria, Poland, and Germany, and it was with enormous pleasure that they finally reached their beloved home at The Hague. The family circle welcomed them rapturously, relieved and delighted to see them again, and their Egyptian cook,

Halib, was quite a sensation. Harriet had had her fill of oriental travels. She would have been more than content never to leave her house again, save for congenial family visiting in Holland and England—at least, so she told herself at the time.

Interest in the still undiscovered sources of the White Nile had been quickening throughout the nineteenth century. Several Egyptian expeditions had attempted the ascent of the river, and one, in 1840, had reached a point above Gondokoro, near Juba, in latitude 4°N, before being stopped by cataracts. In the mid-nineteenth century, missionaries on the East African coast heard from Arab traders about the existence of vast lakes in the interior. In 1858, Richard Burton and John Hanning Speke went to explore these lakes, hoping that they might prove to be the chief sources of the Nile. They disagreed on their findings, and Speke, who was convinced that the lake he called Victoria Nyanza was a Nile reservoir, returned to it in 1860 with James Grant to attempt a descent of the river. There was, naturally, worldwide interest in the subject at the time. One of Anthony Trollope's rural clergymen grumbles about the excessive number of articles on the Nile sources currently appearing in periodicals. If Barsetshire was reading of it, how much more must it have been a topic of conversation at the dinner tables of Cairo, where there had been speculation as to the origin of the life-giving seasonal floods for thousands of years, and where fascinating legends abounded of mysterious fountains, lakes, and snow-covered mountain peaks. Alexine, having explored the lower reaches of the river as a tourist, began to dream of playing some part in the quest for its beginnings. Dreaming led to determination, and Harriet's retirement in the peace and elegance of The Hague was over.

In 1860, preparations were already in train for an ambitious Nile journey. How accurate a picture of their intentions they gave to their relatives is not clear. Anxiety about them seems to have been more on account of their travelling without a suitable gentleman escort than of the dangers of tropical illness and possible hostile peoples. Actually, beyond a vague intention of exploring the Nile, they had formulated no plans. Harriet may have been overpersuaded by Alexine, but she enjoyed the excitement of acquiring what she thought were the necessities of travel beyond the bounds of civilisation. There had to be furniture, including brass bedsteads and a piano, silver, china, and such camping comforts as were then available.

In July 1861, Alexine sailed from Amsterdam for Marseilles with the Dutch menservants, two ladies' maids—grumpy Flora and her own maid, Anna—a number of dogs, and a mountain of baggage. Harriet Tinne went overland to Marseilles with her sister, Adriana van Capellen, Alexine's Aunt Addy, who was suffering from an acute depression. She was said "never to have smiled again" as a result of an unfortunate love affair in Russia, whither she had accompanied her royal mistress, the Queen dowager. Her lover was probably the dowager's nephew, the Czar Alexander II, who was married. She had resigned the royal service and had retired to a life of apathy at The Hague, when the strong-minded Harriet decided that travel in the Middle East might renew her interest in life, and perhaps even bring back her smiles. Her sister and niece were delighted to have her company, but she was not a good traveller, and the enterprise was doomed to tragic failure.

From September 1861 until January 1862, the Tinnes kept a splendid establishment on the outskirts of old Cairo, and they entertained lavishly. Two of the leading families of the European community were the de Lesseps and the de Bellefonds. Members of both families had travelled far up the Nile, and they tried to persuade the Dutch ladies to abandon their dangerous project. Alexine, in reply, and whether teasing or boasting one can only guess, expressed her intention of ascending the river and crossing the continent to the island of Fernando Poo in the Gulf of Guinea. In fact, her plans were not even then at all definite, and they eventually set out for Khartoum with the intention of playing it by ear and deciding where to go when they got there. One possibility was to spend the summer in Ethiopia, and they carried suitable introductions to the Emperor Theodore. Aunt Addy, after some indecision, decided to go with them as far as Khartoum.

A convoy of three dahabiyahs was necessary to transport the expedition upriver. A tremendous throng of Cairo residents and visitors came to give the traditional, and in this case apprehensive, send-off to the party. In the first boat were the Europeans, including the Dutch servants, Halib the cook, the other local servants, and the party of dogs which had been augmented by various stray puppies collected in Cairo. Throughout the voyage, these dogs caused considerable delay, because twice a day the whole convoy had to be halted while they were taken ashore to relieve themselves. Osman Aga, whom they had originally picked up in Palestine, sailed with them as Wakil. There was a great deal of livestock, both for transport and the table, and quantities of fodder for its consumption.

This time the dahabiyahs were lightened in order to be pulled up the cataracts by as many as 200 men. Alexine, who by now spoke reasonable Arabic, remained on board in charge of this operation, and the rest of the party took the heavy baggage round the falls on camels and donkeys. When the second cataract had been safely negotiated and the expedition had been reassembled at Philae, Alexine ordered musicians and dancers for a celebration, and the gaiety went on far into the night. The Tinnes were certainly travelling in the grand manner and were apparently respected for it. From Philae it was only three days' travel to Korosko, where they said goodbye to their dahabiyah fleet and assembled their caravan for the desert crossing to Abu Hamed, which cuts off the great westerly loop of the Nile.

Introductions from the de Lesseps and the de Bellefonds facilitated the organisation of the caravan, and a handsome young Nubian, Sheikh Ahmad, well practised in the desert road, was willing to take charge. There were 6 guides, 30 camelmen, 102 camels, and many horses and donkeys, and Harriet felt proud of her splendid train. A special arrangement of mattresses and cushions was constructed on a camel for Aunt Addy; nonetheless, she loathed the 18 days of hot desert journey. The dogs rode in panniers on the camels, probably disliking it just as much. Alexine, on horseback and escorted by the glamorous young Sheikh who admired her greatly, strayed continuously from side to side of the road in order to see the countryside. Harriet, on a white donkey, was thus always ahead of the caravan, and the first to encounter and pay the tiresome wayside demands for baksheesh. On rejoining the Nile at Abu Hamed, Aunt Addy was put on a boat for her greater comfort, and, pausing at Berber to watch the festivities at the end of Ramadan, the caravan continued to Darbar. There, another large convoy of boats was hired for the journey to Khartoum, which they reached on April 4, well over three months after their departure from Cairo.

A Mudir, or Provincial Governor, ruled at Khartoum on behalf of Ottoman Egypt. The chief business of the town was connected in one way or another with the lucrative ivory trade, and many wealthy merchants were based there. Originally, the trade had been largely a European monopoly, but by the 1850s, it was to a great extent in Egyptian hands. The mechanics of ivory collecting were inextricable from slave trading, and the Egyptian merchants were heavily implicated in it. Being technically Ottoman subjects, the trade was known as the Turkish slave trade. It was probably impossible for the European merchants not to be, at least indirectly, involved in it as well. The European society consisted of merchants, several of whom acted as Consuls, and many of whom had wives or accompanying ladies of some kind, and the Austrian missionaries, the Verona Fathers. In addition, there were occasional adventurous European travellers. When the Tinnes arrived, two Italians had just returned in wretched health from Gondokoro, and it was hoped that before long, Speke and Grant would arrive in the course of their historical journey down the Nile from the source. Many of the residents were experienced in travelling in the south of the Sudan, and as Cairo friends had done, they warned the Tinnes of the all-too-serious dangers. This may have accounted for Alexine's being sulky and even discourteous in the Khartoum society, but it certainly did nothing to discourage her. She was determined to go higher up the Nile.

The Dutch menservants had had more than enough of foreign travel, and they attached themselves to the Italian party returning to Cairo. This meant that the Wakil, Osman Aga, assumed a greater importance, and he assisted with the preparations. Flora and Anna were sufficiently brave, or sufficiently devoted, to continue. Harriet had to send for more money to buy all the supplies necessary for a long period away, and they were swindled on all sides, especially by the Mudir. They were slow to realise what a den of slave-raiding thieves Khartoum was. There was by then one steamer there, and Harriet tried to hire it. It belonged to the Egyptian Governor of the Sudan, who was absent, and all that Monsieur Tanyon, the Frenchman in charge of it, could offer was a steamer tow upriver for a large dahabiyah. The Mudir, for an enormous sum payable in advance, supplied an escort of soldiers who travelled in a second boat with Alexine's horse and donkey. Tents and trading goods were taken for travel in the bush. Finally, an Italian bricklayer was included, because there was a project to build a house on an island site at some-where like Gondokoro. The departure was on May 4, and all the Khartoum friends waited for them a short way upriver and gave the party a gay farewell dinner.

The first part of the voyage was not enjoyable: the scenery was dull and disappointing. Illness began to manifest itself, and Harriet began to realise that she had taken on grave responsibilities. Then, the horrifying sights of the big slave depot at Jebel Dinka overwhelmed even Alexine. Feeling compelled to do something about it, she provided a herd of oxen for thousands of starving wretches, and personally rescued one family by purchasing them. She must have been beginning to realise the immensity of the traffic and the overwhelming power of the traders. Two women whom she rescued by purchase stayed with her, and one, Rosa, was still with her at her death. She may not have realised the extent to which she laid herself open to accusations of impli-cation in the slave trade by these purchases, and, indeed, it was difficult for any Nile traveller to avoid such accusations at the time.

From a camp above Jebel Dinka, Harriet returned in the stea-mer to Khartoum, where she succeeded in hiring it outright but at enormous cost. While there, the Nile explorers Samuel and Florence Baker arrived. They had been travelling in the Blue Nile regions but were now bent on playing what part they could in the main Nile quest. Harriet guessed that Baker wanted her steamer, or at least a steamer tow for his dahabiyah, and managed to slip away without his knowledge. This fact no doubt contributed to the acrimony of his private comments about the Dutch ladies. His main criticism was on the unsuitability of a young, unmar-ried girl circulating amongst the naked Dinka and Shilluk tribes. The triumphant Harriet in her steamer, and towing yet another nuggar full of supplies, rejoined her party above Jebel Dinka in a four-day trip from Khartoum.

For all the evidence of their eyes, the ladies still found it difficult to believe that the courteous Arab gentlemen who came to the steamer to pay their respects were involved in what was becoming almost the main commerce of the river system. At Kaka, five days farther on, dancing was arranged for their delight by a local merchant, only to be followed up by the offer of a partnership in a big slave empire, where, presumably, a Tinne capital investment could have been fruitful. Kaka turned out to be nothing but a vast slave zeriba, or stockade, and they were glad to leave it. As they entered the Shilluk country, in spite of Samuel Baker's comments, the visits of charmingly mannered but stark-naked young chiefs proved very agreeable. An attempt to explore up the eastern Sobat tributary failed, because there were no trees to provide fuel for the steamer's boilers. They returned and sailed up the Nile to Lake No, at the junction of the Bahr el Ghazal and the Bahr el Jebel, or White Nile. Turning south there, they went up the latter, winding interminably through the dense river vegetation of the Sudd, where they had continual trouble with tow ropes. The ladies sat on board under an awning and sewed or painted the passing scene, apparently pleased with themselves.

After three weeks, the cumbersome flotilla reached Holy Cross, where there was a mission station of the Verona Fathers. Many African travellers have experienced the companionship and commented on the unexpected gaiety of Catholic Fathers in the bush, and the Tinnes made great friends at the mission. Good Dutch Protestants though they were, they found the Roman Mass wonderfully comforting amidst the horrid savagery of the river commerce. Two of the Fathers took Alexine exploring, and one of them rode with her in an effort to overtake Mr. and Mrs. Petherick who had passed through Holy Cross southbound not long before. Petherick had come out originally as a mining surveyor in Muhammad Ali's service, but by then, he had acquired his own trading network in Kordofan, while also acting as British Consul. Being well acquainted with the upper navigable reaches of the Nile, he had been given a sum of money, raised in England, in order to arrange for supplies to be available at Gondokoro if and when Speke and Grant should arrive. He had been very much delayed while about his own affairs and was now hurrying south, afraid that Speke would appear before he delivered the goods. His wife, Anne, was with him. Alexine's intention was to offer to take the goods herself in the steamer, and Petherick would probably have been glad to accept, but they were not able to catch up with him.

The Fathers had a terrible tale to tell about the depletion of their numbers through malaria and blackwater fever; one after another of their stations had been closed by the death rate. But the intrepid travellers were not discouraged and regretfully took their leave and sailed on. Just short of Gondokoro, which the flotilla reached on September 29, they suffered the serious loss of Osman Aga, the Wakil who had served them well. He was drowned while trying to prevent one of the dahabiyahs from drifting downstream when the tow rope broke. A quick expedition above Gondokoro confirmed what they must have known: that the river was no longer navigable. They were at a dead end. Several of the party had had fever, and now Alexine went down with it very badly and was delirious for five days. Aunt Addy and the Dutch maids were miserable the whole time. Finally, the splendid hopes of building a residence by the Nile, at almost the highest-known point of its course, were abandoned. They sailed back to Khartoum in three and a half weeks, passing on the way Samuel Baker, who, probably still jealous of the steamer, had some acid comments to make on the excessive tourist traffic then to be met with in those out-of-the-way places.

Harriet and Alexine were far from satisfied, and apparently not at all discouraged. In spite of Alexine's illness, which was probably the main reason for the quick return, they had enjoyed themselves for most of the time. Harriet confessed to loving the "damn-me don't care" sort of life she had been leading, and Alexine's ambitions were far from fulfilled; she had done no pioneering nor blazed any trail. Having failed to get far up the White Nile, they decided to explore the Bahr el Ghazal. Perhaps up this river they would find the great lakes or snowy peaks of legend. Aunt Addy's nerve had gone, either for exploring or for returning to Cairo, so she stayed to worry and fuss miserably in Khartoum. On the other hand, the party had grown by the addition of the Austrian Consul, Baron von Heuglin, a German scientist called Steudner, and a Dutchman, Baron d'Ablaing. They had various scientific interests, and von Heuglin had a brief to watch out for news of the German explorer Vogel, who had crossed the Sahara with the British-sponsored expedition and who had disappeared in the direction of Lake Chad. In agreeing to let them join her party, Alexine made it quite clear that it was her expedition.

They left at the beginning of January. The flotilla this time consisted of the steamer, a dahabiyah, and three nuggars. In addition, d'Ablaing had his own boat. They took provisions for six months and the necessary ammunition for 70 soldiers. Besides the sheep and poultry for the table, there were the transport animals, Alexine's horse, 40 donkeys, four camels, and a couple of mules. The steamer which had proved useful in the Sudd on the White Nile became a liability on the western river. The Nile had been exceptionally high, whereas the Bahr el Ghazal was exceptionally low, and the steamer's paddle wheels were continually clogged with vegetation. It took three weeks to get to the Mashra al Riqq, a broadening of the river where a great many Nile craft were lying-to. Transport from here was normally overland. The rainy season was not far off, and von Heuglin and Steudner went ahead on mules to prospect for a healthy site where the expedition could stay during the rainy months. While at Wau, a hundred miles to the west, Steudner died of blackwater fever, and von Heuglin returned to the Mashra in great distress. Things were not very good there. D'Ablaing had fetched more supplies from Khartoum in the steamer, but porters to carry the mass of baggage seemed to be unobtainable. Petherick's arrival about his trading affairs eased the situation, but even with his help, 500 porters took some finding. None of the Europeans seems to have contemplated for a moment the possibility of foregoing any of their comforts or amusements or the elaborate materials for their several ploys. The great, unwieldy caravan set out in May, with Harriet in a carrying chair and Alexine and the Dutch maids mounted on donkeys.

The rains came early, and dramatic, deluging storms contributed to difficulties and discomforts. The porters were inclined to mutiny over food shortages and deprivations, but Alexine controlled them with formidable authority. Then, the soldiers threatened disobedience, and she successfully dealt with them and made them throw down their arms. She seems to have been ill some of the time and to have travelled on a stretcher, which cannot have been enjoyable. But the country was changing, and nature began to compensate for the discomforts. Wau, where Steudner had died, proved to be a naturalist's paradise. There were thousands of birds on the banks of the Bahr Wau for von Heuglin's ornithological collection and, of especial delight to Alexine, luxuriant wild flowers. In time, a notable collection of the flora of the region, either pressed or carefully drawn, was sent to Vienna for publication.

Moving always westwards in the direction of the Gossinga Mountains, their way led from one slave zeriba to another, and they paused at one belonging to a notorious trader called Buselli. In time, they realised that Buselli was robbing them over food prices and was delaying their progress by every means in his power. Alexine realised that they were probably in some danger from him, and knew they should move quickly. Unfortunately, the report of bad floods ahead made it necessary to set up camp only a few miles to the west. With the arrival of the rains, the regular trading caravans had all departed towards the Mashra and the river transport. The Tinne expedition was, therefore, isolated and without means of communication for some months. But still revelling in the beauty of the countryside, and in spite of outbreaks of illness, the ladies, dressed always, with the help of their ladies' maids, in their unsuitable crinolines, settled down to a camp life of some elegance. All the time they were watching for an opportunity to continue westwards.

Then, in the second half of July, disaster came. Harriet, the one member of the party who had never been ill, went down with blackwater fever. She was desperately ill for days but rallied, and they began to think of moving on. Then, on the morning of July 25, she was found dead in bed. As is so common with death, Alexine was not at first able to take it in; then, the reality all but overwhelmed her. Her relationship with her mother had been one of rare quality: they had shared companionable delight in their wanderings, satisfaction in their achievements, and much laughter. But even if Harriet travelled gladly, Alexine must have known that it was really her mother's great love for her that had brought her to these unhealthy wilds. For the satisfaction of her own ambitions, she had accepted that love quite ruthlessly, and had ruthlessly pressed on in the face of all warnings. Remorse must have added a terrible burden to the miseries of the ensuing weeks and, indeed, of the ensuing years. Her greatest comfort immediately was grumpy, devoted, old Flora, who had travelled the world with them since Alexine was a child. But she did not have her for long; just a month later she, too, died of fever and was buried alongside her beloved mistress.

To return to Khartoum now seemed the only thing possible for Alexine, though she was not able to get away until the early days of 1864. Her own maid Anna was now her chief support and comfort, and both von Heuglin and d'Ablaing decided to go with her. Von Heuglin had hoped to explore the watershed between the Nile and the next river system to the west, towards which the expedition had been heading, and it must have been a bitter disappointment to him to turn back. But both he and d'Ablaing had had frequently recurring bouts of fever and dysentery, and in fact, they travelled most of the way on stretchers. From their own point of view, they were certainly right to return, and no doubt they felt duty bound to escort the desolate girl.

All this time poor Aunt Addy, worrying herself sick in Khartoum, had had no news. The Pethericks had been there from time to time and had showed her kindness, but she was too anxious about her relatives to accept their offer of an escort to Cairo. Speke and Grant arrived dramatically, having successfully made their way from the coast of East Africa and all but followed the course of the Nile from the Victoria Nyanza. Neither of them was a linguist, and they were glad of Addy's English-speaking company in the polyglot society of Khartoum; she was certainly glad of theirs. She consulted Speke about the dangers of travelling up the Bahr el Ghazal, and he was disturbed to hear that her sister and niece were there at the time. His were not the prudish reasons of Samuel Baker. He knew the health hazards all too well, and from his unique knowledge of the lie of the land, he judged that there could not be anything of geographical interest to discover for a long way up the great western tributary. At Addy's insistence, he wrote a letter to this effect to the Tinnes. He also warned them that it was dangerous to proceed with too

large a caravan because of the ever-recurrent difficulties in pro-
visioning it. If they ever received this letter, they took no notice
of even this later caution. Speke and Grant went on their way,
and Addy went on fretting and worrying for months. Eventually,
it became unbearable to remain inactive, and she decided to
despatch a rescue or relief party. With some competence, she
mustered 75 soldiers and considerable quantities of provisions
and despatched them to look for the Tinne expedition.

Alexine's caravan was in dire distress when it met the relief
party at Wau on the homeward journey. Adequate supplies of
food and water had proved impossible to find, and mutiny threatened all the time. The local peoples along the route, associating
any caravan with the slave traders, had frequently been hostile.
It is probably not too much to say that without Aunt Addy's relief
party, the caravan might not have got through. Even with its
help, the journey was desperate, and there was more tragedy. On
January 22, Anna sickened and died. In terrible loneliness,
Alexine hurried on to the Mashra ahead of von Heuglin and
d'Ablaing on their stretchers.

The dahabiyahs she had ordered to meet her there had been
delayed by the Governor of Khartoum, who had exacted an
exorbitant toll before he had allowed them to depart, and also by
unusually dense river vegetation as they came through the Sudd.
But in time, a flotilla was assembled, and all that was left of the
Tinne expedition sailed eastwards. The journey was slow. Long
passages had to be hacked through the Sudd in advance of the
boats, and it was not until March 29 that they approached
Khartoum. The men of the party went on ahead to break the
news of so many tragedies to poor suffering Addy. Petherick was
in Khartoum at the time and went with them. He had been in
touch with Alexine's half brother in Liverpool over the absence
of news, and was anxious to help in any way he could. Cables
were sent to the family, and to the Royal Geographical Society,
which had begun to take an interest in the expedition.

Alexine sailed her boats a short way downriver and remained
on board. Apart from her grief, her situation was embarrassing.
Great kindness was shown her by the local society, but conscious
of her guilt, she must have sensed criticism. Poor headstrong girl,
she had ignored all advice, and she had failed tragically. Her

botanical collection and von Heuglin's bird collection were to prove useful. She had measured the distance between the Bahr el Ghazal stations, but Petherick had thoroughly explored the river system already. For four lives and an expenditure of over £15,000,very little had been added to the knowledge of the Nile waterways. It was only human that she should thrash about for scapegoats: the Governor of Khartoum had deliberately delayed her boats, and his financial demands had been extortionate; Buselli had deliberately delayed her progress westwards. She set complaints in motion through her high-powered Dutch relatives at King-Khedive level. It was probably ill-advised and certainly useless, but to be able to take some action in distress is comforting. Also, she knew that her family and friends might be critical of her, and perhaps she thought it would help to spread the load of blame.

Fourteen months of constant anxiety had put a severe strain on Aunt Addy. She had survived to see her niece's return, but she was already ill. The news of the deaths of her sister and the faithful Dutch maids prostrated her, and within two months of Alexine's return, she died and was buried on an island in the Nile. Alexine was bereft of all the affection with which her life had been surrounded; even her most beloved dogs had perished. Von Heuglin was dutifully attentive, but she never found him congenial. Together they struggled to organise dahabiyahs to go north from Khartoum, which had become abhorrent. The Governor and officials were openly hostile, and it was only with difficulty that they got away early in July. The Pethericks, bound directly for Cairo, went with them as far as Berber. There they camped for two months and organised a caravan to transport their baggage and their precious collections across 250 miles of desert to Suakin on the Red Sea. The Nile route was now distasteful to Alexine, and they may have thought that the desert road and sea transport to Suez was safer for the specimens of flora and fauna.

The desert journey in the late summer heat was an ordeal. Suakin at the end of October brought the comfort of the kindly hospitality of some French nuns and contacts with European Consuls. Travelling with Alexine was a young Sudanese of "deepest chocolate hue" called Abdullah ben Said. He had been

with her on the Bahr el Ghazal expedition and was to stay with
her always, becoming, in time, her most confidential employee.
Years after her death, he maintained that from Suakin she sailed
across the Red Sea to Jidda, the port of Mecca. There is no
evidence of this from other sources, for Harriet had been the
main diarist, and after her death, details of the travels are
missing. If the story is true, it is conceivable that the distraught
girl entertained the mad possibility of travelling to the Holy
Places of Islam in order to restore her self-respect. If it did
happen, von Heuglin was wisely discreet about it, and she must
have returned immediately, because within a few weeks, they
embarked their precious collections on board a cargo ship and
sailed together for Suez. It is, of course, possible that their ship
called at Jidda on the way, and Abdullah, as a Muslim, would have
remembered it especially.

Alexine would have liked to avoid Cairo, with all its associations of happy days there with her mother, but it was not
possible. In the end, she stayed there for 18 months. Her English
half brother, John Tinne, and his wife went out to her as soon as
she arrived, but were quite unsuccessful in their efforts to
persuade her to go home with them. This is understandable. She
knew that she would find kindness with her family, but she
would have been apprehensive of the unspoken criticism which
would have been hard to bear. In a commodious house in old
Cairo, she acquired the aura of a tragic femme fatale. Dressed
always as an Arab women, and surrounded by countless servants
and their wives and children, the inevitable dogs, and quantities
of the ethnographic souvenirs of her travels, she became one of
the sights for exclusive tourists to see. Apart from formal callers
who were always suitably introduced, she does not seem to have
been very sociable. Nor does she seem to have been popular with
Egyptian authorities, and they expressed no sympathy over her
complaints about the Governor of Khartoum. She now wanted
to build a house on an island in the Nile near Cairo. Her long-
suffering brother was told to send out a man of affairs to
negotiate this for her, but she came up against Egyptian
officialdom and was not allowed to purchase the island site. John
Tinne was probably blessedly relieved. Even when she was

settled down in the comparative safety of Cairo, his father's daughter was a heavy responsibility.

It was not to last long. Alexine disliked the heat of her first summer in Cairo, and in 1866 she packed up her house, despatched many of her effects to England, and hired a yacht in which to sail the Mediterranean. Her botanical collection had already been sent to the Imperial Herbarium of the Court of Vienna, where it was used as the basis of a splendid and botanically important publication. Many of her vast household were Negroes, and she could not abandon them to possible slavery in Egypt, so she took them all with her. Abdullah ben Said was now her cook, and her personal maid, a Negress, was probably his wife. The mixed retinue caused quite a sensation at Mediterranean ports, but Europe seems to have become meaningless, if not positively unattractive, to Alexine. She sailed about as the spirit moved her, only making contact with her family when supplies of money and European commodities were needed. The hired yacht failed to give satisfaction, and John Tinne was told to buy one and send it out to her. With the purchase price, fitting out, and the hiring of a crew, it cost £4,000 to deliver at Toulon. She registered it under Dutch ownership with herself as master, and she spent more money on decorating it. But it gave her no more satisfaction than the hired yacht, and she said it was a hideous shape. In a short time, she landed in Algiers, persuaded some of the Dutch crew to stay with her, and told her brother to sell it.

From all accounts, an outbreak of cholera at Algiers temporarily harnessed Alexine's real talents and generosity. Perhaps this shows that her tragedy was the enforced idleness of riches. She passed her time intelligently enough—with her music, languages, botany, and photography—but a real purpose that measured up to her dynamic personality and was yet within her scope did not come her way. The epidemic over, Algiers began to seem too civilised and boring. Inevitably, from the North African coast, it was the Sahara that beckoned. She became interested in everything that she could hear about the Tuareg, and she applied herself to their language, Tamashek, and began to plan a desert journey.

Years later, Abdullah ben Said described the proud emotion with which he remembered watching the great caravan of his Roumi princess passing out through the old Bab el Zoun of Algiers. As he remembered, there were 135 camels and a vast regiment of attendants. Among the latter were the Dutch sailors from the yacht, including the captain and his wife. They were all dressed as Bedouins. They left in late December 1867, and the first day of 1868 found them in the bitter cold of the Saharan Atlas Mountains, crossing the low range between Djelfa and Laghourt. The caravan was proving no easier to command than any other, with the Dutch sailors as troublesome as anyone, and the Dutch captain and his drunken wife the most troublesome of all. From the Atlas range, there were tremendous and enticing panoramas of the Sahara, but Alexine turned eastwards and went to Touggourt. She may have intended to go south from there, but relations with the Dutch captain had become intolerable, so she turned north, and after another bitterly cold mountain crossing, reached the coast at Philippeville, where she finally disbanded the caravan.

The Dutch captain and most of the sailors were sent home, not without apprehension as to the mischievous stories they would probably tell in Holland. Abdullah ben Said became her principal adjutant and confidant. With one of his wives and a child, he went with her on a shopping expedition to Malta in the summer of 1868, and they rejoined the rest of the household in October, this time at Tripoli. This proved much more congenial to Alexine than Algiers, though, in what was then a Turkish dominion, the trans-Saharan slave trade was even more harrowing than that on the Nile. It was, in fact, the location of Tripoli at the head of one of the main trans-Saharan trade routes that was its main attraction for Alexine, for she was determined to go across the Sahara. The plan she had formulated was to travel south to Bornu and Lake Chad and then to turn east towards Darfur, possibly reaching Khartoum by way of the Bahr el Ghazal. This journey in reverse was one of the original plans she had had when ascending the Bahr el Ghazal. Except for its tragic associations, it is easy to understand that she may have wanted to give some meaning to that disastrous episode. Possibly after an inter-

val of time, the associations may even have been an added induce-
ment. She had left some lonely graves along the route.

Alexine's stay in Tripoli coincided with that of Gustav Nachtigal. Originally a doctor in the Prussian army, ill health had
brought him to North Africa some years earlier. He had been
physician to the Bey of Tunis and had studied Arabic and Muslim
customs. He was now planning a journey to Kuka, the capital of
Bornu, at the request of the King of Prussia, who wished to send
presents to the Sultan of Bornu as a token of gratitude for the
Sultan's kindness to German travellers. It was natural that he
and Alexine should discuss their plans together, but in Tripoli,
though he helped her in some ways, she remained the aloof
aristocrat of Cairo report. He was relieved that there was little of
"emanicipated woman" about her, and he was shyly respectful of
her position and her travelling experience, but he was apprehensive of joining forces with her.

In Tripoli, and later in the desert, she was known as the
enormously rich *Bent el re*, or king's daughter, and she still ignored
Speke's advice about large caravans organised regardless of cost.
Amongst other things, she had some elaborate metal tanks constructed for transporting water in the desert. Nothing like them
had been seen before, and they provoked a lot of curiosity.
Nachtigal was aware of the gossip about her, but Ali Riza, the
Governor-General, reluctantly admitted that he had some jurisdiction over the Fezzan and as far south as Murzuq, and that
there was probably no great danger in Alexine's going there. So
he let her go ahead on January 30, 1869, and followed in his own
inconspicuous way a fortnight later.

Once again, Abdullah proudly watched a great caravan get
under way. It passed out from the white minarets of Tripoli,
through the Bab el Mesheya, along the avenues of feathery
palms, and out into the desert. Two of the Dutch sailors had
remained, Kes Oostermans and Ary Jacobse. Besides them, there
was the usual retinue of Arabs and freed Negro slaves. Nachtigal
later was critical of her servants, but the party seems to have
been the most congenial ever commanded by Alexine. As she
went, she collected wild flowers as usual, and from time to time,
at desert sites, Roman potsherds. Only the horrid spectacle of the

northbound slave caravans marred the pleasantness of the journey, and they reached Murzuq in just over a month. Alexine was the first white woman to go there, and the world press noted the fact.

When Gustav Nachtigal arrived at the end of March, he was warmly welcomed by Alexine, whom he found installed in a large house in the principal part of the main street. Her household had been added to by more freed slaves and by the concubine of a peculating official, who wanted the lady kept safe from his other household effects threatened with confiscation. A very large and handsome dog was another important member of the entourage—perhaps, to Alexine, the most important. His breed is not known, but he was old, and it is possible that he was a survivor of the Nile journey. Nachtigal found lodgings a few doors away, and the two young, cultured Europeans—he aged 35, she 34—isolated in a little Muslim desert fortress city, developed an affectionate friendship. His own words best describe the relationship:

> At sunset I used to sit with Alexandrine Tinne on the terrace of her lofty house, refreshing myself with her in the fine evenings which provided such a comforting contrast to the windy, dusty and often burning hot days....Our animated conversation about our future plans, and the rich experiences of my friend's past, about our home and the rest of the world, felt the influence of the enchanting tranquility and gradually died away. The more profound our silence, the deeper were we absorbed in dreams, until the melancholy sound of the drum, calling from afar throughout the night, summoned us back to reality, and reminded me that it was time to depart.[1]

Alexine had malaria in April and then, in May, developed serious intestinal inflammation. She almost died of this, and by ill luck Nachtigal was himself too ill with malaria to attend to her at first. When he recovered, he found her desperately ill, in severe pain, and terribly emaciated. She had not eaten for days, and he scarcely hoped that she could recover. Indeed, without his professional assistance, it is unlikely that she would have. But she must have had a reasonably good constitution, and under his tender care, she returned to her normal health. She started forthwith to make plans for further exploration of the Sahara.

Both travellers wanted to go to Bornu, and both were interested in the desert peoples, Alexine especially in the Tuareg. It was evident that the most practical way of reaching Bornu would be to join one of the occasional large southbound caravans of merchants. There seemed to be no prospect of such a caravan for the moment, and they decided to wait until the autumn. Then, if there were still no signs of merchants assembling, they would hire an armed escort and go together. In the meantime, Alexine arranged to despatch the faithful Abdullah to Tripoli to purchase more camels. He was also to collect a consignment of Maria Theresa dollars that she had asked John Tinne to obtain for her, along with a quantity of presents for the sheikhs she would encounter as well as for Sultan Umar of Bornu. For the latter, she was in rivalry with the handsome royal gifts from Prussia, and rather than expensive and splendid offerings, she had ordered European novelties such as ice-making machines, simple cameras, and sewing machines. She had even asked for a very early model of something like the "Teasmade," in which an alarm clock ignited a candle as it went off. Her list would assuredly have given great pleasure.

With the Bornu journey still some months off, it seemed best for Nachtigal and Alexine to go their own ways for the summer. He undertook the negotiations about their journeys with the local officials. For himself, he had decided to visit the Tubu-speaking people of Tibesti who lived to the southeast of the main road to Kuka. He sensed that Hajj Brahim ben Alua, the courteous Sheikh of Murzuq, disliked the idea, as the Tubu were considered dangerous. He nonetheless gave polite and helpful cooperation. For Alexine, with her all too evident wealth, he considered the project unthinkable. But Ali Riza at Tripoli had given introductions to Ikhnukhen, the aged chief of the Asgar Tuareg in Ghat, to the west of Murzuq. He knew and trusted him and considered him the only Tuareg chief likely to prove friendly. Alexine had communicated with Ikhnukhen, and had received courteous encouragement from him. He offered to come to meet her and to escort her amongst his people. He had been known and trusted in Tripoli for many years, and under his protection, her safety seemed assured. Nachtigal felt that he could reasonably encourage her, but he began to suspect that Hajj Brahim disliked having her on his hands at all. His superb manners had disguised this from her and, at first, from him also, but before long, he had no doubt that she was reckoned a very hot potato.

According to Abdullah, she rode out into the desert in all directions when she was well enough. This alone made her a responsibility. But in Murzuq itself, she was regarded as a very unnatural phenomenon. Rich king's daughter she might be, but as a solitary, apparently unmarried woman, she was incomprehensible and therefore a mystery. Some thought that she was married to Nachtigal, which was probably harmless. A great many more thought that there was a sinister relationship between her and her adored and adoring dog. There was even a rumour that she turned him into a man at night. Her passionate grief at the dog's death in May seemed to confirm this possibility. Nachtigal did his best to paint a picture of a noble, generous-hearted woman who loved above everything to travel in Muslim lands, and whom it should be a privilege to entertain, but he doubted if he did any good.

On June 16, Alexine's caravan was encamped outside the western gate of Murzuq, having made the customary false start on the journey to the rendezvous with Ikhnukhen in the Wadi el Gharbi. Nachtigal, who was leaving next day on his much more hazardous journey to Tibesti, rode out to the camp with Alexine, and there they parted. "...we bade farewell to each other, a very cordial farewell, for while we had been at Murzuq I had learnt to value equally highly the intellect and the courage of this lady."[2] The lady proceeded westwards and arrived at the Wadi el Gharbi in five days. Ikhnukhen advanced to meet her down what she described as "a stern wild valley and greeted her with apparent pleasure. He had a vast escort of Tuareg, and their appearance came up to all expectations. Wearing black veils with eye-slits, coloured robes, and with their camels gaily caparisoned, they approached in a dramatic camel charge, only brought to a halt when collision seemed inevitable.

Alexine wore her most splendid robes and conducted the interview from a palanquin slung between two camels. Her knowledge of Tamashek was a priceless asset during the ensuing four days of social activities. Abdullah said they were there for ten days, but he was not always accurate, and it is doubtful he was even there; he may have already gone north on his errand to Tripoli. She certainly had time to make contact with Ikhnukhen's family and with many of the lesser chiefs, and the Tuareg had time to inspect her effects, including the iron water tanks. Ikhnukhen is said to have expressed great admiration for her, and he offered to escort her through his own country and to take her as far as Kano if she wished. For some reason, she told him that she had to return to Murzuq for presents for him. It seems unlikely that these had been forgotten, and to other people, she said that she wanted to consult with Sheikh Hajj Brahim. An elderly Tuareg, whom Ikhnukhen said he trusted as a son, was sent with her as guide and escort.

Whenever it was that he departed for Tripoli, Abdullah was not with Alexine when she left Murzuq for Ghat the second time. His place as her adjutant was apparently taken by someone known as Muhammed of Tunis. Some other Arabs seem to have been recruited, as well as an additional 27 camels. While at Murzuq, a party of eight Tuareg visitors called formally on Alexine, having heard that she was a distinguished traveller about to visit their country. Tuareg visitors were apparently a rarity there, but Alexine was starry-eyed about the race and delighted to see them. They did not try to obtrude themselves on her but put their services at her disposal should she wish them to travel with her. Among them was a nephew of Ikhnukhen's, who was probably his heir-apparent but who was thought to be nursing a grievance against his uncle at the time. When Alexine finally departed, they went with her and camped each night, not in her camp, but in the near vicinity.

The journey went easily and agreeably until the morning of August 1, when disaster came. The events of the day were subsequently pieced together by Nachtigal, on his return from Tibesti, by Abdullah, and by Alexine's nephews. The details from each account conflict, but Nachtigal's is probably as near to the truth as possible in the circumstances. In the early morning, while the preparations for the march were at their height, a disturbance broke out among the Arab camel drivers over the arrangement of the baggage on their beasts. The ensuing commotion seems to have been out of all proportion to the difficulty,

though the kind of Arab employed for the work was reputedly
emotional. The two Dutchmen, whose riding camels were waiting already saddled and loaded, were superintending the preparations, and Oostmans went to see what the trouble was and to
calm down the drivers.

This was the signal, almost certainly prearranged, for the
escalation of the rumpus. The eight Tuareg were watching the
proceedings, and one of them shouted to Oostmans to leave
Muslim affairs to Muslims, and forthwith decapitated him with
one sabre cut. Jacobse ran to get his rifle from his camel and was
felled to the ground and then killed. Pandemonium reigned
throughout the camp and brought Alexine to the opening of her
tent. She raised an imperious hand and commanded silence, but
the carefully generated chaos was beyond her control. Her hand
was severed by a sword, and Nachtigal maintains that it was an
Arab who first attacked her. A moment later she was struck on
the head by a sabre and stunned. Unfortunately, her silk scarf
and her thick plait of hair deflected the blow, and she was not
killed outright. She lay wounded on the sand for many hours, and
her Negro servants were forceably prevented from giving her
comfort. When she was dead, the Tuareg looted her effects,
which, after all the rumours circulating among the desert peoples, proved disappointing.

Survivors of the caravan returned to Murzuq and reported to
the Sheikh. Soldiers were sent to the scene of the murders, and
they buried Alexine in the desert sand, with her faithful Dutchmen one on either side of her. The news reached Tripoli and was
telegraphed to Liverpool. Alexine's nephews set out at once to
try to ascertain what had happened and to wind up her affairs.
They attended the long Court of Enquiry commissioned by the
Governor of Tripoli in the early months of 1870, but it was
wholly unsatisfactory and inconclusive. Language difficulties,
added to the unreliability of most of the witnesses, caused hopeless confusion. As a result, the responsibility for the grim tragedy
remained largely a matter for conjecture. Greed for Alexine's
riches, probably especially provoked by the iron water tanks that
were rumoured to be filled with treasure, was almost certainly
the largest factor. Despite the apparent spontaneity of the fighting, it was thought that the episode had been planned in advance,

and that many in the caravan were involved. Abdullah blamed his deputy, Muhammed of Tunis, who distributed the loot after the murders. But in all likelihood, the principal villain and leader of the conspiracy was the ambitious young Tuareg chief, Ikhnukhen's nephew. Certainly, both Tuareg and Arabs were involved.

The Tinne munificence continued after Alexine's death. She had left instructions that her servants and dependants were to be cared for, and these were generously carried out. Fourteen years later, an English traveller, the Reverend A. W. Boddy,[3] met Abdullah in Tripoli. He was then a Hajji and a leading citizen, and was still receiving a handsome monthly pension from the Tinne family. Many of the other servants were living in Tripoli, and they too were pensioned. Abdullah said that the young Tinnes had gone to great lengths to trace and ransom a Negress called Jasmina, whom the Tuaregs had sold into slavery. In Europe, legends grew that the mistress was not dead: that, having married an African ruler, she had become a great "She who must be obeyed" somewhere in the interior. But, though the desert sands quickly obliterated all trace of the lonely triple grave, there can, in fact, be no doubt as to the reality of Alexine's tragic fate.

NOTES

1. Gustav Nachtigal, *Sahara and Sudan*, vol. 1, trans. Alan G. B. and Humphrey J. Fisher (London: C. Hurst & Co., 1974), p. 96.

2. Ibid., p. 195.

3. Alexander W. Boddy, *To Kairwan the Holy* (London: Kegan Paul Trench & Co., 1885).

3

MARY KINGSLEY:
Explorer and Scientist

Mary Kingsley was born in London in 1862. When her father, George, Charles and Henry Kingley's less famous brother, died 30 years later, the *Dictionary of National Biography* gave him a short notice. The entry, which describes him as a writer and a traveller, ends with a brief sentence on his private life: "He married in 1860 Mary Bailey, who died in 1892, leaving a son Charles, and a daughter." Within five years the unnamed daughter was one of the most famous women in England. Within eight years she was dead. The achievements of the short span of years between anonymity and fame and death were indeed formidable.

The Kingsley family had for many generations been country gentlemen, soldiers, sailors, or parsons. The three brothers shared a great interest in travel and adventure and also in natural history. George qualified as a doctor and made a profession for himself as medical attendant to young noblemen of sufficient affluence to equip expensive expeditions to little-known places. He and a young Earl of Pembroke sailed in the *Albatross* to the Polynesian Islands. They recounted their experiences gaily in a travelogue called "South Sea Bubbles" by the Earl and the Doctor. It was also as "The Doctor" that he became a contributor of natural-history articles to *The Field*. A would-be ethnographer, a

An earlier version of this chapter appeared as "Mary Kingsley" in *African Affairs* 70 (1971), pp. 222-35. Reprinted by permission of the Royal African Society.

passionate naturalist, and above all a happy adventurer roving the world almost continuously, he achieved a life he loved and for which he probably sacrificed a successful career in England.

While he wandered, his delicate wife, his daughter Mary, and her younger brother Charles had to get along without him as best they could. They lived for many years in a small house in Highgate, and subsequently in Cambridge. The mainstay of the household was Mary. Her devotion to her family was almost a religion to her, and on meagre means it was a hard life. She must have suffered in seeing her mother so frequently deserted, and knew that the long, amusing, and affectionate letters that came from distant places were wholly inadequate as compensation. But she would have understood her father's wanderlust, which she shared, but which it was apparently not her lot to indulge. Her role in life was that of the dutiful Victorian daughter, and being Mary Kingsley, she did it exceptionally well.

Except for some German lessons, taken in order to help her father with his ethnographic researches, she had no formal education, whereas £2000 were spent on educating her brother. She was given a copy of Craik's *Pursuit of Knowledge under Difficulties*, and it proved the more fruitful investment. Presumably, her mother helped her to literacy, and she read copiously in her father's library. Her tastes were hardly typical of Victorian girlhood. She read widely in science, Burton's *Anatomy of Melancholy* was among her favourite books, and she was a true Kingsley in her love of the literature of exploration and piracy. For pets she had a couple of fighting cocks, and she was skilled in their management, though their tactless, strident crowing irritated her father when he was at home. In spite of a delightful intellectual companionship, her relations with her father were frequently stormy, due to his temper and to his complete lack of domestication. She was quite capable of being a little unscrupulous with him, as when she watched him hunting for a book on solar physics that he wanted to lend to a friend; she had herself hidden it, in order to be sure of finishing it before it left the house.

When the family moved to Cambridge in 1886, it was for the benefit of Charles, who was up at the university. But here a broader life opened for Mary among sympathetic friends, especially scientists, and she had access to the best of scientific libraries. It was during the Cambridge years that she became what she described as her father's "underworker." This was overmodest. For all his talents, George Kingsley was uncoordinated, and had the reputation for being a bad finisher. She followed dutifully in his fields of research, but she almost certainly had the greater mastery there.

Mrs. Kingsley's health had never been good, and the long years when her husband was away visiting cannibals in the Pacific, or involved in Indian wars in North America, had not helped her. In 1888 she became a hopeless invalid, and there followed for Mary four years of devoted day-and-night nursing. Not long before the end, her father returned, himself in poor health as a result of rheumatic fever contracted overseas. One morning in 1892, after her long night watch with her mother, she found him dead. Within a few weeks her mother too was dead, and in her thirty-first year, her life as a daughter was ended. Less than 18 months later, in August 1893, she sailed alone for the Guinea coast and beyond, where in one of the deadliest climates in the world, she was destined to wander alone along forest trails, in friendly contact with strange peoples.

In retrospect, this apparently amazing departure seems logical. She had had some idea of becoming a doctor but thought, rather strangely, that it was too individual a profession for her. Her life's work was to assist others, and it seemed natural to continue assisting her father, whose ethnographic *magnum opus* lay unfinished. Some years later, she wrote in an article in T. P. O'Conner's *Weekly*:

When there were no more odd jobs to do at home, I, out of my life in books, found something to do that my father cared for, something for which I had been taught German, so that I could do for him odd jobs in it. It was the study of early religion and law, and for it I had to go to West Africa, and I went there, proceeding on the even tenor of my way, doing odd jobs, and trying to understand things, pursuing knowledge under difficulties with unbroken devotion.[1]

But in the secret places in her heart, there was another reason for going to the white man's grave. Her whole life had been conditioned by her devotion to her parents, and without them she no longer had a positive wish to live. She did not reveal this at the time, but her friend and biographer, Stephen Gwynn, was surprised to discover, after her death, a letter to a friend of later days, which gives an indication of her state of mind: "My life has been a comic one: dead tired, and feeling no one had need of me any more, when my mother and father died within a few weeks of each other in '92, and my brother went off to the East, I went down to West Africa to die."[2] She was probably being a little overdramatic, but she evidently went there expecting to die, but certainly meaning to live and die usefully.

The exuberant gaiety with which she set about her preparations is in great contrast to the secret melancholy of her going. Travel and adventure were the spice of life, and with her first taste of freedom, she was off to have her share of it, and she felt, as she says herself, "like a boy with a new half-crown." Her friends no doubt thought her mad, but at least happily mad. Few of them knew more of West Africa than that was where Sierra Leone was, and Sierra Leone was the place where the "sad trials" in families were sent on remittance. The "sad trials" had a convenient way of not returning. There were others who bombarded her with haphazard and irrelevant advice, and she had to pick her way among the rubbish and make her own decisions. She consulted doctors and they were not encouraging. They showed her a map of the geographical distribution of disease, and it was painted dramatically black from Sierra Leone to south of the Congo. She reacted by taking a short medical course in Germany. Many were the suggestions made to her about suitable clothing, but she remained fixed in her determination to make no revolutionary changes in the Cambridge fashions of the 1890s. She always maintained that she owed her life, and certainly her comparative comfort at the time, to her voluminous black skirts, when she fell into a game trap and found herself impaled on a bed of carefully pointed stakes. For luggage, she merely added a waterproof sack to her customary portmanteau and black bag. This was for her blankets and boots and suchlike. In a humid climate it served her well, but she confessed that she was throughout apprehensive that it would disintegrate and leave her without her comforts. One other important part of her luggage was some inexpensive equipment for collecting beetles and fishes. After long discussion with Dr. Günter of the British Museum, she had come to the conclusion that these were the best natural-history pursuits that she, with her slender finances and her lack of training in natural sciences, could profitably follow. For her ethnographic work, she had behind her her father's experience, and many years of wide reading, relevant to what she was seeking.

She sailed from Europe in a cargo ship, the *Lagos*. It was commanded by Captain Murray, a battered old seaman, who became her friend and tutor, not only in the lore of ships, but also out of his great experience on the Liverpool–West Africa run, in the ways of the "Coast." One wonders what Captain Murray and his crew thought of the thin, fair, shy but quite unshockable spinster they carried as passenger. She had a gift for coaxing friendliness in unlikely milieux, and the sea was far from an unlikely milieu for a Kingsley. One gets some idea of the kind of tuition she attracted to herself from the fact that she was able to claim later that she had on three occasions taken a 2,000-ton ship across the Forçados Bar of the Niger, and up the Forçados Creek as a pilot.

It was with a "thrill of joy" that she first sailed into Freetown. From her knowledge of the literature of exploration and of piracy, she "knew the place so well." She recognized the mountains where the thunder, rumbling like roaring lions, had given rise to the name Sierra Leone, and also the bays that had harboured the pirates. Anyone who shares with her the experience of the first impact of West Africa will enjoy her picture of Freetown. The air laden with the heavy, sweet scent of tropical flowers, not unmixed with that of nonexistent drains; the whitewashed market where the goods would take the "pen of a Rabelais" to catalogue; the local inhabitants dressed in skimpy assortments of rags, surely only adhering by capillary attraction, and carrying on their heads tea trays of merchandise surmounted by their hats; the ladies, just as colourful, but more *soignée,* and "Oh! Allah! the circumference of them"; the splendidly robed Muslims; the city slicker, pathetic emulator of "rubbishy white culture"; the delapidated row of vultures, West Africa's blessed scavengers, sitting on the cathedral, apparently nursing hangovers from some bloody feast: it is all so vividly painted that one must regret that she wrote no consecutive account of this first journey. It can be pieced together only from incidental references in her books and articles.

Calling at a selection of the Guinea ports, she sailed as far south as St. Paul de Loanda in Angola, which, already 400 years old, she thought the loveliest town in West Africa. Here she apparently made friends with members of the Portuguese colony, and she began her scientific pursuits. How she travelled north from Loanda is not clear. It was certainly very simply and with no grand white man's caravan. She probably already carried the necessary goods to do a little trading as she went, which became her invariable practice. It made her acceptable to Africans and it helped with the finances. However she went, she visited the ancient kingdom of Kongo, and explored both shores of the Congo River estuary, getting as far up river as the Pallaballa Range above Matadi. Belgian commercial enterprise, both royal and private, was already in full swing, but she never wrote of what she saw. It is possible that she had to give an undertaking not to do so, in order to get permission to go so far into the Free State. There are, however, slight references in her books that leave no doubt that she was bitterly shocked at what was happening. Later she became a great friend of E. D. Morel, who led the campaign for reform in the Congo, and it is clear that she supplied some of the evidence for his brief.

From King Leopold's Congo she passed into French Congo, which she found more congenial. There she did her first detailed ethnographic research amongst the Fjort before continuing her journey to the Oil Rivers Protectorate, where she spent some time at Old Calabar as the guest of the High Commissioner Sir Claude Macdonald. She reached England again in January 1894.

Her journey had been an excellent apprenticeship to West Africa, and she had proved, for herself at least, that it was possible for an impecunious Englishwoman to travel alone in the West African bush. Her collection of fish, and to a lesser extent of beetles, had proved her competence as a collector. She was no longer an amateur, and the British Museum was prepared to equip her adequately and to brief her for further research in the field. And she had discovered something that was to colour her whole attitude of West Africa. She had found that the English traders, the much abused "Palm Oil Ruffians," who acted as agents for the merchant companies, were doing excellent work in their country's interests, and that they had many admirable qualities.

At the end of 1894, Mary Kingsley sailed again for West Africa, this time in the *Batanga*, commanded by her old friend Captain Murray who had transferred from the *Lagos*. She had an agreeable travelling companion in Sir Claude Macdonald's wife, who was going out to join her husband. It was a rare undertaking at the time for English wives to brave the health dangers of the Guinea Coast, and it was natural that Sir Claud should have arranged for them to travel together. Once Lady Macdonald had been persuaded that kindly meant efforts to talk about fish were quite unnecessary, they became great friends. The rest of the passengers were mostly "Old Coasters," in whose company she now took a robust delight.

On her first voyage there had been reciprocal suspicions; she had been told that they were all desperadoes, and that she must avoid their company. They had put her down as a fanatic going out to get some "shocking statistics" on the liquor trade for the World's Women's Temperance Association. She had heard frequently the classic fable of the "Coast," of how Satan got ready to vacate the infernal throne every time a trader died. And die was what they mostly did, and before they did it, they talked interminably about it. By now on the way to becoming an Old Coaster herself, she well knew the dread truth and therefore the tremendous courage that underlay the macabre jesting. They swapped statistics of the malarial and yellow-fever epidemics that wiped out whole European communities; of the horrid refinements of the variants of fever; and of the fly-infested corpses that travelling agents found in up-country factories. She later recounted the stories with a ghoulish detail that shocked some of her friends. But she was quite unrepentant. She had taken the traders under her special protection, and she was determined to speak out in their interests.

The fact that Lady Macdonald was the wife of a Commissioner meant that the two ladies were given VIP treatment on the Gold Coast, which was already a British colony. At Cape Coast, Mary Kingsley chose to see the centuries-old town and its slave forts with some Wesleyan missionary friends. But at Accra, after a hazardous passage through the surf bar in a canoe, both ladies were taken in state, in rickshaws with cummerbunded retainers, to Christiansborg Castle. There the malarial statistics and the recurrence of white funerals vied with the last race meeting and the affairs of Ashanti as conversational themes. Young officials claimed that they walked in the cemetery daily to accustom themselves to their all-too-likely future surroundings. In the cemetery, two ready-dug graves underlined the reality.

After Accra, the next port of which we hear was Old Calabar, where a splendid reception and a fireworks display greeted the Commissioner's lady. It chanced that Sir Claude Macdonald had immediate business in Fernando Poo, and intended crossing there in the *Batanga*. His wife decided to accompany him, and Mary Kingsley went with them. It was a brief visit, but she explored the lovely, fertile volcanic island and learned a little of the Bubis, the shy Bantu-speaking people, who had not passed out of the Stone Age when the Portuguese discovered the island in the fifteenth century. Back on the mainland she stayed for over four months , for the most part as the guest of the Macdonalds. A great deal of time she spent looking for fish up the devious, mangrove-bordered waterways. She also studied the indigenous religions of the region, but though there are frequent references to them in her books, which show proof of considerable knowledge, she did not consider that she had done enough work to publish on them. She clearly intended to return to the Oil Rivers at some time for further research.

Perhaps the most interesting event of her stay there in 1894 was her visit to Miss Mary Slessor in the Okoyong district. This Scottish mill hand, who had become a Presbyterian missionary, had established for herself a position of great influence over peoples virtually uncontacted by Europeans. While endeavouring to attack the more barbarous customs inherent in the local religions, she nonetheless proceeded with respectful tact. She well understood that these customs were dictated by centuries of religious tradition, and that changes must come slowly. Mary Kingsley found this admirable. It is interesting to picture the meeting between these two great women who shared so much, including a love of laughter and the friendship of Sir Claude Macdonald, whom Mary Slessor always addressed as "Laddie."

Alone in a grass hut by the lowering Cross River, deep in the
Nigerian forest, they sat and talked far into the night. Happily
there exists a record of the visit, in a letter written by Mary
Slessor after Mary Kingsley's death. It was in reply to a request
for information about her political views:

But, O dear me!...To give you an account of Miss Kingsley and her stay
here—you may as well tell me to catch the clouds with their ever-
varying forms, or catch the perfume of the forest jessamine, or the
flashes of the sunlight on the river. Miss Kingsley cannot be portrayed.
She had an individuality as pronounced as it was unique, with charm of
manner and conversation, while the interplay of wit and mild satire, of
pure spontaneous mirth and of profoundly deep seriousness, made her a
series of surprises, each one tenderer and more elusive than the foregoing. No! there was only one Miss Kingsley, and I can't define her
character by speaking in this way, in the terms we speak of one another;
or gather up the beauty and instruction and joy of those days of companionship, and say, There! she gave me this or that other impression or
impulse or idea. It is like the languorous glamour of a summer's day in
which one bathed, and lay still, and let life go by in a sweet dream.[3]

Mary Kingsley's brief from the British Museum had included a
request for a collection of fresh-water fish from above the tide
line of a tropical river. For this purpose she had intended to go
north from the Oil Rivers Protectorate into the territory of the
Royal Niger Company. She had corresponded with its Director,
Sir George Goldie, who had expressed his willingness to make
arrangements for her on the Niger, and on its tributary the
Benue. Then, for what she called "certain private reasons," she
changed her mind. Her reasons were a matter of some delicacy.
There was hostile rivalry between the Protectorate and the
Chartered Company.[4] This had recently been brought to the
boiling point by trading reprisals, carried out into the Company's
zone, by the native traders of Brass. Sir Claude Macdonald was in
sympathy with the reprisals, and was altogether opposed to
Chartered Company rule for West Africa. Mary Kingsley, on the
other hand, was developing into its most formidable protagonist.
She admired Sir George Goldie, though she had not met him at
the time; but both the Macdonalds were her friends, and she
owed them a considerable debt of gratitude. In these difficult

circumstances, she decided to keep herself as free as possible from any involvement in the political scene. She chose instead to go to French Gaboon, to ascend the Ogowe River as far as necessary for her ichthyological purposes, and to find her way from the Ogowe to the Rembwe River, and thence to the Gaboon estuary. From the point of view of literature, it was a fortunate decision. She describes the Gaboon journey in greater and more consecutive detail than any other part of her travels, and the result is a superb travelogue.

To get to Gaboon, it was necessary to start westwards and to change ships off Lagos bar. There is a lively account of what Mary Kingsley would have called the Lagos palaver—the elaborate and frequently dangerous arrangements, then necessary, for landing passengers at Lagos. It is with the art of a novelist that she brings to life the many characters incidental to West African travel. The local lady, a minor merchant princess in the chicken business, getting very much the better of the young ship's officers over her freight dues; the government official in a continuous fuss at being kept from his important duties on shore by the late arrival of the eastward-bound *Benguella,* are memorable figures. Even the small craft of the French companies that plied for trade up the Gaboon rivers develop personalities. Having arrived in the *Benguella,* it is in the *Mové,* a "fine little vessel," that Mary Kingsley sails out of Libreville early in June en route for the mouth of the Ogowe and Lambarene. "Food is excellent, society charming, Captain and Engineer quite acquisitions." An overnight stop is made alongside the *Fallabar, Mové's* predecessor on the run, now anchored at the mouth of a sombre creek as a trading hulk, because, though reputedly a fine little ship, she 'wouldn't steer'. Then on the day-long run between the *Fallabar* and Lambarene Island, the gay, good-humoured asperity subsides before the overwhelming beauty of the river scene. The passionate nature lover takes over, and the splendidly colourful Ogowe forests and broad, winding river itself are vividly painted for the reader.

Mary Kingsley spent a couple of weeks at Kangwe, the station of the Protestant Mission Evangélique, on the north shore of the river opposite Lambarene Island. As usual, she collected fish and took notes on native religion, and she wandered among Fan villages. These people, conquering immigrants of comparatively recent origin,[5] had a probably exaggerated reputation for awkwardness and also cannibalism. The considerable contact she made with them while in Gaboon was something of an achievement.

Towards the end of June, she proceeded upriver in the "charming little stern-wheel steamer" *Eclaireur*. Once more her description of the company is a delight, from the gay, sophisticated French official, whose destination was 36 days' canoe journey beyond Njole, *Eclaireur*'s turning point, to the furiously argumentative French captain, with whom her lack of French precluded her from engaging in hostilities, to their "mutual regret, for it would have been a love of a fight." A delight too is her picture of the excited disembarkation of deck passengers at a riverside village, while *Eclaireur* slips downstream, broadside on "as though she smelt her stable at Lambarene," and a delight, as always, the passing scene, as the great river valley thrusts deeply into the Sierra del Cristal.

From Talagouga, below Njole, where she was again the guest of the Mission Evangélique, Mary Kingsley succeeded, not without difficulty and discouragement from missionaries and French officials, in mustering a canoe and a crew for a journey up through the Ogowe rapids above Njole. The exceptional interest of the collection of fish that she had made at Talagouga had suggested the usefulness of a further collection from higher reaches of the river. Her crew was made up of Igalawa, because the local Fan were unwilling to encounter their reputedly wicked relatives in upriver Fan villages. The trip was undoubtedly a very dangerous enterprise. Through wild water and tearing smooth water, bypassing, not always successfuly, whirlpools, rock-shoals, and sandbanks, it took two days to reach their destination at Kondo Kondo Island, and perhaps they were lucky to get there at all. She summed it all up as playing "a knock-about farce before King Death, in his amphitheatre in the Sierra del Cristal."

On 22 July, after revisiting the Mission Evangélique at Kangwe, Mary Kingsley started on the overland crossing from the Ogowe to the Rembwe. This was probably the most adventurous of her many adventurous journeys, and for much of the way, she must have been the first European to travel along such paths as there were. She started by canoe down the O'Rembo Vongo, the arm of the Ogowe that flows on the north side of Lambarene Island. For crew she had four Ajumba, an aristocratic and reputedly honest people. They proudly and gaily shouted "Rembwe" to enquiries as to their destination from other canoes, but Mary Kingsley on this first day was lying prone at the bottom of the canoe with a splitting headache. The party was completed by an interpreter who could not interpret and who was a miserable traveller, and by a passenger who had begged a lift. They branched off the O'Rembo Vongo on the second day, and went north along the Karkola River. This in time led them to Lake Ncovi, where there was a Fan town on an island. Like all Fan towns, it was of evil repute, but the success of the whole expedition depended on some cooperation from its people. Two of the Ajumba claimed trading acquaintances there, but there were twenty anxious minutes while the whole hostile-seeming population scrutinized the party from the beach, and while the existence of the acquaintances was verified. It all went according to plan, they stayed the night, and three Fan were added to the party for the overland carry to the Rembwe. The usual route, via Lake Ayzingo, was said to be barred by some especially "fearful Fan"; they were not, apparently, mutual admiration societies. Mary Kingsley herself, while well aware of their shortcomings, got on very well with the three who joined her party. She came to have some respect for them, and they seemed to respect her, which was endearing; though she thought there was probably a "better to drink with than fight with" element in their relationship. They proved a liability in the three other Fan villages in which she spent the night, as old murder- or women- or debt- "palavers" were apt to catch up with them.

In the event, none of the villages really lived up to their reputations for wickedness, and she was always provided with some crude accommodation and a little privacy. In one village, the unpleasant smell emanating from some little hanging bags in her guest hut tempted her to investigate the cause. They contained some affectionate mementoes—ears, toes, a hand—of a cannibal dinner. At another, she had to set up as the village apothecary, and at another, she was awakened in the small hours to adjudicate at a bankruptcy trial. All the way, the path was scarcely trodden, frequently treacherous, and very arduous. There were grave dangers, too, from the forest fauna. Eventually, on 27 July, she reached the Rembwe, at a point downstream from the trading station which had been her target. It was a splendidly courageous journey.

While still in Gaboon, Mary Kingsley sailed to the island of Corisco, where she made a collection of shellfish. After that she took ship westwards to begin her journey home. Sailing past Mungo Mah Lobeh, the great 14,750-foot peak of the Cameroon mountain, she felt again the longing to climb it which she had experienced on her way down the coast in 1893. She stopped off at the German colony of Kamerun in order to do so. She had had several distinguished European predecessors in the venture, but she was the first woman to reach the summit. It required considerable force of character to persuade her porters to come sufficiently high on the mountain for her purpose. They deliberately left the water behind in the hope of sabotaging the climb, but she sent them down to fetch it. The rain, on one of the wettest mountains in the world, was incessant, and frequently of tropical-storm proportions. One night was spent in the open in drenched blankets. But the only thing that the indomitable but nonetheless Victorian spinster found too daunting was the possibility of accepting the offer of a hot bath from the German official at Buea. His house had no doors, nor adequate window covering for her modesty. She caught one of the worst colds imaginable. When she finally reached the coast at Victoria, she sat on the verandah of the German Governor's palace and watched and listened to the enchantment of the tropical night, and she asked herself why she had come to West Africa. "Why!" she told herself, "who would not come to its twin brother hell itself, for all the beauty and the charm of it." It was all but her last look at West Africa, and in November 1895 she reached England. The press was at Liverpool to meet her, and she found she had become a celebrity.

The preparation of *Travels in West Africa* was her first preoccupation. It was published in 1897, and as a brilliant account of exceptional travels, it was an immediate success. But it was a book of far greater significance than a mere travel journal. In

over 700 pages, alongside and intermingled with the travel descriptions, there is crammed a wealth of information on an
immense span of subjects relevant to West Africa, in a literary
style that races headlong and is spiced with good-humoured wit.
The great importance of the book at the time was the fresh or
even revolutionary interpretation of the peoples of West Africa
that reached a large public and quickened their interest. And it
was of enduring importance also, because many of those who
followed her to West Africa in the years when British interest
was paramount in much of it went there aware of her new-found
concept of "African personality," equipped with some of her
formidable knowledge, and influenced, surely, by her sophisticated tolerance.

There had been pioneers in the ethnological field already,
notably Sir Richard Burton, who had come to the fundamentally
wrong conclusion that Africans never matured out of childhood.
The questioning of this misconception was Mary Kingsley's
achievement. Africans, she maintained, matured as other men,
but she considered they were living in the thirteenth century.
But if Africans were of normal adult intelligence, she yet considered them to be a different human species. She considered them
less material and more spiritual than Europeans, in that religion
was more completely in charge of all aspects of the lives of
African peoples. Unsuitable though some of the manifestations
of African religion were, it was far from all bad, and gave to
society an essential moral code. In short and in spite of Kipling,
then at the height of his popularity, the African was neither "half
devil" nor "half child." Where she was wrong was in thinking of
Africans as a different human species, and where she was also
wrong was in considering them to be quite uncreative. She did
not know that some of the world's greatest sculpture was lying
either stored or buried, within a hundred miles of the Oil Rivers
Protectorate. She is unlikely, of course, to have met many educated Africans.

As a result of her first book, the previously unknown, shy
spinster of four years ago became an important public woman in
Victorian society. She was still conservative in her dress and
generally unconcerned about her appearance, but it must have

been at about this time that an artist rebuked Stephen Gwynn for describing her as plain. He, the artist, thought her the most beautiful woman in a crowded room. Certainly, some of her photographs show a touch of that elusive quality that can only be called beauty, and she was without doubt a striking personality. She dined at the tables of the great and lectured up and down the country to learned societies, to Chambers of Commerce, or to schools such as Eton or Cheltenham. The sophisticated young gentlemen at Eton were quick to assess the courage that her splendid flippancy all but concealed, and less exacting audiences were just as enthralled. But there was a deliberate plan about everything she did, for she had by now formulated strong views about English commitment in West Africa, and she was preparing to do battle for them.

To begin with, she had become extremely critical of two of the most important forces operating there. The first was the official colonial administration, where it existed, and the second was the Christian missions. The basis of the criticism in both cases was the ignorance of African society, which was combined with a wish to interfere with it unnecessarily. She set out to "show how absolutely worthless from all sides our Crown Colony system is."[6] She made great play of the Hut Tax rebellion which broke out in Sierra Leone early in 1898. She argued that for an African, this particular tax was the equivalent of enforced payment for something which was by tribal custom completely his own; one of his wives could be taken from him with less injustice. It was a good illustration for making her point, but she made it too vehemently. There is just a hint that young government officials may have patronised her as an oddity and failed to realize the calibre of her expertise. But she had known, and correctly valued, at least one great colonial administrator in Sir Claud MacDonald, and however tiresomely she may have been put in her Victorian woman's place by ignorant young officials, she allowed herself to become too prejudiced.

As regards missionaries, in spite of great personal respect for some individuals, she thought they were a seriously disrupting influence in an ordered, if not perhaps wholly well-ordered, society. The philosophy expressed in a popular missionary hymn with the refrain:

Just a little chat with Jesus
makes it right, quite right

was a dangerous one for Africans, especially when they were
being persuaded to break away from the strict rules of their own
traditions. Though owning to a belief in God, and claiming to
"yield to none" in her admiration for Jesus Christ, she was no
admirer of Christian churches. She had also been prejudiced
against missions by her father. In her eventual plan for West
Africa, however, she was prepared to allow missionaries an educational role, and the heat of battle once again led her to overstate
her case against them.

On the positive side of her argument, she overstated it even
more. It was to commerce that she wished to entrust the commitment of Great Britian in tropical Africa. Admiration for their
courage, gratitude for countless kindnesses received, a tremendous personal interest in trade itself, and the lively pleasure of
defending a despised breed of men had already made her the
champion of the trading agents. She now became the intimate
associate of the firms that employed them, especially those based
in Liverpool. Largely owing to Sir George Goldie, of whose policy
of indirect rule she approved, she had decided that Chartered
Company rule, as that of Goldie on the Niger, was the right form
of English involvement. She played a considerable part in recon-
ciling the merchant firms with the Chartered Company, hitherto
mutually hostile, and she worked for their ultimate amalgama-
tion into one, possibly Nigerian or possibly even West African,
Chartered Company.[7] She lobbied everywhere, and she talked
at length with the Colonial Secretary Joseph Chamberlain, who
respected her greatly. They were both imperialists, but Mary
Kingsley's imperialism was to be exercised by commerce, given
sufficient ruling powers to protect and nourish its interest. African society, still ordered by its traditional rulers, would, she
thought, coexist peacefully with the European merchants. Naturally, the commercial firms were in agreement with her, and the
party she was largely responsible for coordinating was a formidable one. But the forces of official imperialism were in the ascen-
dant, and she failed completely. The deciding factor was the
European scramble for Africa, which demanded official interven-

tion and the ultimate sanction of military forces. The British taxpayer would scarcely have financed such forces for purely commercial enterprise.

In *West African Studies,* the second of her two major books, Mary Kingsley gives her political arguments at length. She delayed its publication in the hope that she would win her case and that it might become impolitic to restate it. But when she sensed that she was losing, she published it in 1899. It contains at some length her "alternative plan" for West Africa, an alternative, that is, to both Crown Colony and Chartered Company rule. A Grand Council in England, composed of representatives of the Chambers of Commerce, and responsible to the Crown, was to appoint one Governor-General for all the British spheres of West Africa. He was to spend half of his time travelling and inspecting, and half reporting back to the Grand Council. There were to be two subcouncils: one in England of experts, lawyers, and doctors; and one in West Africa of native chiefs. A very small number of highly expert officials would represent the Governor in very wide districts, but a few coastal towns would be administered by Europeans, and serve as examples of urban excellence. The whole system was to be funded by a tax on the trade, levied at the British, or, as necessary, European ports. The plan, which was worked out in great detail, would thus accomplish Mary Kingsley's two paramount ideas: trade would be unimpeded by inexpert officialdom; and African society would be left comparatively undisturbed. The fact that she considered it as an alternative to straightforward Chartered Company rule shows that she had some later misgivings as to the latter, but the safeguards that she tried to build in against its likely abuses seem quite inadequate. It does not do her much credit.

As a great fighter, believing passionately in her cause, she can be pardoned her prejudices. Her misjudgement, with all her knowledge, is harder to understand, though it is easier to say that after an interval of 80 years than it would have been at the time. She was born too soon, and died too soon, to realize that the long centuries of Africa's isolation from world development were coming to a close. African peoples had to be tutored into the twentieth century at a far greater pace than she ever envisaged. It is probable that the colonial period, with missionary education working within the colonial framework, provided as good conditions as any in which the transition could easily be made. But her overenthusiasm and her misjudgement did little or nothing to detract from her stature. Her two great handbooks to West Africa had struck a new note with compelling authority, the note of understanding and tolerance that was the essence of Mary Kingsley. And "people shed their prejudices under the warmth of her humour and humility,"[8] which was beneficial both to her own country and to West Africa.

In 1900, the South African war was in progress, and instead of returning to West Africa, she went out to Cape Town to offer her services. She was assigned to a horrid task, which she tackled gallantly. This was at the hospital at Simonstown where Boer prisoners were dying of enteric fever in large numbers, in chaotic conditions. Between them, she and a doctor achieved some order in the shambles. But in two months, she herself caught enteric, and she died of heart failure after the ensuing operation. Her dying wish was to be buried at sea, and she was accorded full military honours. A regimental band accompanied the gun carriage carrying the coffin to the pier at Simonstown. There it was placed on board a torpedo boat which sailed southwards to Cape Point. Just as when she first sailed into Freetown harbour only seven years before, from her great knowledge of Portuguese exploration, she would have known "the place so well." There, at that great milestone of ocean history, called the Cape of Storms by the first Europeans to sail past, and renamed the Cape of Good Hope by Vasco da Gama returning from his first voyage to India, her body was cast into the sea.

She was only 38, much the same age as was Jane Austen at her death, and she left her admirers with the same sense of loss of what there might have been to come. Eighty years later, though she is not widely known, those who do read her books seldom fail to become her admirers, and they suffer the same sense of loss and regret at not having known her. Her writing brings her own personality vividly to life, and to many she seems made of the purest gold. Of the tenderness and the sense of justice, perhaps only her contemporaries could speak. Of the intellectual span, the courage, the poetry, the laughter, and the deep underlying seriousness, her readers will speak for a long time to come.

NOTES

1. Autobiographical sketch published in T. P. O'Connor's *Weekly*, May 1899, cited by Stephen Gwynn, *Life of Mary Kingsley* (London, 1933), p. 17.

2. Gwynn, *Life,* p. 26, letter from Mary Kingsley to Sir Mathew Nathan, March 1899.

3. Gwynn, *Life,* p. 278, letter from Mary Slessor to James Irvine, 12 December 1903.

4. See J. E. Flint, introduction to *Travels in West Africa,* by Mary Kingsley, 3rd ed., p. xi.

5. P. Alexandre, "Proto-histoire du groupe beti-bulu-fang," *Cahiers d'études africaines* (1965), pp. 503-60.

6. J. E. Flint, "Mary Kingsley, a reassessment," *J. Afr. Hist.* 4, 1 (1963), p. 102, citing a letter from Mary Kingsley to John Holt dated 1 October 1898.

7. J. E. Flint, "Mary Kingsley," p. 97.

8. Gwynn, *Life,* p. 5.

4

MARY SLESSOR:
Missionary and Magistrate

Southern Nigeria to the east of the Niger River is seamed with waterways. Near the coast they are mostly merged into monotonous, brackish mangrove swamps, but further inland they have an intense and rare beauty. They flow between walls of sombre, tropical, forested cliffs, and the dark, slow-flowing waters shimmer in the heat; when still and calm, they mirror profoundly the greens of the forest trees. It is lowering, haunting but unforgettable beauty. Chief among the waterways are the Cross River, the Enyong Creek, and the Calabar River, and there are many more. They drain the great rain forests down into the Bight of Biafra and the South Atlantic.

Divers peoples inhabit these riverain and forest lands, and until the middle of the nineteenth century, they lived in societies with social rules powerfully enforced by deep-rooted tradition, which were abhorrently cruel to Western eyes. There was domestic slavery, not in itself necessarily evil, but carrying the perpetual threat of ugly death. For there was human sacrifice, and slaves were offered as propitiation to ancestral gods, or condemned to execution by proxy, or subjected to the poison ordeal for uncommitted crimes, or despatched to accompany their dead masters into the next world for their greater convenience and glorification. There was also the foreign slave trade, and down the lovely rivers, men, women, and children were carried in chains to the coast, where the greedy white man was waiting with his ships to buy them and transport them to his plantations in the New World.

The little sailing ships, with the slaves inhumanely rammed into the holds, took many months to cross the Atlantic. The conditions on board were appalling, and the human casualty rate on the passage was enormous. But for some of the survivors, it proved a grim road to a first contact with civilisation at the Christian missions in the West Indies. And it was the tales that they told of their homeland to their Presbyterian pastors in Jamaica that inspired the first idea of a mission to the peoples of Calabar in Eastern Nigeria. It was first mooted at a meeting of the Jamaican missionary presbytery in 1840, two years after the emancipation of the slaves in the West Indies. Enthusiasm grew rapidly, although it took some years to convince the Missionary Council in Scotland that a mission to unknown Calabar, with its almost lethal climate, was remotely possible. But the money for it came in freely from a public anxious to expiate the sins of the slave trade, and early in 1846, the Reverend Hope Wadell and a party of six from the Jamaica Mission, some white, some coloured, sailed for the coastal towns of Calabar. These towns had had a long and reasonably peaceful association with Europeans, but an association based on the barter of guns and spirits for human beings had scarcely been civilising. The cruel social customs continued unabated among the native peoples. The foreign slave trade was, however, dead or dying, sternly suppressed by England, so long one of its chief participants. Legitimate trade, mainly in palm oil, was replacing it. In this situation, the chiefs of the coastal towns welcomed the missionaries as likely to help them into a future where the principal former source of their prosperity was denied them. They wanted to "learn book" and be like the white man.

In 1876, 30 years after their first arrival, the missionaries were joined by a young, red-haired Scotswoman named Mary Slessor. She was 27 years old. In her background was the small Scottish farm, the croft, which has produced many distinguished people, including at least one British Prime Minister. Some of her cousins had gone to university, but Mary's father was a hopeless failure and an incurable drunkard, and she grew up in desperate hardship in Aberdeen and, later, in Dundee. There she joined her delicate mother, working in the mills when she was 11. The money she earned was needed to help feed and clothe her brothers and sisters, who were all delicate. As well as the long hours at the looms, the mill provided, for a few hours each day, some elementary schooling, and Mary acquired sufficient literacy to become a great reader on her own initiative. Like her hero David Livingstone, she used to prop her book, frequently the Bible, on her loom, ready to take advantage of a chance idle moment; she was even seen reading as she walked through the slum streets on her way to work. She was very intelligent and wrote with statesmanlike clarity about the affairs of the mission, and poetically when describing the forest rivers she grew to love.

In the ugliness of the Dundee slums, the Scottish Church, with all its austerity, provided an oasis of beauty for Mary, her mother, and her brothers and sisters. It was a blessed refuge from the persistent horror of her father's drunkenness, which she and her mother strove to hide. It was also a window to a wider world that she knew little about, and it was where she first heard of a place that sounded infinitely glamorous, Calabar. Her eldest brother expressed a firm resolve to go there himself as a missionary, but she was too modest to dream of it for herself. There was, in fact, plenty of missionary work among the poor mill hands and their families, who, in the sixties and seventies, were frequently unemployed, hungry, and living in distressing sqaulor. Timid and diffident by nature, she found the courage for this work, which often took her amongst dangerous roughs. The story is told, and will be retold forever in Dundee, of her being assailed one night by a gang of hooligans out for mischief. Their leader showed off by swinging a heavy lump of lead on a string closer and closer to her face. She held her ground, though it would very soon have been hurting her badly. The boy gave in first, shouting "she's game lads" to his friends, and on the memorial to her in Dundee, the words "she's game" are printed as her epitaph. They would not be easily translated into Efik, the language of Calabar, but a similar sentiment was expressed for decades to come among the Efik peoples.

Mary confessed that her own first surrender to the Christian Church was brought about by the threat of hell-fire. But the gospel she herself preached in the slums of Dundee, and later in the forests of Calabar, was a gospel of love. From many descriptions, it is clear that she possessed that rare essence of radiance often associated with a great nun. It was doubtless this quality that carried her message across, despite her extreme shyness. A wry Scottish humour seldom deserted her, and for all her gentleness, she had a disposition to tomboyishness even in early middle age; some would have said later still. Tree climbing was quite irresistible to her. Though she was frightened of fireworks and of cows, her phenomenal courage was to be tested and proved almost daily throughout her life, and perhaps never more so than when, at the death of her brother, she resolved to take up the mission he had set his heart on. In 1876, a neat but shabby little Scotswoman with a gentle, intelligent face and bright, carroty hair sailed from Liverpool for West Africa. The ship carried a vast cargo of casks of spirits, the hard liquor that had caused so much of the hardship of her young life and had ruined and finally killed her father.

Since its beginnings in 1848, the mission had waged a long and bitter fight against the cruel practices inherent in the local society. Progress had been made at the estuary towns of Duke's Town, Henshaw's Town, and Creek Town. At the latter, the local chief, King Eyo Honesty, and his son had been especially sympathetic. But inland, human sacrifice, the poison ordeal, twin murder, and the tyranny of the secret society known as Ekpo were part of the daily life. There was as yet no colonial authority, though Calabar was considered a British sphere of influence. The British Consuls to the Bights of Benin and Biafra, with their considerable prestige, had given valuable support to those who were opposing the cruelty of the local laws. But not even at the coast had there been much progress towards professed Christianity. Neither polygamy nor slave ownership was easily given up, and their abandonment was, of course, a prerequisite of church membership.

It had been wisely decided to let conversion develop within the framework of the more peaceful society. That was the missionaries' first aim. It was realised that only with the aid of native evangelists could a church be founded in Calabar, and their training was inevitably slow. The first two actual converts, one of them the son of King Eyo Honesty, had been made after seven years. In 1876, when Mary arrived, there were 174 communicants in the whole mission area, though thousands attended the church services on Sunday. Hope Waddell and Hugh Goldie had written down the Efik language, compiled a dictionary, and translated some books, which had led to some reasonably good schools. The total achievement in nearly 40 years was not perhaps very great, but the Christian foothold was slowly and surely growing. The casualty rate through illness had been enormous. Many had died and many more invalided home forever. The team that Mary joined consisted in all of 12 Europeans plus some wives, one trained African, and eight native agents. It was a tiny company for the size of the job.

Duke's Town, where Mary landed in 1876, was a squalid little estuary settlement, but on Mission Hill, above the town, there was orderly and convincing civilisation. Cool, whitewashed houses, church, schools, and dispensaries stood amongst lush fruit orchards and gay flower gardens. Not long before, the hill had been a tangle of dense bush which had served as the town refuse dump and where the rotting corpses of the less important were thrown. Her first home was with "Daddy" and "Mammy" Anderson, who were both outstanding characters in the history of the mission. He was well-loved, though given to fierce outbursts of temper at behaviour he disliked. But it was Mammy who ruled not only on Mission Hill but also down in Duke's Town. A strict Calvinist and a highly efficient Scotswoman, she was among those who prompted the comment of an old Calabar chief, "Them women are the best man for Mission." Mary found the orderliness soothing, but the debilitating climate and the strangeness of Africa caused her both physical and mental strain. She was often sick and lonely, and Mammy Anderson's strict discipline scarcely eased her early days. She nonetheless admired Mammy and grew fond of her, and when her lack of punctuality was punished by being deprived of her dinner, Mary was convinced that Mammy knew that Daddy was privately supplying her with biscuits and bananas. Years later, when he was a widower, he returned from retirement to visit Calabar, and died in her arms.

Her first work was in the Mission School, and for this she had to learn Efik as quickly as possible, since the primary class was in the vernacular. She was also sent out along the bush trails to visit Old Town and Creek Town to get some knowledge of the missionary organisation. These adventurous walks with just a guide or, when necessary, a porter seem to have made a congenial change from the rigid daily round at the Andersons. The paths were rough, there were hills to be scrambled over and streams to be jumped, and everywhere splendid trees to be climbed. She climbed many of them, and this was often the cause of her tardiness. What the local population thought of this particular activity is not on record, but they were probably very amused.

In time, her work included visiting in the women's compounds in all the estuary towns, and it was here that she began to comprehend the immensity of the task that the small band of missionaries was tackling. Centuries of feminine subservience had bred apathy and unattractive indolence. Social customs had enforced filth and cruelty. Women lay around on the ground, everlastingly doing each other's hair, in apparent ease and luxury, but always under the threat of the atrocities which were only superficially suppressed. Widows were confined in small filthy huts until their husbands' lengthy obsequies were over. Mothers of twins were cast out in shame into the forest, their babies battered to death or thrown out to die. Work was not arduous for the free women, but they were more restricted than the slaves. This was the horrid picture that Mary had to assimilate. She saw that much of her work would lie among the women, and she knew that it would not be easy to make an impression. She also knew that it was work well worth doing, and that for God and her Saviour she must do it.

More than at any other time, Mary suffered from homesickness in these early days of her apprenticeship to Calabar. Those who serve overseas generally agree that the first tour is the worst. To her longing for her beloved family, Mary added anxiety about their welfare. She had contributed to their support since childhood, and she knew that her widowed mother must be struggling desperately. Her own salary was £60 a year, but a substantial proportion of that had to be paid to the Andersons for her board and lodging at European standards, and she could send little home. In 1879 she had her first leave, during which she moved her family to a village on the outskirts of Dundee. Many people would probably have thought that she ought to have stayed with them, but the Christian message is clearly not that.

Her mother used to say that God had given her Mary and that she gladly gave her child back to God's service.

While at home, she asked the Mission Council of the Church if she could be sent to a station on her own. She was essentially an individual person, but her main reason, which she did not give, was that on her own, she could live entirely on native food and at an African level in all things, and thus save a larger amount of her salary for her family. On her return to Calabar in October 1880, she was told that she had been appointed to be in sole charge at Old Town, a place that had had an unhappy record in missionary terms. It was under the supervision of Duke's Town, a few miles away, but to Mary it was a command at last. She never confessed to apprehension or fear about the solitude or danger. It is possible that she was too proud to admit that the financial side was so important to her, and that she had to overcome them.

Her work at Old Town included the care of two other small villages, and at all three places, she taught in schools, ministered to the sick, comforted the suffering, and, of course, preached. Overcoming her intense shyness, she faced congregations of black people who, firm in the grip of their ancient religion, might have been hostile. Her passionate message of faith rang out, and her radiant personality held them spellbound. The quiet, little woman was transformed by the strength of her belief into a formidable and moving orator. The crowning event of the week was the Sunday evening service at Old Town, when vast crowds assembled in the chief's compound. It began at dusk and ended by the light of lanterns. As they left in their hundreds to go down the dark trails to their homes, many of them would approach her and bid her a friendly goodnight. Some would hold their lanterns high to light her way to her own house. Maybe they would not embrace the Church for years to come, but they were touched and stirred by a profound respect for her, and really wished for her friendship.

Mary's home at Old Town was a derelict mud-and-palm-thatched hut, without any comforts. She ate only the local food, and when there was scarcity and people around were hungry, she ate only the poorest and plainest of that. She always went bare-footed and, even in the tropical sun, bareheaded. It was a completely African way of life that she lived almost the whole time from then on, and no doubt it contributed to the closeness of her contact with Africans. But though she could not afford the elegance of the mission houses at the other estuary towns, she never let her way of life preclude an emphasis on beauty and refinement, to which she was convinced Africans were susceptible. Like other missionary households, hers very soon included a little group of children and babies, the first of many such groups of "bairns," some of whom grew up to work in the mission field. There were a few whose parents wanted them to have the advantage of growing up near this white woman. Many more were destitute waifs, the victims of violence of one kind or another; some were rescued twins. This latter problem incensed Mary, but she realised that it was a deep-rooted superstition that would not be easily eradicated. Even the mother who had borne the twins thought of herself as unclean.

The people around her at Old Town came to consider her their own special possession, and they were always apprehensive, probably with good reason, when she wandered alone in the forest. There were already signs that the "untouched millions" of the hinterland were stirring her imagination; but she was still serving her apprenticeship, and undermined by the persistent death rate, the mission had no plans for expansion. She did explore a little way up the Cross River, and towards the end of her Old Town years, she answered the call of Chief Okon at James's Town, 30 miles down the estuary on the west bank. She had struck up a great friendship with old King Eyo Honesty, and to his great delight, Mary's mother, who had often heard of him at missionary meetings in Dundee, had written to him. Hearing that Mary was going to James's Town, he lent her his own canoe, and she embarked with all her bairns, knowing that she could not safely leave them. She found a friendly welcome and was regarded as a great curiosity, crowds following her everywhere.

While there, a bad soaking in a tropical storm that had blown the roof from the house where she was lodging resulted in an attack of fever, and at one moment she thought she was dying. When she recovered, she learned that four young girls were in trouble for what seems to us like a trivial bit of naughtiness. Two of them, the wives of a chief, had left the yard to which they were officially confined, and had visited friends in another yard. This was rigidly tabooed, and the girls, with two others who had connived at the incident, were condemned to the potentially lethal punishment of 100 lashes each. Mary went to see Chief Okon and persuaded him to let her speak to the tribal elders. She knew by now that many of the evils of West Africa were due to a strict adherence to tribal laws, and she began by telling them that they were certainly within their rights in sentencing the girls as they had done. This they found gratifying. She then criticised them about the iniquity of the laws themselves and of the system that confined young girls to this harem existence at the age of 15 or 16. This did not please the elders at all, but she fought on and succeeded in getting the punishment reduced to ten lashes. She judged that she must go no further, and be satisfied with this. Mary went miserably to her hut to prepare such medicaments as she had to alleviate the girls' pain.

Still in the aftermath of malaria, Mary left James's Town after a few weeks, and Chief Okon and his principal wife accompanied her in the canoe. In the course of the voyage, there was a sudden, dramatic tropical storm, and they were all but shipwrecked. Under Mary's orders, they made for the bank and, from the tossing boat, held on grimly to overhanging trees. The storm subsided as quickly as it came, but Mary had had another drenching. It left her shivering with ague, and only the large, warm body of Okon pushed firmly against her on one side and that of his fashionably fat-besmeared lady on the other side restored her circulation. She reached home safely with her equally sodden bairns, but the malaria returned, and she ailed more or less continuously until she was invalided home in 1883.

Mary was so ill and weak that she had to be carried on board the homeward-bound ship. Also carried on board was a tiny black baby girl, whom she was taking with her. A trader had found the baby lying crying in the bush, and Mary, guessing the facts, traced her boy twin and took them both into her care. The mother was a slave who was very ill, but before she died, she managed to bring about the death of the boy, possibly in order to purge her own impurity. There would have been little chance for the girl's survival if she had been left behind in Calabar, but there were also grave risks in taking her home to Scotland. Mary was scarcely strong enough to care for her, and might easily not have lasted the voyage. There are also many risks involved in completely detribalising a child, but they would be for later in the child's life.

The Scottish Mission was sometimes criticised for adopting these outcast babies, but quite apart from the humane impulse to rescue the helpless and give a tiny life a chance, there were other sensible motives. If the Africans could see with their own eyes that twin babies grew up into normal human beings and not into monsters, it would help to undermine the superstition; and the more intelligent children, growing up in an educated white home, were potentially valuable native staff for the mission. To some extent this proved true, though, inevitably, there were some failures and one or two tragedies. This baby girl of Mary Slessor's lived to have an interesting and useful life. She was christened Janie, after Mary's sister, in the Wishart Church in Dundee. Then, Mary took her on deputation work, the almost obligatory lecturing and money-raising round for missionaries on furlough. Apart from being an asset to Mary in overcoming her shyness, she proved a star turn everywhere. Most Scottish missionary subscribers would have heard of twin murder, and it was both exciting and moving to see for themselves this picaninny, the actual survivor of twin murder. As events turned out, she was a mischievous little girl of 3, speaking broad Scots, before she returned to Calabar. Not long after her return, Mary discovered that the father, whom she had thought was dead, was trying to get a glimpse of his child without actually coming near her. Mary almost hurled them into each other's arms, saying, "Hoots man, what harm could the wee girlie do you?" He was enchanted with her and brought her many little presents until he died a few years later.

On the protracted leave that began in 1883, Mary was herself in dire need of a rest in a healthy climate. She also found illness in her family. Her beloved sister Janie was already an advanced consumptive, and the harsh, smoky air of Dundee was killing her. Mary conceived the idea of taking her back to Calabar with her. Just possibly the sea voyage might have helped the invalid, but the intense humidity of the river settlements could hardly have done her any good, and the whole idea savours of desperation. Poor Mary's strongly felt loyalties were conflicting. The mission, perhaps rightly, turned down the proposition, and in the circumstances, Mary could not herself go back to Africa. She took herself off the strength of the mission, as she felt she was not entitled to the salary when she could see no immediate prospect of going back to work. Her sister Susan was by then contributing to the family budget, but it was naturally frustrating for Mary to be kept at home.

Then, a chance visitor from the south suggested that the milder climate of Devonshire might help Janie. Clutching at a straw, Mary forthwith took the two Janies to Topsham on the Exe estuary. She found a cottage, and the local Congregational Church community welcomed them kindly. Janie rallied well and when Mrs. Slessor joined them, there was a peaceful, happy time in surroundings of great beauty. Mary regularly attended Exeter Hospital to widen her medical knowledge for when she could go abroad again. Then, Susan Slessor died quite suddenly on the doorstep of a house in Edinburgh. It became imperative for Mary to have a salary again, and the mission was only too glad to reenrol her. She was appointed to Creek Town and given a sailing date in November. But Mrs. Slessor fell ill, and Janie had a relapse, and it was obvious that they could not be left alone. Mary wrote an impassioned appeal to an old Dundee friend to come and help. She came at once, and, with the baby Janie, Mary sailed on time, knowing that her mother and sister would be well cared for.

Neither of them had, in fact, long to live. Mary heard the news of her mother's death in February 1886, and of Janie's death three months later. She had lost the first great focus of her life, the care of her very dear family, who were now all dead, and she was desolate in the loss of an affectionate home to think back to and to which she could pour out her heart and her "nonsense" in letters. But for the first time, she was free of responsibility and able to pursue any venture that she thought worthwhile, whatever its dangers. She had long been dreaming of thrusting deeper into Africa, and her dreams might now come true.

The Okoyong were comparatively recent arrivals in the country that lies between the Calabar and Cross rivers. They had apparently come from the direction of the foothills of the Cameroon Mountains, and they had pushed the former inhabitants to the other side of the Cross River. They were, therefore, regarded with hostility as very wicked people, and the hostility was reciprocated. They spoke a Bantu tongue, an unusually westerly example of the great Bantu language family. Some of them must have known some Efik, because, although ostensibly outlawed from the local trade, and certainly excluded from the busy commerce of the coast, they did manage somehow to import guns, spirits, and chains. None of these commodities was conducive to a peaceful way of life. They were organised into large chief's households or villages, and were mutually hostile, except when united against the foreigner. They had had no direct contact with Europeans, and tribal law was absolute.

Mary spent another two years at Creek Town, consciously preparing herself for what was to come, and living, for once, in some state in one of the European houses. She even mixed with what she considered very cultured and high-class society: consular officials, doctors, ships' officers, traders, and missionaries. All the time, the possibilities of a station in Okoyong were being explored. She went with three different reconnaissance expeditions, and found the people sullen, inhospitable, and armed. Each time on her return, she admitted that she found the whole thing very frightening. But like Mary Kingsley, she had no one left to live for, and for such a cause, she considered her life expendable. On her fourth visit, she went alone to negotiate for facilities for residence. She considered that a woman by herself was less likely to provoke hostility, but her courage was nonetheless formidable.

In Creek Town, Mary's friendship with King Eyo Honesty had flourished. She helped him with advice on matters of administration, and he helped her in any way he could. So, once again, it was in the elegance and comfort of his state canoe that she embarked on her long voyage up the Calabar. The inland river was beautiful, the boatman sang improvised songs, and, lying on luxurious cushions, she was able to relax and indulge her great feeling for nature. Already, she loved the forest rivers. She landed on the west bank of the Calabar and walked four miles through the forest to a village called Ekenge. She was greeted by hundreds of local people who were eager to see and, if possible, to touch the white "Ma." Her instinct in coming alone had proved sound, because they seem to have admired her courage and possibly have been a bit awed by it. Edem, the village chief, was by good fortune at home and sober. He was very civil and accommodating about a site for a house and a school, and, of paramount importance, she was able to negotiate the promise of sanctuary rights for refugees in her compound. In her short visit, Mary struck up a friendship with his widowed sister, Ma Eme, which was to prove enduring and very valuable.

After a night on a bundle of corn husks and dirty rags in a rat-infested hut in the women's yard, she walked a few miles farther on to the village of Ifako. Once again, she was successful in negotiating the accommodation and the sanctuary rights she required. Then, more hopeful than she would have thought possible, she returned downriver to Creek Town to prepare for her permanent move to Okoyong. Everyone tried to dissuade her. It was said that Okoyong could only be civilised by a Vice-Consul with a gunboat and troops. What chance would a humble little Scotswoman have in opposing the powers of witchcraft by herself. Five years later, when the British Government was gradually assuming control, the battle was going so well in the lone hands of the little Scotswoman that she herself was the obvious choice for the Vice-Consulship of Okoyong. She had never had, nor did she ever need, a gunboat.

The final departure for Okoyong was in August 1888, exactly 12 years since Mary had started on her missionary apprenticeship. The embarkation was emotional, because many people thought she could not survive the venture. The calmest and most encouraging of her friends was old King Eyo. He installed her under the canopy of his canoe himself, together with her five current bairns, aged from 1 to 11 years, and all the baggage. Her friend, Hugh Goldie, was so distressed when he saw her about to leave by herself that he asked for a volunteer from the mission to go with her and help her to settle in. Mr. Bishop, the mission printer, a recent arrival, stepped forward gallantly. Then, the gathered well-wishers, many of them weeping, saw the canoe glide away in blinding rain, a drummer beating monotonously in the bow.

It was still raining in the evening when the party landed on the beach four miles from Ekenge. Mary and the children, carrying light rations, set out on the swampy forest trail to fetch porters for the rest of the baggage. The smallest baby rode on her hip in local fashion. Darkness came while they were still on the march, and the children were overtired and frightened and cried all the time. She sang little Scottish "nonsense" songs to try to keep them going, but it was a sorry, half-drowned little band that escorted the future "white queen of Okoyong" into Ekenge. She found the place deserted. Everyone had gone off to some drunken junketings, probably a funeral, some distance away. It was then that she blessed the presence of Mr. Bishop. When he realised that something was wrong, he hurried up from the beach, but as a newcomer, he was unable to persuade the tired crew of paddlers to act as porters for the baggage.

She left him on guard with the children, and, tired though she was, she almost ran, bare-footed for greater speed, to the beach. It was Saturday night, and as a good Scottish Presbyterian, she could not have her effects moved on a Sunday, and had to get them up to her lodging that night. The crew were all asleep under the awning, but she went in among them and almost pushed and pulled them to their feet. Once aroused and in spite of, or maybe because of, her teasing Scots tongue, they were cooperative, and she was installed before the Sabbath dawned. The hut set aside for her in the women's yard was filthy and rotten, and it rained throughout her first Sunday. The revellers were still away, and sitting in lonely squalor, she admitted that her confidence sank to a low ebb. Fortunately, her faith in her mission was powerful.

Mary had to continue living in the women's yard for some time, and it was a horrid experience. The free women had less liberty than the slaves, and the frustration made them vicious. One was a compulsive scold with a harsh voice, who flogged her sickly slave girl daily. To the efficient, vital Scotswoman, the very lassitude was nauseating. The huts were filthy, the children neglected, and the children of slaves stole their food where they could. But Mary was never the nagging, scolding missionary woman. The squalor was awful, but it was only part of a whole social structure in which there were far worse evils. More important than hygiene and indolence was the saving of life and the prevention of cruelty, and they were formidable tasks, because killings and torture on ritual occasions were of deep religious significance.

Mary Slessor set about her task in the full knowledge of the depths of the problem. She did not condemn and she exercised tact. She knew that, apart from the humane side, the rules of society were amounting to slow tribal suicide as the death roll from human sacrifice and the poison ordeal was decimating the population. Her supreme gift for her task was courage combined with compassion. The courage was so shining that it intimidated, and slowly, over the years, the high officers of this most conservative of societies came, first, to respect and, then, to submit to her. The Missionary Council in Scotland might be waiting to hear of hundreds of good new Presbyterians, all decently dressed in their own cast-off Sunday best, but Mary knew that that goal was a long way off, and was by no means the first priority.

As well as her faith, anger was sometimes the inspiration of her courage. But the anger often had to be controlled. A boy who had assisted her in her first few days was accused of betraying the old ways, and before she realised what was happening, he had boiling oil poured on his hands. The watchers, inured to such things, and some probably enjoying them, had no idea of the passive courage Mary needed to watch this happen. She was passive only because she was too late to prevent it, and from then on she was seldom too late. Ma Eme, Chief Edem's sister, became her great ally and, in the strictest secrecy, her informant of threatening disaster. A messenger with an empty medicine bottle and a request to refill it was the signal. Ma Eme had herself been lucky to escape death by poison ordeal when her husband died. She was both compassionate and brave, but though her friendship with Mary was real, she never actually embraced Christianity.

It was in her early Okoyong days that Mary set out on a journey of many hours through the forest, because she heard that one of the Okoyong chiefs near the Cross River was dying. Everyone in Ekenge warned her of the danger of going into strange country and strange villages, but a chief's death meant a holocaust of killing, and, albeit with apprehension, she felt impelled to go. Most probably, she welcomed the chance to reach out beyond her own two villages. When Edem realised she was quite determined, he provided her with an escort for the journey. Much of the march was in drenching rain, and, one by one, she

took off her soaking garments, which were hampering her progress. She arrived dirty and dishevelled in her chemise, and
wondered if she had lost her European prestige irretrievably. In
fact, her persistence and stamina were remembered with admiration for a long time. She certainly was "game."

The chief was still alive, but there was nervous apprehension
among the watchers in the yard. Nobody knew who and how
many the witch doctors would accuse of responsibilitiy if he died.
The poison ordeal or some other death would follow for some of
them, and perhaps more would be killed to swell the dead man's
entourage in the next world. Mary could not at that time have
stopped the killing. All she could do was to try to save the chief's
life. She managed to obtain some necessary extra medicines from
a mission station on the other side of the Cross River, and after
some days of continuous nursing, she knew she had won her
battle. Not only the chief's life, but also countless other lives
were saved.

It was but one of many similar episodes in her years in
Okoyong, but it spread her reputation, for the first time, beyond
her two initial villages of Ekenge and Ifako. It also gave her some
assurance that, in spite of the warnings of her mentors in these
villages, it was possible for her to travel abroad in the rest of the
country. Soon after her return to Ekenge, Chief Edem was
seriously ill with an abscess in the back, but the witch doctor took
charge of the case before she could see him. Hostages against
Edem's death were already chained to posts in the yard, and he
showed Mary extraneous articles, ostensibly extracted from the
abscess, as proof of the necessity for them. She could do nothing
this time but pray, and, fortunately, her prayers were answered.

While she was still living in Edem's yard, a primitive school was
started. For the first few weeks, it was socially essential for all
ages and social ranks to attend it, but when the novelty wore off,
attendance was reduced to more manageable proportions. A few
learned the Efik alphabet, and many more enjoyed the hymn
singing. Mary was accepted with tolerance when she did not
interfere too much, but Edem was showing no signs of building
her a hut in her own domain, and still less in building a church
and house. The neighbours at Ifako were doing better, and a big
hut for church or school with occasional sleeping facilities was

soon completed. This was the fourth year of her tour, and she was in poor physical condition, but she started to clear the bush with her own hands on what was to be her compound. This served as an inspiration, and a two-room hut was erected quickly by local labour. It was made out of red mud, or swish, which also did for the furniture. It would one day, perhaps, act as an out-building to a more suitable mission accommodation. Chief Edem liked her but was not sufficiently assured of her importance to give her this. What finally advanced her social status enormously was her involvement in commercial diplomacy.

Okoyong was singularly isolated from the outside world. One of the few manufactured commodities that arrived was hard liquor, and the people had little else to do but drink it. Mary worked hard to get them to dispense with it at tribal palavers, and she had some small success. A few people agreed with her that it was nicer if no blood was shed on these occasions, especially since bloodshed always generated bloodshed. The wish for peace, even on this slight scale, was encouraging. But Mary realised that to reduce the consumption of liquor significantly, some alternative occupations were necessary. She had many African trader friends at Calabar, and she asked them to come up to Okoyong with their wares in the hope of stimulating the production of some crops for barter. The traders refused emphatically, because the Okoyong were known to be bad people, and they knew that they would not be safe among them.

Then, she had recourse to her old friend King Eyo, who always kept a watchful eye on her from a distance. He agreed to invite some of the Okoyong chiefs to come with her to Calabar for peaceful discussions about possible trade. Both he and Mary understood that they were to come unarmed. The idea caught on among the chiefs, and there was great enthusiasm to go until they learned that guns, and what they called their cutlasses, were to be left behind. This was unthinkable. They never went among strangers unarmed, and they told Mary indignantly that she was trying to make women of them. Quietly but firmly she called the whole thing off. There was bitter disappointment, but Mary knew that persistence always paid, and before long, a small party agreed to hand their arms to their women before leaving. A canoe was then loaded with some produce—a barrel of oil, plantains, and yams—but there was no skill in loading weight, and it sank. The cargo in the next canoe was so badly distributed that there was danger of capsizing. Mary ordered a rearrangement, and in the course of it, she noticed a pile of cutlasses under the produce. To the accompaniment of lusty Scots opprobrium, she threw the swords overboard one by one, and it is a measure of the growing confidence in her that the party continued the journey.

At Creek Town, King Eyo rose magnificently to the occasion. He thought of the Okoyong as rude savages but treated them courteously, and he talked to them for their own good, reminding them that they now had the means of listening to the Gospel in Okoyong, and they must not fail to do so. Then, Mary gave them a conducted tour of the King's palace and the European missionaries' houses and the other glories of Creek Town, which they found overwhelming. In the evening, King Eyo addressed them in the church on the text "to give light to them that sit in darkness and in the shadow of death [and] to guide our feet into the way of peace."

The chiefs were greatly impressed by the King and anxious for his friendship, and a window onto a seductive new world had opened for them. On their return, they waxed enthusiastic and maintained that the wonders of Calabar were within their reach in Okoyong, as they had their very own white Ma Slessor. They had seen her treated as an equal by this great King at Creek Town, and by all these amazing Europeans. The first thing they must do was to build her a house commensurate with her importance, and it must be started without delay. In fact, she awoke on the morning after her return to the sound of the preparatory forest clearing.

Before long, Mary reported home that she had got a "beautiful building," but without doors or windows, which were beyond the scope of the local building talent. In March 1889, the Scottish missionary journal, *The Record*, published an appeal for a carpenter with an interest in missionary work who would go to Calabar. As a result, three months later, Charles Ovens walked into Mary's yard while she was dining outside with all the bairns, and greeted her in broad Scots. He had been on the point of returning from Scotland to America, to which he had emigrated, when he was told of the advertisement. He had never heard of Miss

Slessor, but he rewrote his luggage labels, and sailed for West Africa instead. Apart from his carpentering skills, he was a great delight to Mary. She loved laughter, and his humour was akin to her own. He sang old Scottish songs as he worked, which caused her nostalgic but not unhappy tears. He had not imagined that conditions could be quite as primitive as he found them, but he was more amused than bothered by them.

The noises of the African forest have a rhythm to which the ear becomes attuned, and a break in the rhythm is instantly noticable. When Mary's fine mission buildings were nearing completion, a sudden break in the rhythm one day made her apprehensive. She was sure that something was wrong. She listened intently for a moment, and then, with something of the instinct of a wild animal, she knew the direction to go in, and she ran like the wind into the forest. Etim, the eldest son of Chief Edem, was engaged in building a house for his bride-to-be. While fetching timber from the forest, a big log had fallen on him and had virtually broken his back. Charles Ovens found Mary kneeling by the unconscious body, and quickly constructed a stretcher on which Etim was carried to his mother's hut.

Then, Mary began a two-week-long fight for his life, and probably many other lives, because violent death would have to be punished. The people of Ekenge watched and waited with terrible apprehension. It was a hopeless case, and at the last, some unsuitable treatment by local practitioners hastened his death. The diviner was summoned, and he decreed that a certain village was to blame. The armed freemen of Ekenge marched to this village and captured all those who had not taken refuge in the forest. They sacked the village and brought back their prisoners, a dozen men and women, and chained them to posts in the chief's yard.

Mary knew that if she was to have any chance of saving their lives, she must be as helpful as possible over some of the death ritual, and she cooperated in the adornment of Etim's body for the grave. She dressed it as splendidly as she could in swathes of silk and a new suit she had made for Edem. A turban on the head was further crowned with a feathered hat, and it was propped on a chair under an umbrella, with a mirror placed in front for self-admiration. When the spectators were allowed in, they found it wildly exciting. They yelled and capered and skirmished round the gorgeously costumed corpse and around the prisoners. They started to drink and continued drinking for days. Mary and her carpenter ceased work on the buildings, and watched over the prisoners in alternate day and night shifts. It was a harrowing vigil. Three of the women had small babies, and one had a 15-year-old daughter, who either clung to her or knelt at Mary's feet, asking her to help. Charles Ovens, who a little time before would not have thought such things possible, became desperate and threatened to free the prisoners with hammer and chisel. But Mary's experience dictated patience, and they watched and prayed.

When she sensed that the time of the poison ordeal was approaching, she went to see Chief Edem and his brother Ekenyong, and told them that they must not kill the prisoners. They were not prepared to listen, and found her arguments absurd. Only the guilty would die; justice demanded their lives; and the relatives were entitled to them. She went on pestering them ceaselessly, and they became cross and told her that she was abusing their hospitality by interfering in the sacred matters of the tribe. She sat down in Edem's inner yard and said that she would not move until the prisioners were freed. She was aware that, for whatever reason, her presence was inhibiting. Under cover of darkness, the first woman was unchained and led to the table on which the mixture of poison beans was ready. Mary was expecting this and she acted instantly. She snatched the woman's hand, and bolted with her to her own enclosure, but the watchers, stupified with drink, reacted too slowly to stop them.

Mary continued her pestering, knowing the corpse was deteriorating rapidly, and would soon have to be buried and with some attendant corpses. First, two and then, five more prisoners were released after taking the Mbiam, an elaborate oath to a remote god, and drinking a nonpoisonous but sacred libation, with the impassioned plea to be dealt with if they lied. Mary was winning, but three prisoners remained. One was an ailing woman with a tiny baby, and it was Ma Eme who successfully begged her brothers for her life. Edem was now wracked with guilt, because he was failing to do the right thing by his own dead son, who might have to suffer in the afterworld for his fault. Mary Kingsley used to say that West Africans would have a better under-standing of the Antigone of Sophocles than would Europeans.

In Ekenge, it was a poignant drama that was being played out between the old chief, with his sacred obligations to a dead freeman, and the little Scotswoman who so well understood his agony. Edem was being pushed to take a first terrible step away from age-old darkness. Mary was sympathetic, but she was inex-orable, and she continued her pleading until the last man was freed. One woman remained and Mary despaired for her. The burial was urgent, and the starving woman was herself asking for death. But late that night she crawled into Mary's yard in her chains, which she said she had broken herself. Mary was con-vinced that it was not she, but Ma Eme, who had done so, not wanting it known among her people. The burial of a freeman finally took place for the first time in Okoyong history, without a single death. What must have been especially encouraging to Mary was the evidence of a stirring of compassion, in Edem himself, and in some of the women, that she knew had helped her in her battle.

The episode did not quite finish with Etim's burial. Drunks on their way home started shooting each other; one man was killed, and a small war of vengeance was threatening until Mary inter-vened. Runners from the mysterious Ekpo secret society arrived, calling for revenge for Etim, but their antics, though often vio-lent, appear curiously fatuous. Ekpenyong, Edem's brother, was then accused of his nephew's death, and Mary actually had to snatch the poison beans from him when he determined to dem-onstrate his innocence. But after many weeks, the whole distur-bance died down.

Charles Ovens wrote a detailed account of the episode to the home mission, and perhaps for the first time, they were made aware in Scotland of what Mary was really doing. He also gave a picture of her daily life that astonished them. At one moment, the gentle, ministering angel cares for the sick and tends her refugee bairns; at another, the caustic but good-humoured Scotswoman taunts her neighbours for some stupidity; at another, the little red-haired termagent boxes a drunkard's ears, and topples him over to keep him from the gin bottle. From time to time, she steps between the opposing forces when an armed brawl is getting under way, and orders them to lay down their arms. Ovens saw people angry with her, and he saw organised drinking bands of women jeering at her, but never once was a hand laid on her.

One of the many advantages of adequate mission buildings was that Mary could now more easily be relieved to go on furlough. She had been nearly five years in the country, and the last three had been superhumanly strenuous. She suffered continuously from malaria, and the treatment at the time was in itself debilitating. Frequently, she was up all night, nursing the sick or making her lightening dashes through the forest to intervene in some potentially dangerous happening. She went downriver at times to Calabar for a short rest, but much more than that was needed if she were to survive. Fortunately, a Miss Dunlop was willing to fill her place for a time, and she did so gallantly, though she was appalled at what she found, and she lacked, perhaps, the knowledge of the real significance of the evils she saw around her. Mary packed for home, and, of course, Janie was to go with her. Many Okoyong friends came to wish her goodbye, and to bring her humble little farewell offerings. She promised them faithfully that she would return, and bade them be good while she was gone.

At the last moment, against all advice, she ran once more all night through the forest, because a small fracas was rumoured to be escalating into a full-scale war. For once, she shed a little of her defencelessness, which had frequently proved a protection, and asked for the escort of an Ekpo society drummer. When she reached the battle zone, and confronted one of the opposing forces, the chief, whose life she had saved near the Cross River in her early days in Okoyong, stepped forward and knelt to greet her. She had indeed cast her bread upon the waters that night when she had dashed half naked through the rain to his supposed deathbed. He now begged her to make peace, and after a tediously long palaver, it was achieved. She had another strenuous effort to make: to prevent the ratification of the peace treaty in gin. She managed to cut the ration down to one glass for each person, and impounded the rest under the protection of the Ekpo drum until blood had cooled. She only just got back to Ekenge in time to embark by canoe and catch her steamer to England.

At home she went straight to Topsham to visit her mother's and sister's graves. She rented a cottage and stayed with wee Janie for several months. It was a kinder climate than Dundee in which to recuperate; she had friends in the Congregational Church community; and she loved the Devon scenery. Though her friends were unaware of it at the time, a tremendous personal happiness had come into her life. On her recurrent visits to Calabar from Okoyong, she had met a young missionary schoolmaster called Charles Morrison, and a great intellectual friendship had grown up between them. Nowadays, Mary Slessor would probably have read English literature at a university. Even with the rudimentary education that she had sandwiched in between the long working hours at the mill, she had gone on to read enough to develop a fine critical taste. And so it had been a great delight to her to experience, occasionally, the companionship of someone who shared her taste, and who could help her to broaden her reading. He had provided some of Dickens's novels for her to read on the voyage home. For his part, he was an ardent admirer of her character and her work. He had been up to Ekenge to stay with her, and had marvelled at it at firsthand. When she passed through Calabar on her way to England, he had proposed to her, and she had accepted him on condition that he joined her in Okoyong. He was 24 and she was 42.

During her year at home, they made an application for a joint posting to Okoyong, and there seemed to be a great deal to be said for it. Mary was badly in need of help, and it was not easy to find anybody suitable for her who would come to know the people as she did. They would be able to man the station for each other when away, and they would nurse each other when sick. Mary was reasonably confident that the application would succeed, and she announced the engagement and wore a ring. With her boyishly cropped hair, she looked younger than her age, and for the most part, her friends and Charles's relations took a favourable view of the affair.

The Mission Council was less enthusiastic; in fact, for the moment they turned down the application. Charles was too valuable a teacher to be spared from Calabar, and in Okoyong, Mary had only scraped together the rudiments of a primary school. She could have been appointed to Duke's Town to join

Charles, and he hoped that she would accept the posting. And yet, he must have known that she had made promises to the Okoyong people to return that she would consider binding. Her references to him are so formal, he remains "Mr. Morrison" in her letters, that one can only guess at the measure of her disappointment, and she accepted the decision with formal dignity. They still hoped to marry one day, but Charles's health deteriorated rapidly, and he had to be sent home from West Africa. He went out to stay with his brother in the backwoods of North Carolina, and, after a literary manuscript on which he was working burned in a fire, he died there. It is said that in the letter that Mary wrote to his parents at his death, it was clear that she had loved him dearly; there is no doubt that he had loved her and needed her.

It is understandable that missionary effort should have been directed towards literacy. Missionaries tended to be reasonably educated people, and they generally thought that the seed they were sowing would only gain a lasting hold in a moderately literate society. In this way, the teaching of the semi-skills of the manual worker had been perforce neglected. It is easy for attitudes to harden conservatively, and in 1891, there were missionary voices expressing the recurrent theme "they're not ready for it," with reference to Africans being taught to use their own raw materials with their own hands. It was said that, accustomed to acting by force of necessity only, they would never have the persistence and stamina to learn carpentry and other crafts. At the coastal towns, there was some scope for the semiliterate, but in Okoyong, virtually none.

Mary went from Topsham to Edinburgh, and was sent on deputation, speaking at meetings all over Scotland. While there, she wrote an anonymous letter to *The Record*, emphatically repudiating the "not ready for it" theory. It was lucidly and cogently argued, and it was addressed over the head of the Missionary Council to the Church of Scotland. She suggested that a small delegation of experts should go at once to Calabar to make a study of the desirability and feasibility of sending out artisans to train Africans in their trades. It was impossible for such a statesmanlike letter to be ignored, and a delegation was organised at once. One of the delegates was Dr. Laws of Livingstonia, who had founded famous schools for technical training in central and southeastern Africa. The result was the Hope Waddell Institute in Calabar, which was an outstanding success. Mary Slessor, having initiated the idea, and having been formally consulted about it before she left Scotland, was not again involved with its administration.

During Mary's year at home, the situation in Eastern Nigeria was changing. Hitherto, there had been a single British Consul posted to what was known as the Oil Rivers, to the Cameroons, which were in the process of German settlement, and to Fernando Poo. This Consul, though influential, had no official jurisdiction. In 1888, a survey was carried out by Sir Claude Macdonald, a one-time soldier, whose outstanding administrative ability had led him by chance into the service of the Foreign Office. His recommendations had led to the first African Order in Council, giving the Consul jurisdiction over an area yet to be defined. Finally, the British Niger Coast Protectorate was declared, Lord Rosebery disliking the oleaginous sound of Oil Rivers. Macdonald had been appointed Her Majesty's special Commissioner and Consul-General, the consular part still being relevant to the Cameroons and Fernando Poo. British colonial rule had now really commenced. Macdonald was an enlightened and imaginative administrator. He was also a Presbyterian Scot, and sympathetic to the Scottish Mission.

The advent of colonial rule necessitated better facilities at the coast, and this was Macdonald's first preoccupation. Three quarters of the white population had died in a blackwater-fever epidemic in 1890, but now good drainage, improved sanitation, and more efficient hospitals gave a better chance of survival. Macdonald then turned his attention to the extension of the British rule of law into the hinterland. He had a small military force and a gunboat, and he recruited young men from England to act as vice-consular agents in up-country districts. They were, for the most part, quite inexperienced, but under Macdonald's guidance, British jurisdiction was slowly established. When he went up to Okoyong, he found Mary anxious that some raw recruit was going to come among her people and upset them.

It did not take him long to realise that the Okoyong people, reputedly the hardest to deal with in his area, already stood in awe of this little, red-headed Scotswoman, who addressed him as "Laddie Dear." Her knowledge of the local customs and laws was unique, and the respect in which she was held was of inestimable value, and he did not want it to be wasted. He made the inspired but well-reasoned decision to appoint her his Vice-Consul and District Magistrate. Sir Clement Hill, at the Foreign Office, was outraged at the idea of a woman holding such office, but Macdonald knew what he was doing, and was not discouraged. Mary, after deep thought, and some criticism from her missionary colleagues, decided that it was in the interests of the work to which she had dedicated her life to accept the appointment. After all, David Livingstone had accepted consular status, on condition that missionary considerations would always come first.

Mary presided over the local Okoyong courts within the terms of reference dictated by the Doctrine of Repugnancy, which recognised native law and custom except insofar as they were repugnant to civilised standards of natural law and justice. Some missionary colleagues were shocked at her involving herself in anything so heathen and sometimes obscene as native customs, probably having little idea of the extent to which she was already involved. She was, of course, extremely well qualified for the job. She usually "sat" in the open, on a wickerwork chair by a small table, on which was the book in which she recorded her own judgements. If supplies from friends in Scotland had been good, there was also a bag of her favourite toffees. Ranged on either side of her were a few of the local chiefs, who got their ears boxed if they talked in court, and behind her stood a uniformed court official, or native policeman. Certain categories of cases, such as murder or those involving strangers, she sent straight to the higher courts sitting in Calabar.

Mr. T. D. Maxwell, the Chief Magistrate at Calabar, who later became Justice of the Supreme Court, described his first official visit to "Miss Slessor" as a magistrate. He found her sitting in a rocking chair on the verandah, nursing a small baby. She was evidently expecting him, because she was wearing the only bit of finery she was known to possess, a little gossamer Shetland shawl, over her head. Her welcomes were always a delight, and Maxwell admitted to being rather naively surprised at the richness of her Scottish accent. He got his first vivid flash of the way she ruled Okoyong when he was partaking of some refreshment before the court opened.

Suddenly she jumped up with an angry growl: her shawl fell off, the baby was hurriedly transferred to someone qualified to hold it, and, with a few trenchant words, she made for the door, where a hulking over-dressed native stood. In a moment she siezed him by the scruff of the neck, boxed his ears, and hustled him out into the yard, telling him quite specifically what he might expect if he came back again without her consent. I watched him and his followers slink away very crestfallen. Then, as suddenly as it had arisen the tornado subsided, and (laced shawl, baby and all) she was again gently swaying in her chair. The man was a local monarch of sorts, who had been impudent to her, and she had forbidden him to come near her house again until he had not only apologised but done some prescribed penance. Under the pretext of calling on me, he had defied her orders...and that was the result.[1]

Maxwell came to know her court work well and wrote of it with both admiration and envy:

I have had a good deal of experience of Nigerian courts of various kinds, but I have never met one which better deserved to be termed a Court of Justice than that over which she presided. The litigants emphatically got justice—sometimes, perhaps, like Shylock, more than they desired—and it was essential justice unhampered by legal technicalities.[2]

On one occasion, she had to find for the plaintiff in a case involving a small claim for debt. She knew very well that he was a rogue, whereas the defendant had a good reputation. She allowed the debt on the evidence, but she gave the defendant the right to thrash the plaintiff in public. The judgement gave enormous satisfaction locally, and Maxwell said that during his life as a judge, he often wished that he could follow it as a precedent.

In 1895, Mary had a delightful treat. Mary Kingsley, who was travelling in West Africa mainly in the interests of her ethnographic studies, walked into the yard unannounced one afternoon and stayed for several days. She arrived in the middle of a twin palaver. An Ibo slave, much valued by her mistress, had given birth to twins, and her hitherto reasonably secure position was instantly changed. She was violently abused, her clothes torn, and most of her effects smashed. The rest of her possessions, including the two babies, were rammed into an empty gin case, and when Mary Slessor ran to her rescue, she was staggering along weakly with this and a skillet and some calabashes on her head. She would most probably have been killed but for fear of Mary Slessor's anger. Mary quickly relieved her of her load, and turned with her in the direction of her own compound. But she did not go straight there along what was the main market road. She made a detour and waited in the hot midday sun while a path, just sufficient for herself and the mother of the twins to pass along, was hacked through the bush to her house. This was supremely tactful, for had the main road been polluted by the passage of the unclean woman and her unnatural babies, another road would have had to be made through dense forest.

The whole episode was of tremendous interest to Mary Kingsley, who was already enquiring about the origin of the abhorrence of twin-birth among many of the West African peoples.

I arrived in the middle of this affair for my first visit with Mary Slessor, and things at Okoyong were rather crowded one way or another that afternoon. All the attention one of the children wanted...the boy for there was a boy and a girl...was burying, for the people who had crammed them into the box had utterly smashed the child's head. The other child was still alive, and is still a member of Miss Slessor's household of rescued children, all of whom owe their lives to Miss Slessor.[3]

These two outstanding women were instantly attracted to each other, and the temporary social ostracism due to the twin episode left them in peace to talk for many hours of each day. They were both very able and both, to a large extent, self-educated. Mary Kingsley had had the advantages of living in an intellectual world and of access to good libraries. Mary Slessor, on the other hand, had infinitely deeper knowledge of the peoples of that part of Africa, and she had a great deal to teach Mary Kingsley. Both women were infinitely serious people who could, nonetheless, laugh uproariously. Mary Kingsley could not quite be called inhibited, and yet, in comparison with Mary Slessor, she had her little complications. Had she found herself encumbered by her long black skirts in a tornado in the forest, she would have clung tenaciously to the drenched trappings of respectability rather than undress to her chemise.

Even with the great difference of background, they had much in common, with one big fundamental difference. Mary Kingsley was not a believer, and with the exception of Mary Slessor and one or two other missionary friends, she was critical of Christian missionaries. On the vexed question of drink, they would also have disagreed, but more on matters of fact than of belief or opinion. Mary Kingsley was perhaps overanxious to repudiate the impression she was apt to make in West Africa that she was a member of a women's temperance society, collecting data on the wickedness of the liquor trade. She maintained that she was not looking for drunkenness, and what she did not see she could not write about. She had noticed more drunks in London than she ever had in West Africa, and she preferred not to discuss the matter. Mary Slessor could have justly put her in the picture, but she was too well-mannered to go against her guest's wishes. It was a pity, because as a result, the soundness of Mary Kingsley's judgement of how West Africa should develop was impaired.

Mary Kingsley gives a good appraisal of Mary Slessor's life up to 1895, though, very curiously, she omits to say that she was both a missionary and a Magistrate.

This very wonderful lady has been 18 years in Calabar; for the last six or seven living entirely alone, as far as white folks go, in a clearing in the forest near to one of the principal villages of Okoyong District, and ruling as a veritable white chief over the entire Okoyong District. Her great abilities, both physical and intellectual, have given her among the savage tribe, an unique position, and won her from white and black who know her, a profound esteem....This instance of what one white can do would give many important lessons in West Coast administration and development. Only the sort of man Miss Slessor represents is rare.[4]

Mary Kingsley described her visit as "some of the pleasantest days of my life." Mary Slessor, after Mary Kingsley's death, wrote more poetically of "the joy and instruction of those days of companionship...like the languorous glamour of a summer's day in which one bathed, and lay still, and let life go by in a sweet dream."[5] There was "something" that they planned to do together in the future, but Mary Kingsley's tragic early death intervened, and, except for a brief farewell visit a few months later, they never met again.

The rest of 1895 was not a good year. Mary had been in a malarial climate too long, and she was exhausted. There were tragedies among the bairns, and several old friends at the coast died. The local Okoyong were drifting westwards in search of more fertile lands, and Mary herself moved to Akpap in order to remain as central as possible to the people. Akpap was six miles from Ikonetu on the Cross River, and that was now her main route to the Calabar bases. She had to live primitively for some time before new mission buildings could be built. Her health suffered, and she was far from well when a smallpox epidemic broke out in 1896, though she threw all her strength into fighting it. She vaccinated hundreds, and when her supply of vaccine ran out, she scooped the necessary lymph from sore vaccinated arms with a penknife in order to continue. It was during this epidemic that she went to Ekenge to see how they were faring there. When she found her old friend Edem dying quite alone, she nursed him and later buried him by starlight.

Early in 1898, Mary's carpenter friend, Charles Ovens, came up to join her at Akpap in order to work on her new mission house. She was able to avail herself of his presence to go, at long last, on her desperately needed leave. There remained the problem of what to do with the bairns, because she could hardly leave them all for Ovens to look after. Finally, Mary took three of the children under 5 with her to Scotland, and, of course, Janie, now aged 16. She almost dreaded the return to civilisation after years on her own in the bush, dressing as she pleased, eating as she pleased, and doing anything she needed to at a moment's notice. Friends who went to Edinburgh station to meet her were certainly taken aback at the appearance of the large party that climbed out of the railway carriage. She took refuge immediately in a small cottage near the sea, where the completely bush household aroused no little comment from the neighbours, and where Mary literally shivered with cold. They were rescued from unfriendly suburban neighbours and biting east winds by a Miss Adams. She was a rich woman who spent most of her money rehabilitating missionaries on leave, and she installed the whole

party in a house she owned at Bowden St. Boswells in Roxburgh-
shire. It was warm and comfortable, and they passed happy
months, roaming the Scottish countryside, climbing the Eildon
Hills, picnicking, and meeting the country folks. Janie was
accorded the honour of carrying the minister's baby boy at his
christening. He was called Dan, and Janie, who had a strong
affection for Scotland, was delighted with herself.

After some months, Mary's health improved, though it is
doubtful if she was ever a really fit woman again. She had to start
out on the usual arduous deputation work, and gave lectures all
over Scotland. Mary was still shy, expecially of male lecture
audiences, which is surprising in a woman who could stand in
between opposing armed forces, or reason with tribal elders over
cruel funeral rites, or tell the High Commissioner to "see and be a
guid laddie." But if there was only one male Scot in a lecture
audience, she hated it, and she was thankful when her passage to
what she now called home was booked. In December 1898, the
party embarked on the *Oron*. Mary was already a well-known
personality, and the ship's company went to great lengths to
provide a specially enjoyable Christmas for her and for the little
girls.

Mary's main plea to her missionary audiences in Scotland had
not been for money, which was coming in fairly well, but for
personnel. She herself had worked miracles in Okoyong, and had
singlehandedly gained a very real foothold for Christianity. Her
mission, however, had never followed it up: there had never been
an ordained minister for more than a brief visit; there was no
teacher and no dispenser; and she had no assistant. She would
herself have acknowledged that she was a difficult person for
whom to find a lady assistant, as her ways were very much her
own. Also, she lived with too little comfort for most of the
missionary ladies, who balked at the absence of amenities, and,
with good reason, at the presence of rats, mosquitoes, and cock-
roaches in her house. Some of them were critical of her way of
life, though most of them admired her intensely, and not a few
were completely devoted to her.

She was prepared to do an enormous amount herself, but it
was impossible to carry out the real work of consolidation without the necessary officers—above all, without a minister. The

mission, of course, was always short of staff, and the casualty rate from death or physical breakdown was still very high, and the unique position of respect and trust she had won among the Okoyong was being wasted. The British Government had, in fact, made much better use of her genius. What she wanted was a complete team to take over Akpap and leave her free to go farther afield. She knew she was not at her best in the administrative organisation of a mission station, and though she had become devoted to her Okoyong, she felt that solitary pioneering for Christian footholds was her real vocation. In this, just possibly consciously, she much resembled David Livingstone.

No relief or consolation team came, and she struggled on by herself. The task was overwhelming, and she was so ill in 1899 that a doctor, sent up specially to see her, threatened to invalid her home permanently, which worried her to distraction. But all the time, her great role as arbiter among the people, supported by her legal authority, was producing ever better results. It must have been a gratifying moment when she heard that at a funeral which she had not been able to attend, the only casualty had been a man so drunk that, on being refused his request for the poison ordeal, hanged himself in an ecstasy of expiation for a crime he had not committed. Ill health frayed her temper, and once, in court, after listening to an interminable, lying defence by an important chief, she was seen to take his umbrella and clout him over the head. Apart from trying to rescue the babies, she moved slowly against the evils resulting from the twin-birth superstition. Her colleagues at Calabar urged her to use legal authority to stamp it out quickly, but she saw danger in that.

Nonetheless, she was progressing, and she was delighted when the star pupil at her mission wanted to marry Janie, even though he was aware that she was a twin. The marriage apparently was a success, and the husband even allowed Janie, who had changed her name to Jean, to bring twin babies from the mission into her compound. Then, a baby boy who was born to them died immediately, and the old superstition came rushing back. Jean had to return to Mary, who had, of course, been missing her very much. She was thus able to feed an orphaned baby boy that a chief had brought to Mary to save. This boy was named Dan after the son of the Manse at Bowden St. Boswells, and Slessor after

Mary. He is proud to bear the name to this day, and he speaks of an exceptionally happy childhood. As the first boy to be adopted by Mary, he had a special place in her affection, and the local name for him meant "Ma's eldest son."

It was to the "untouched millions" on the other side of the Cross River that Mary was impatient to go. Between the big western tributary, the Enyong Creek, and the sea, there were the Ibibios, who spoke an Efik language. To the north and west were the Aros, a tribe of the great Ibo race. For centuries, they had been known as exporters of slaves who were, for the most part, sent down the Cross River to the sea. But by 1900, their export outlet was of necessity confined to the trans-Saharan slave caravans to the Mediterranean. They were a very intelligent, powerful people, and their power was reinforced by a far-famed sacred oracle known generally in pidgin English as the Long Juju. The deity was the great Ibo god Chuku, and the cult was centred on a gorge known as Arochuku, and was watered by a stream not far from the head of the Enyong Creek. The priests of the cult travelled far and wide, persuading frightened people to make their pilgrimage to Arochuku to solicit the advice and blessing of the oracle. Once there, having paid heavy dues, they were either sacrificed to Chuku, or, much more frequently, marched by devious ways to a slave market. It was, in fact, a slave trap.

Roger Casement had gone 15 miles up the Enyong Creek when he was a Vice-Consul in 1894, and had been lucky to escape with his life. But no European had reached Arochuku, and no Europeans knew very much about the goings-on there, with the possible exception of Mary. She had talked with Aro slave traders who sometimes passed through Okoyong, and had not hesitated to tell them that their ways were wicked. They taunted her and challenged her to come and reform them. Also, being herself in many ways a famous oracle, people from as far away as Iboland came to consult her, and she questioned them and began to have some understanding of what went on at the Arochuku shrines. She had considerably undermined the mystique of the Ekpo secret society in Okoyong, sometimes tearing off the silly masks with her own hands. Had anyone arrived at Akpap to relieve her, and had she been fit, she would almost certainly have gone to see what horrors were being perpetrated in the gorge. She might have been killed and that prospect would not have worried her. But such was her reputation that the oracle of truth might well have proved a match for the oracle of fraud. In the end, it was the government that took action.

In 1899, Sir Ralph Moor, who had succeeded Sir Claude Macdonald, received a report on the discovery of a wandering group of over a hundred emaciated and dying persons. They were the survivors of a party of 800 pilgrims who had come from a great distance, and had been led by roundabout routes to the neighbourhood of Arochuku. From there, parties of about 20 at a time were taken to consult the oracle and never reappeared. It was said that Chuku had demanded their lives, and the stream below the gorge had been seen to run red with blood, probably that of goats. It was thought that the survivors owed their escape to the wretchedness of their condition, which rendered them unfit either for sacrifice to a great god or for long journeys in slave caravans. Both Macdonald and Moor were against the use of force, but this event revealed the scale of the activities at Arochuku, and the great distances at which the priests operated. They decided to prepare a military operation to wipe out the whole business. By August 1901, a base had been established at the confluence of the Cross River and the Enyong Creek, and an advanced unit was stationed some way up the latter. The government then summoned all the missionaries to Calabar for their greater safety during the military operations. Mary did not want to go and said that she trusted her people completely, even in disturbed times, but she was firmly rounded up and taken down to the coast in the government launch. The High Commissioner wanted to lodge his valuable proconsul in one of the grand European houses, but for her own reasons, she preferred to live in one room in the hospital. Here, many puzzled and apprehensive up-country chiefs came secretly to ask her to explain what was happening in their country, and to advise them how they should best react in the changing situation.

Three military spearheads converged on the sacred grove of Arochuku on Christmas Eve 1901. The battle was short, and on New Year's Eve, the ravine, which was crammed with the grisly relics of its former function, was dynamited. Many of the priests fled, so the spiritual cult was not eliminated, but their enormous powers over innocent men's lives were ended, and the military took over the administration temporarily. The Scottish Mission would have liked to have been the instrument of ending the Long Juju by more peaceful means, but they had never had the necessary resources, and they realised that the urgency probably justified this short, sharp military operation.

Mary fretted in the enforced idleness of Calabar, and yet she, probably more than any other European, had her finger on the pulse of feelings in the interior. As soon as the news of the capture of Arochuku reached her, she set off for Okoyong without waiting for leave. In the first part of 1902, when Sir Ralph Moor was travelling everywhere, consulting and negotiating with the inland chiefs, she filled a vital role of interpretation. A stream of messengers came to her house from all directions to ask her to come to advise. The Cross River area was never to be the same again, but the trust the local people placed in Mary's wisdom is thought to have been a considerable factor in the reasonably peaceful transition, once the brief military episode was over.

To press on just to take hold wherever it might seem feasible was now the driving force of Mary's life. She realised that the mission ought to follow quickly in the wake of the military takeover, and early in 1903, she left Jean in charge at Akpap and set out by canoe up the Cross River with three young trainees from her own school. At Itu at the entrance to the Enyong Creek, she found the chiefs welcoming, and she was offered a fine site for a station on high ground overlooking the river. She plotted out the usual church with living accommodation, and stayed to supervise the building, skillfully mixing all the concrete for the foundations herself. Once, in Scotland, she was asked whether she had been taught how to do this, and she said that it was quite easy. She mixed it just like porridge and told God it was for Him, and it was sure to come out all right.

She found the people congenial, and commented on the friendly, laughing mixing of the sexes, which was like Scotland, but which did not happen in Okoyong. She had to return to Akpap, but for what it was worth, she left her three young apprentices to pioneer on their own. She would have maintained that youngsters with far less education than they had were worth a great deal. The local people begged her to return soon, and she wrote a report to the Mission Committee, persuasively advocating Itu as a site for a big mission station. The geographical features that had made it the greatest inland slave market commended it. Reactions to her arguments were not as wholehearted as she hoped, but a medical mission was established there and, in time, the Mary Slessor Hospital. She professed to being a bit embarrassed about this, but it was evident to those who knew her well that she was really delighted.

In the meantime, she kept a watch on her three little missionaries from Akpap. Once, by chance, when she hailed the government launch from the beach at Ikonetu in order to get a lift there, the military commander was on board and invited her to go to Arochuku with him. She had no luggage with her, but, of course, she accepted. Having known so much about the place, it was natural that she should have a sense of awe on entering the notorious gorge, but 18 months of military occupation, helped abundantly by tropical nature, had obliterated all traces of the sacrificial altars and the horrid relics of the ceremonies. She was surprised to find a considerable population in the neighbourhood, and the people were friendly. Some of her old slave trading acquaintances greeted her with the assurance that they knew she would come one day. The main local commerce was utterly dead, and a way of life probably unquestioned for centuries was ended. There was now a demand for knowledge of a new god, for new commerce, and for book learning.

Mary had been in Okoyong 15 years, and for many of them she had virtually ruled it. Yet so dilatory had been the response to her calls for official reinforcement that no one had been baptised. Then, in August 1903, on the anniversary of the lonely, wet first Sunday in Ekenge, a minister came to visit, and 12 young people were baptised, and the first communion service was held. The visible rites of the Church were something the people had never seen, and the crowd that collected to watch was apprehensive of witchcraft. Even some of Mary's most devoted adherents preferred to let others try the experiment first.

For Mary, the first communion service signalled the end of her work in Okoyong. She was over 55 and looked older. The gay, cheeky red hair was silver grey, and the boyish crop had given place to rather carelessly pinned-up hair. The round, challenging face of girlhood had changed very much; it was now spare and lined, but with the lines of wisdom and of suffering. It was both resolute and compassionate. The eyes remained powerful and, by many accounts, memorable. The quirk of humour never left her. Her biographer, W. P. Livingstone, says "her religion was a religion of the heart, and her communion with her Father was of the most natural and childlike character."

For years now she had travelled a religious road quite alone, without priest or habit or rule, except for an early morning hour spent exploring the Bible she already knew so well, and which was covered by comments in her own impressive handwriting. She found it easier "to do than to pray" and yet believed passionately in prayer, saying, " the dynamic lies that way to advance the kingdom." She had no doubt that sick or well, her destiny was to advance. She could no longer live in Scotland; she had none of her "ain folks" there. Her ain folks were now these "unlovely unwashed savages" whom she could not desert. However poor her health, she could not retire, because it had to be in Africa, and Africa would never let her retire. She would be besieged by petitioners who would respect neither her rest nor her privacy, and who would know that whatever barriers she contrived, human or otherwise, she would not fail them if they were in serious need.

Mary was due to go home on leave in 1904, but she wrote to the committee in Calabar for permission to spend that leave pioneering westwards. They heard that she was ill and were, naturally, hesitant to grant her request. The matter was referred to Scotland for decision, but probably everyone knew that Mary Slessor was no longer really under orders, and there was a compromise offer of six months' local leave. She recovered her health, but her illness left her both nervous and rheumatic, which was a serious handicap from then on. But she went down to Calabar and formally resigned her legal office. Then, she loaded several canoes with cement, hinges, locks, and planks, the sophisticated finishing touches for the simple missionary buildings she intended to erect wherever she could, wherever her wanderings took her.

Two women arrived at long last to take over at Akpap, and in 1904, Mary, Jean, and the usual household of babies moved to Itu. She was aware that her health might now sometimes make it inadvisable to go pioneering with a canoe full of babies, and she planned to leave them at Itu with Jean if necessary. She went for an emotional reunion at almost the end of her life, but it was now that she really said goodbye to Okoyong forever. The final leave-taking was heartrending, both for Mary and for the thousands of weeping Okoyong on Ikonetu beach. The farewell presents all but sank the mission launch, and a great wail went up from the throng on the shore as it pushed out into the stream. Mary was seen to be shaking with emotion. Her voluntary abdication of her Okoyong status is one of the yardsticks of her greatness. It would have been only human for a tired, sick woman to have rested on her very substantial laurels among the people she loved and who loved her. But she knew that the future of the Okoyong must lie with other missionary hands than hers.

In the end, Mary spent the whole of her year's leave exploring in the Enyong Creek, as she had, perhaps, always intended. She looked for possible footholds where she could leave someone versed, if only slightly, in the word of God. The barely initiated ministered to the wholly uninitiated, as in the early days of the Christian Church, and here and there the tiny nucleus of a Christian community formed itself. This "outreaching" was not the usual policy of the Scottish Mission, but the committee at Calabar was tremendously interested and impressed by the reports she sent them. They could but think of her as a valuable forerunner. She was costing them nothing, and by now, they were better equipped to follow up and consolidate her work. She hoped so much that it might be the seed of her own evangelical faith that was first sown among these newly contacted peoples. And her mission had certainly staked a claim west of the Cross River. But if its personnel and means were insufficient to take advantage of these rights in the terms of intermissionary agreement, she thought it wrong to keep others out. Her own personal religion was above denominational differences, and, for a member of the Kirk, she was even quite tolerant of Roman Catholics. After all, "they'll nae take them tae hell," she used to say. And she had some good Catholic friends among the growing European community.

Long ago, the unfavourable reports of the Okoyong had been a factor in her wish to go among them. Now, accounts of the

Ibibios to the south and west of the Enyong began to interest her, not so much because of their dangerous reputation, but because of the contempt in which they were held both by the Aros and by the coastal peoples. A dense population had been raided for slaves for centuries, and with every neighbour a predatory enemy, they were sullen and evasive, with a sense of social inferiority.

By now, there were government administrators everywhere in the interior, and in 1904, the Ibibios were fortunate in the arrival of a District Commissioner called Charles Partridge. He was one of the breed of scholarly proconsuls that existed not infrequently in the British Colonial Service. At Cambridge, he had read theology, followed by anthropology, then in its infancy as an academic subject. He had published a travel book illustrated with his own photographs, and he was a Fellow of the Royal Geographical Society. With quick perception, he realised that the Ibibios, in spite of their long history of oppression, had good qualities. He was also quick to perceive Mary Slessor's qualities, and it was largely he who harnessed them for his Ibibios. His district headquarters were at Ikot Epene, 25 miles to the west of Itu, to which a road was in the process of being built. Good roads, which were a revolutionary innovation, were reaching out everywhere, and, in land that had never before seen wheels, District Officers were riding bicycles along them. So, too, at the age of 56 was Mary Slessor. Charles Partridge first wooed her with a present of an English plum pudding, a rare treat indeed, and then with a bicycle, the first she had ever ridden. She was as excited as a 10-year-old would have been, and wondered what her Scottish friends would think of her.

But plum puddings and bicycles were just the preliminaries to a great creative friendship that built up between them. They went prospecting through the bush together, which resulted in Mary's acquiring two useful sites, one at Use, which she designated for a project she had long had in mind, and the other two miles away at Ikot Obong, which was to be her base. Officially, she was still stationed at Akpap, but this did not stop her starting to build at Ikot Obong. She knew that whatever her orders were, she would remain in Ibibio, if necessary under her own steam financially. Certainly, her letters made it plain to the mission and were too impassioned to ignore. " Whether the Church permits it or not, I feel I must stay here and go on even further as the roads are made...I dare not go back," she wrote. Realising that she was utterly committed to "outreaching," the mission finally gave her official status as a "pioneer missionary."

In May 1905, a letter arrived from "His Excellency the High Commissioner," asking if she would accept the status of permanent Vice-President of the native court. It was a similar office to that which she had held in Okoyong, but everything was now more official and formal. The letter continued: " His Excellency is desirous of securing the advantage of your experience and intimate knowledge of native affairs, and sympathetic interest in the welfare of the villagers." She accepted, but refused the salary, saying, "I'm born and bred and am in every fibre of my being a voluntary." Charles Partridge had probably had a hand in the appointment, and, as District Commissioner, he presided over the next higher court to hers. For her convenience, he moved the native court from Itu to Ikot Obong. As in Okoyong, she could give sentences of up to six months' imprisonment, but fines were much more usual, and she frequently allowed the culprit to work off his fine in her own employment. By 1907, the government was reporting a marked decrease everywhere in the number of divorces on account of twin birth, and was attributing it to Mary Slessor's influence. Her own court became famous for its justice to all female litigants. There were even signs that abused categories of women, such as the mothers of twins, were organising themselves into something like unions confident that grievances articulately aired would get a sympathetic hearing there.

Charles Partridge only remained in Ikot Ekpene for two years, part of which he was at home on sick leave. While he was away, and for many years afterwards in his subsequent postings, he corresponded with Mary. Unfortunately, she destroyed his letters at a moment when she thought she was dying. Years later, he deposited hers in the museum in Dundee, and they are a sheer delight and tell much about her. When he had evidently complained of a lapse into "Dear Mr. Partridge" and asked if they were still friends she addressed him as anything from "Dear Patient old Chief" or "Dear old Boss" to "Oh You Dear Duffer. Will that do?" She gossips amusingly and recounts many an episode with the sure knowledge of what will make him laugh.

There is the cow she has bought, "Ma Slessor's coo," which tugs her and her household mercilessly in quest of adventure, but which is yielding to friendly treatment and even submitting to being milked. There is the prudish and pedantic letter from an African clerk, complaining about the disgusting nakedness of some of the local ladies. There are hints about the inferiority to Partridge's successors as District Commissioner.

More and more, there are depressing reports about her health, which was deteriorating, at times dramatically, though she protests that she is doing quite a lot of the things he has told her to do, such as wearing a hat, filtering her water, and sleeping under a mosquito net. There is advice to the young administrator that bespeaks the knowledge that over 30 years of identification with the peoples of Eastern Nigeria has given her. "See how much more likely they are to fear you than to give themselves over at once...If you can discriminate between fear and stubborness you have won half the battle."[6] There is also a moving plea for women's rights, as she saw them. When he was at home, she had virtually commanded him to return with a wife, preferably an heiress, and expressed her intention of acting as "Auntie" to them both. But he had, perhaps naively, pleaded the unfitness of West Africa for women in extenuation of his disobedience to her orders. "I need not say I do not share your opinion about men marrying who are engaged here," she writes. "Women are as eager to share in all the work and sacrifice of the world as men, and it is their privilege to share in it, and is their mission to be the motive power in a man's life, and so you are keeping some good woman out of her place of privilege and work, and are depriving yourself of God's greatest gift outside the spiritual world, in refusing to accept it."[7]

Charles Partridge was by no means her only friend and admirer among the officials, traders, and technicians who worked in the Niger Protectorate. Besides her invaluable knowledge, she was splendid fun to visit, very witty, well read, and, thanks to a steady supply of newspapers from friends everywhere, abreast of the world news. She also had a rare gift of sympathy, which was welcome to the white men, who led lonely lives in West Africa in those days. It was in the white men's clubs that she had been called the White Queen of Okoyong, and the white men who sat at her feet were known as "Mariolaters." They used to tell her that she deliberately broke their hearts in order to get her own way, and she responded gaily to flirtatious teasing. The Niger Coast Protectorate developed into Eastern Nigeria, and the High Commissioner became a Governor, who duly arrived on an official visit to Use. Mary made a firm resolve to show him suitable respect, but she was not entirely successful. However, her "Hoots my dear laddie—och I mean Sir" gave great pleasure, and he told her to take care of herself because "We need you."

One Christmas night, she presided over a dinner party of eight men, who had foresworn drink for the day in consideration of her principles. The junketings went on far into the night and ended emotionally with hands joined in "Auld Lang Syne." She was often careless in her dress, and she cannot have been very prepossessing. But she was always properly attired in court and, apparently, when she had official visitors, because their warning message was apt to read, "Get your shoes on Mary, I'm coming to tea." An unexpected caller found her one day astride her roof, hammering on new palm mats, and quite evidently uninterruptable for frivolous reasons. He took off his hat and said, "Please Ma'am, I'm your new D.C." She still glared ferociously from the rooftop and he added, "But I can't help it." Then, she melted into laughter and gave him one of her famous hospitable welcomes.

In 1907, she was so poorly and so crippled with rheumatism that at last she consented to go home to Scotland. She even confessed to a great longing to see her native land once more, and she probably knew it was for the last time. She left her wonderful Jean in charge at Use, and took 7-year-old Dan with her. He had the time of his life, and met and made friends with his namesake at Bowden St. Boswells. She had not turned 60, but the friends who went to Edinburgh station to meet her this time saw a desperately sick, tired old lady, who walked with difficulty. But as usual, her native air worked wonders, and before she went back, she was able to show off her bicycle riding. She complained that she was being made to submit to a lot of pulling about to get her into what she called "society shape," and she wrote to tell Charles Partridge that her mind was running on nothing but frills and furbelows. There was never any question of her not going back. She was pining and anxious for her large family and her African people the whole time she was in Scotland, and was glad when her sailing time came. She travelled now as a VIP and was handed on from official to official. At Lagos, an A.D.C. came on board to pay the Governor's respects, and to give her suitable presents. She was certainly a West African celebrity, and, indeed, judging from the breadth of her correspondence, a world celebrity.

It was perhaps inevitable that the last seven years of her life had their sadnesses, though they were seldom occasioned by the Africans with whom she was now completely identified. Much of her life had followed the pattern of David Livingstone's; but for her, there was no Nile source to look for, no mysterious disappearance into unexplored Africa and discovery by sensational journalism, and no dramatic martyr's death. She would not have wished it. She just had to struggle on in aching sickness, knowing that as long as there was a motherless bairn to nurse, she would do so as a matter of course.

New officials came and went rapidly, sometimes too rapidly for them to appreciate what she was, and one or two were even a little ashamed to be seen with the inelegant old lady who occasionally mislaid her teeth. One D.C. completely neglected to call, and she was far from used to that. Nor was she used to opposition in court matters. She was thinking of resigning the magistracy, not because she felt unable to carry out her judicial duties competently, but because she sometimes had to be in court for ten hours in a day, and the physical strain was too much. Then, a very young and new D.C. disagreed with a verdict of "accidental death" on a woman who had bled to death after cutting an artery chopping wood in the forest. Rightly or wrongly, he thought it was murder, but there had been no appeal, and while she was the official District Magistrate, she thought it was not his affair. She argued with him hotly and reminded him that she had known the peoples of Eastern Nigeria intimately before he was born, and had given her judgement in the light of this experience. Then she resigned. She had not meant to go on much longer, but she was, nonetheless, privately very angry when her resignation was accepted, and she poured it all out in a letter to Charles Partridge.

Most people thought it was solely on the grounds of ill health, and those grounds certainly made it desirable, if not absolutely essential.

The mission had taken over Ikot Obong, which she had pioneered, and before the end of her tenure of the magistracy, she had moved the district court to Use, which was now to be her principal base until the end of her life. She had long seen the necessity of an industrial training school for women who were barred, for one reason or another, from marriage. The unexpected receipt of a large cheque from a friend made it possible to start this valuable work even without the promise of financial help from the mission. She was prepared to take the responsibility herself, and it is evident that she was now a free agent, at least whenever she thought it desirable. Some of her colleagues in the mission were critical of her and thought her missionary pioneering untidy, if not indecorous.

Occasionally, perhaps, she was a little indecorous. One story, that when some chiefs had called to take her to select a building site and she had gone in her night dress, had shocked them deeply. Her excuse that they probably thought it was just her evening dress had not been soothing. Missionary officials came regularly to inspect at Use, but it was largely as a matter of form. Night dresses apart, they were immensely proud of her and respected her, though they often disagreed with her on fundamental matters of policy. She once had a vehement argument with a missionary inspector that ended in her storming out of the room. Of necessity, he was staying in her house, and he faced the tête-à-tête evening meal with some trepidation. They took their seats on opposite sides of the table in silence, and he said grace. When he looked up, her face was bubbling with fun, but she was sticking her tongue out at him to make it quite clear she was unrepentant.

Around her at Use, there was the usual household of adopted refugee babies, many older children, and by now, many grandchildren. At least two of the girls had married good Christian husbands and lived nearby with their families. And, of course, there was Jean, whom she called her right and left hand, and from whom she had scarcely been parted since she had rescued her from death as a baby. Jean had developed into a fine woman, and she shared a little of Mary's Scottish background. She was also an avid reader of the Scottish newspapers that always arrived in the parcels of good things from Scotland.

A horrid illness made 1909 a bad year. Painful boils broke out all over Mary's head, face, and neck, and the necessary treatment was very painful. Temporarily, she lost all her hair, and Charles Partridge was so shocked at her description of herself that he almost commanded her to go home. She refused, and the following year she was riding a brand new bicycle that he sent her from Lagos, and making more plans for adventuring in virgin fields. A deputation from Ikpe, of which she had never heard, came to ask her to go to them. It was far up the Enyong Creek, above the Arochuku gorge, and well beyond the reach of any civilised amenities. She was unable to return immediately with the delegation, but she promised faithfully to go as soon as she could. Her rheumatism was bad, and she planned to have a wooden box fixed to four wheels so that the children could pull her about. But friends in Scotland were only too delighted to send her a wickerwork bath chair, with a shaft.

And so, paddled by canoe and pulled in the wheeled chair, she went off to Ikpe in 1910, and lived once again in the conditions of Ekenge in 1888. She founded the nucleus of a mission there, and another at Ikpe Odoro nearby, to which, before long, a motorable road was constructed. Instructions were given for all government transport, including one of the first motercars to arrive, to be at Miss Slessor's disposal as and when she needed it, which made frequent visits to her two new stations possible. But even with the comfort of the motorcar, she was a sick woman, and it was killing her. Then she found she had for once met her match in a new young doctor named Hitchcock at the Mary Slessor Hospital at Itu. He had thought at first that he just had a cranky, old missionary body on his hands, but he rapidly succumbed to her charms, and was quick to realise that it was a valuable life he had in his care. When he could not stop her from going up to Ikpe when she was ill, he said he was going to close down the hospital and go with her. She knew he meant it, and she had to give in.

In 1912 a rich Scottish friend offered Mary a holiday in the Canary Islands, with Jean for company, and she was prevailed upon to accept. A quantity of material arrived from Scotland, and

the ladies at Calabar set to work to make her a suitable trousseau
to wear in the hotel, and they exacted a promise from her that
every dress would be worn once. While at Las Palmas, she forgot
her promise, but she redeemed it by wearing a new dress every
morning on the boat going home, which very much puzzled her
fellow passengers at the captain's table. The holiday was a tremendous luxury and a happy, recuperative time in a kind climate.

When she arrived in Calabar, Sir Frederick Lugard, the Governor of a now-united Nigeria, was there on a state visit. He
expressed a wish to see Miss Slessor, and his biographer,
Margery Perham, describes the meeting as between "two kinds
of authority." One gets the impression that the splendour of the
proconsular feathers did not really upstage the modest little
Scotswoman, who, on the right occasion, had all the dignity that
derives from an intensely lived life. He took her hand, saying that
he was proud to do so, and quite certainly meant it. His brother
Edward was with him, and he records in his diary that her life
story, which he had just had occasion to read, in the course of
drafting a request to the Foreign Office for a recommendation
for some honour in recognition of her services, had brought a
lump to his throat. "The long years of not *quiet*, but fierce
devotion—for they say she is a tornado—unrecognised and without hope of, or desire for, recognition . . . " She was duly elected
an Associate of the Order of St. John of Jerusalem, and was
commanded to go down to Calabar to receive the emblem, a
white enamel Maltese Cross. She was given a near royal reception, and was presented with a magnificent bouquet of red roses.
But though she carried it off with dignity, she sat with her hands
completely covering her face throughout the citation, and was
very moved. Back at Use, she planted a rose from her bouquet in
her garden on the chance that it would take root, and it grew into
a fine bush.

Mary had not always behaved decorously at Government
House. Once, a visiting lady journalist who was staying there
asked to see Miss Slessor, and Mary was invited to lunch. With
difficulty her missionary friends persuaded her to accept, and
there was a roundup of suitable attire from among the ladies.
The bright green Government House picture hat that one of
them lent her does not seem to have been a success, but she was

so rebellious about the whole thing that she did not care in the least what she looked like. There was some apprehension about the look in her eye when she departed for the engagement in the Governor's car, but the full extent of her naughtiness was not known until some months later, when the journalist's article appeared in the *Morning Post*. After wondering "who could have dressed her," the lady went on to give an account of a fine piece of acting that Mary had apparently put on for her benefit, on the lines of "I've failed, I've failed, my bairns would all be better dead." Finally, she placed Mary among the world's most tragic martyrs, those who have suffered grievously to no purpose at all. After the luncheon, the Governor had tried unsuccessfully to correct the writer's impression, but she had probably heard, or thought she had heard, just what she wanted for her brand of writing. And certainly, Mary herself was largely to blame.

In July 1913, Mary went back to Akpap for the opening of a fine new church. She took all her unmarried twins with her to demonstrate what normal people they had grown into, and in general, they were much admired, though some of the old folks were still too superstitious to go near them. She had a very moving reception, and found Akpap an orderly and prosperous mission station, which must have been a great satisfaction to her. She sat and held court on the verandah of the main house for several days, and old friends came from great distances when they heard that Ma Slessor was there. She was so excited at seeing them all again that she could scarcely be persuaded to eat. And above all the rest was Ma Eme, her "dear friend and almost sister," with whom she had collaborated so fruitfully in "those dark and bloody days" of long ago. The old lady was still a pagan, and paid her devotions to a private idol erected in her own house, but she was the same humane and significant aristocrat who shared so many of Mary's own values.

In her 38 years in Nigeria, Mary had been a great pioneer missionary among the "untouched millions." She had administered official justice to the complete satisfaction of both the colonial government and the local population. Within the limits of her knowledge and supplies, she had practised medicine. She had fought and won again and again, and all the time she had steadily increased the trust in which she was held.

And yet, with all this, more than half of her life had been devoted to children. The white administrators who sat at her feet were called Mariolaters. More seriously, was there possibly an unconscious element of Mariolatery in the trusting submission she won from dangerously hostile peoples? She knew that the dissipation of fear was all-important, and there is perhaps little that would so easily dissipate the fear that antagonises than the sight of a woman nursing a baby, even if that woman was seemingly without fear herself. The babies never appeared in court; she would have thought that wholly unsuitable, but they were never very far away. She slept regularly in bush huts with five or six little ones dangling in hammocks from the rafters, each with a string leading to her own bed so that she could rock the hammocks when they cried. Some diaries written in her last sick years make it plain that crying babies added a terrible burden to her own pain-wracked nights. But right to the end, the children were the first concern of her life.

Identified with Africans as she was, the black ones came first, but she had friendships and correspondence with children everywhere, and greatly valued the letters from

. . . the darlings, with their perfectly natural stories and their ways of looking at everything out of a child's clear innocent eyes, and the bubbling over of the joys of a healthy life. It is a splendid tonic, and just a holiday to me, too, taking me with them to the fields and the picnics and the sails on the lochs. Oh, one can almost feel the cool breeze and hear the shouts. Don't you think for a moment, that though I am like a piece of wrinkled parchment my heart is not as young as ever it was, and that I don't prefer children to grown-up folks a thousand times over. I would need to, for they have been almost my sole companions for 25 years back. . . . I don't say that I don't love black bairns better and know them better than white ones, for I do. But one must confess to the loveliness of the Scottish girls.[8]

The last child correspondent was a small crippled boy with whom she had made friends in the Canaries. The letters are charming, as usual, and one written from the boat returning to Calabar shows clearly wherein lay her genius with children, because it assures the boy that it is he that has had something to give. " . . . How good it was to meet you. It will ever live as a picture in my heart and memory the times we spent with you, and it was very good for Jean to know you....″⁹

Mary was at Ikpe Odoro with several of her family when she heard the news of the outbreak of war in Europe in 1914. She had probably never heard the word, but she was surely a pacifist, and the knowledge of the bitter suffering to come affected her greatly. In fact, already ill, it prostrated her, and the children decided they must get her back to her home at Use as quickly as possible. They carried her in a stretcher to a canoe, and she was paddled down the Enyong Creek for the last time, and slept under the stars on the landing beach for Use. They carried her home the next day. She struggled on until Christmas, when the present of a plum pudding from Charles Partridge gave her special pleasure, because his letters had inevitably become less frequent. By the New Year, most people knew she was dying, and towards the end, she was heard asking God—in Efik, now her most natural language—to release her. On January 13 she died.

The body was quickly conveyed by government launch to Calabar and carried the next day in a mahogany coffin to the cemetery on Mission Hill that overlooked the harbour. Police lined the route, flags were flown at half-mast, and offices and schools were closed for the day. The fine church was packed for the funeral service; every proconsular dignitary was present; and the tributes for a great life were eloquent. A cutting was planted on her grave from the red rose bush at Use that had originated in her bouquet when she was decorated, and in time, a tall granite cross was erected.

But there were those who wondered if all the pomp of the funeral was quite right for Mary Slessor. On the other side of Africa, when the body of Mother Kevin was passed on from one solemn ritual to another, it seemed both fitting and very moving. But Mary's devout Christian life had been lived without any ritual, and in this way she was unique. She loved, indeed, her "Father's house," and many times her own tired hands had stirred up the concrete and hammered on the beams and plastered on the mud so that some visible edifice could be available for worship to thousands who were without it. Perhaps, she should have been laid to rest near one of her own little mud churches away in the forests where, indomitable in her defencelessness, and powerful in her love, she had lived her life, and where she was best remembered. Many years after her death, the face of an old chief was seen to break into a delightful smile when her picture was projected onto the screen at a magic lantern show at Ikpe. His comment, in pidgin English, makes a fitting epitaph, because it seems to come from the heart of an African: "I liked dat woman too much."[10]

NOTES

1. W. P. Livingstone, *Mary Slessor of Calabar* (London, 1915), p. 130.
2. Ibid.
3. Mary H. Kingsley, *Travels in West Africa* (London, 1897), p. 475.
4. Ibid., p. 74.
5. Stephen Gwynn, *Life of Mary Kingsley* (London, 1933), p. 279.
6. Carol Christian and Gladys Plummer, *God and One Redhead* (London, 1970), p. 162.
7. Ibid., p. 165.
8. W. P. Livingstone, *The White Queen of Okoyong* (n.p., 1916).
9. Ibid.
10. Christian and Plummer, *Redhead*, p. 183.

5

MOTHER KEVIN:
Missionary and Foundress

David Livingstone, wandering alone with his four devoted servants, died in the swamps of Lake Bangweolo in 1873.

His dying prayer was that others would take up his self-imposed task of opening up the dark, unknown continent, then miserably ravaged by the slave trade. One of the first to respond to the message of his death was Henry Morton Stanley, who had come under his influence in the few months they had spent together after their dramatic meeting by Lake Tanganyika. Stanley decided to go again into the interior, to pick up Livingstone's trail, to solve the mystery of the great African rivers, and, if possible, to cross the continent. In the course of this journey, in April 1875, he reached Buganda, the ancient and powerful kingdom on the north of Lake Victoria. His reception there by the able but despotic young monarch, Kabaka Mutesa, and the courtesy and intelligence of the people, impressed him greatly. He talked to them of Christianity, and at Mutesa's request, he sent a letter to England asking for missionaries to be sent to Buganda.

This letter was carried by Linant de Bellefonds, an emissary of General Gordon, whose visit to Mutesa's court coincided with Stanley's. De Bellefonds took the letter to Khartoum, whence it was forwarded to London, and on November 15, 1875, it appeared in the *Daily Telegraph*. It aroused tremendous interest. But the idea of sending a mission into the deep interior of East Africa, where as yet missionaries had only nibbled at the coasts, was all but unthinkable. Then came the formidable challenge of large sums of money donated specifically for just such a mission, and the Anglican Church Missionary Society accepted the challenge. In 1878, two of their missionaries reached Mutesa's court, and Cardinal Lavigerie's White Fathers followed them within 18 months. A great missionary story, or perhaps, regrettably, two great missionary stories, had begun.

In that same April 1875, when Stanley reached Buganda, a little girl, Teresa Kearney, was born on a small farm in the Wicklow hills in Ireland. Her home was not far from Glendalough, where, dotted around lovely lakes, are seven churches that once testified to the glory of God and to the veneration for the hermit Saint Kevin. It was as Mother Kevin that this baby girl was destined to play one of the greatest parts in the missionary story of Buganda: to export the name Kevin from the Wicklow hills to great popularity throughout East Africa, and to found two religious congregations.

Teresa's father had been killed not long before she was born; her mother died ten years later. The great influence of her childhood was a wise and kindly grandmother who loved her and with whom she lived. From family recollections, the child appears gay, generous, impulsive, boyishly mischievous, at times given to temper and occasionally to jealousy. It was the grandmother who taught her that the help she would need in life in disciplining the temper and the fierce Irish pride would come to her proportionately as she loved God. Some of the temper stayed with her throughout her devoted life, and perhaps contributed a quality to the passion with which she pursued her objectives and fought her battles against stupidity, ignorance, or injustice.

The grandmother died when Teresa was only 17. She was by then earning a living as a comparatively untrained teacher in Dublin, and suffering some of the indignities of the lowly governness of the time. She was drawn to teaching and would have liked to qualify professionally but family finances prohibited this. The terrible loneliness she suffered after her grandmother's death was met ostensibly with gay courage, and before long, to the delight of her family, she seemed to be moving towards marriage with a young Dublin bank clerk. Then, something changed the direction of her life. Family legend, presumably founded on fact, maintained that she had a dream, or possibly a recurrent dream, in which an important black man was beckoning her to come to the aid of his people. Her Father Confessor cautioned her against belief in dreams, but, however it happened, the seed had been sown, which grew, in time, into a strong conviction about God's purpose for her. And it was this conviction rather than any devotional attraction that led her, after two years of consideration, into religious life.

Little Teresa Kearney arrived at the formidable gates of the Franciscan Convent at Mill Hill in November 1895. She had been accepted as a postulant and a volunteer for the congregation's special mission, which was to North American Negroes. She was on her way to the black people whom God had directed her to help. The Franciscan postulancy and novitiate are arduous and exacting, and they were especially so for an impulsive, young girl who had spent most of her life in the freedom of the Irish countryside. The physical hardship did not worry her greatly, but she needed tremendous determination and deep spiritual devotion to carry her through moments of doubt and moments of stormy rebellion. In later life, she told her young African aspirants that she had found it disheartening and lonely at times. In 1897, she donned the Franciscan habit as a novice, and a year later, she made her professional vows and became Sister Mary Kevin. She was 23 years old, "five foot nothing in height, slim and slight with dancing brown eyes and a ready tongue, gallant and generous."[1] The lay Sisters in the convert called her "Little Kevin."

To her great disappointment at the time, Sister Kevin was not included in the first batch of Sisters who left for the American mission field after she became a nun. The attention of the congregation was then directed to an entirely new field. The missionary story of Buganda had started with quite extraordinary success. In 1886, there was powerful witness to this in the martrydom by fire of 22 Buganda youths, some Catholic, some Protestant, who died for Christianity and for Christian morals. Then, the very strength of both Catholics and Protestants involved Christianity in internal political troubles. The labels "Catholic" and "Protestant" were given to opposing political factions, and civil war broke out, which was terminated by English military intervention. Since all the Catholic missionaries were French White Fathers, and all the Protestant missionaries were British Anglicans, Catholicism was thought of as French, and Protestantism as British.

The White Fathers' bishop saw the danger of this, in a country patently coming under British influence. An appeal was made to Cardinal Vaughan to send some Fathers from the St. Joseph's Missionary Society, whose college at Mill Hill was a near neighbour to the Franciscan nuns. The Propaganda created a new Vicariate of Upper Nile especially for the Mill Hill Fathers, and in 1894, Bishop Hanlon, a great missionary traveller, went out with the first party. He returned in 1902 and reported the urgent need of missionary Sisters in the new Vicariate. Cardinal Vaughan had long been interested in St. Mary's Abbey, and he lent his support to the Bishop in approaching the Abbess, Mother Agnes. Her nuns were already in too short supply for the American mission field, but the eloquence of Bishop Hanlon in expressing the crying need of Buganda was irresistible. Amidst great excitement, six nuns were chosen to go. When Mother Agnes sent for Sister Kevin and told her she was to be one of them, it is said that she lost all her newly acquired monastic decorum, threw her arms round the dignified Abbess, and waltzed her round the room. The pioneer party, led by Mother Paul, an American, left with Bishop Hanlon and some Fathers early in December. Sister Kevin had been seven years in the convent, and the departure was poignant.

It was late evening when the last goodbyes were said. The night was crisp and cold and full of stars, as the carriage turned out of the drive. The great iron-studded gate stood open. Sister Kevin remembered her feelings at the first sight of that gate seven years ago. It had opened then to unknown joys and sorrows. Now it opened again, and she passed through it to her promised land.[2]

The party crossed on the night steamer from Harwich, and sailed in a German liner from Rotterdam to Mombasa.

Only a short time before the arrival of Bishop Hanlon's party, at the beginning of January 1903, the journey of over 800 miles from Mombasa to Lake Victoria would have had to be done on foot. This was, of course, a considerable adventure, and subsequent generations of Uganda missionaries used to confess to a feeling of inferiority towards the "bloods" who had "walked from the coast." But even in 1903, the journey was far from luxurious, and certainly not lacking in some danger. The much-derided railway line running inland from Mombasa was already in operation as far as Nairobi, a day's and a night's journey. The route lay through one of the world's great natural game parks. A view of herds of giraffe and zebra, an occasional collision with a rhino, and reports of attacks by lions at wayside stations contributed tremendously to the excitement of the journey. The nuns boiled their own tea on the train, and collected a curry meal from Indian traders when the stop was long enough for it to be ordered and cooked, before returning helter skelter to the whistling train.

In spite of a speed of about ten miles an hour and frequent halts, there were not many dull moments. From Nairobi on to the lakeside port of Kisumu the real hazards began. The line had been laid all the way but was not yet in use. There were three formidable escarpments to be negotiated: the steep descent to the eastern Rift Valley, the equally steep climb out of it up to the Mau summit on the west; and finally, the rather more gentle drop down to Lake Victoria. The first test of a train on the line had ended disastrously, when a coach failed to grip the rails on a sharp bend and the whole train fell down the Mau escarpment. Another attempt was about to be made, and free passages were offered to the Bishop and his party if they were prepared to act as guinea pigs and travel on the test train. The saving of 12 fares, or the elimination of many weeks of walking from Nairobi to the lake, was too good to refuse, and the Bishop accepted. The train went so slowly that the Fathers, at times, walked beside it for exercise. When descending and ascending the tortuous gradients, the nuns were told to stand out on the step gripping the carriage handles in order to be ready to jump clear at a warning shout. Thus, sometimes hanging on like birds on a cliff face, they covered the 200 miles to Kisumu. The only casualty was some of the nuns' gear, which was in a luggage van that parted from the rest of the train en route.

The next stage of the journey was by water. An antiquated steam launch, the *Percy Anderson*, which had seen service on other African lakes, was available for hire, but the only crew with any

experience that could be found was one African. He was quite
willing to undertake every nautical office but proved to have no
knowledge of navigation. Fortunately, Bishop Hanlon realised
that he was taking a course down rather than across the lake, and
to everyone's astonishment and relief, Sister Kevin produced a
compass, a chance parting present from one of the nuns at St.
Mary's Abbey. Without this, and with food aboard only for the
four or five days' run to Buganda, they might have been in
serious trouble. The food was a skinned and dried sheep's car-
case, from which pieces were cut daily and cooked up with onions
and potatoes. The fuel, of course, was wood. The nuns were
given the cabin, which measured 15 feet by 9 feet, and they slept
head to feet on narrow benches. At night, they anchored in coves
or bays near the shore, which they shared with surprised and
curious hippos and crocodiles. The only real privacy was the
darkness. Early on the last morning, when they were nearing
their destination, the Bishop, knowing that there would be a
great reception, decided that he wanted his nuns to arrive in their
white tropical dress. The blessed privacy of darkness was over,
and they were all in black. Each Sister, in turn, crawled under the
table, and, with the boat rocking and pitching, and frequently
banging their heads, they contrived to change in time for the
state arrival.

An elderly Muganda who had witnessed the arrival of the first
white woman in Buganda, once confessed to the Anglican
Bishop, albeit reluctantly, that the sight of the bleached white
faces had made him quite literally sick. By 1903, most people in
the vicinity of the capital at least would have seen white faces.
The arrival of the Franciscan nuns was, nonetheless, a considerable event. The landing was at Munyonyo, and as they approached,
they could see that the shore was black with human beings.
When they had anchored and had transferred to a canoe, as
decorously as circumstances permitted, a horizontal section of
the black wall on the beach seemed to break off suddenly from
the rest. Young Africans swarmed into the water, and the canoe
was seized by many hands. Thus, lifted triumphantly shoulder-
high and lurching and swaying, the nuns were borne ashore, and
only put down high up on the bank. After a hot and dusty
seven-mile walk to Nsambya, the headquarters of the Mill Hill

Fathers, accompanied by hundreds of Africans singing improvised marching songs about the nuns as they went, the long
journey was over. The nuns knelt in thanksgiving at the alter rail
in the thatched cathedral on "penitential and irregular baked
bricks." Then they retired to their convent to rest well on camp
beds gallantly sacrificed by the Fathers, who alone realised that
the nuns' beds had been in the luggage van that had broken loose
on the Mau escarpment.

The little convent that had been built for the Sisters was of
low, sun-baked brick walls, overhung by a preponderance of
insect-ridden thatched roof, and with a mud floor plastered with
cow dung. It was divided in three sections: a tiny chapel, a
dormitory, and a community room. The kitchen was in a mud
hut, and the nearest water supply was two miles away. Yet it was
their own little *portiuncula*[3] in the heart of Africa, and they felt
sure that the Blessed Francis would approve of it. High on Nsambya Hill, the view of the lush Buganda countryside made rich
amends for the poverty of the dwelling. The flat-topped Buganda
hills surrounding them still had little pockets of tropical forest,
and were endlessly patched with the rectangles of banana planta-
tion; the young trees trim and lively bright green; the old ones
tatty with the falling, yellowing leaves disintegrating into com-
post for the next crop. Here and there, in contrast, was a flame
tree or a deep blue jacaranda or a yellow-flowering acacia, Nsambya Hill's own speciality. Down in the valley bottom, the pale
green mop heads of papyrus waved in the breeze, and everywhere tall, red stalagmites testified to the ant population of
Africa. And for most of the daylight hours, "Brother Sun" shone
brightly over everything.

The pioneer days and, indeed, years that followed the nuns'
arrival imposed a hard physical ordeal. Even Sister Kevin, with
her energy and her gay courage, found it daunting at times,
though in later years, she used to say, "Those were the grand
days." The art of survival in a strange land had to be learned
without delay if they were not to be a burden on the overworked
Fathers. For some time, the daily fare was boiled bananas, and to
unaccustomed palates, it is a forbidding diet. The monotony
would have been cruel had it not been for a biweekly present of a
tough bit of sheep or goat from the Fathers.

As the nuns became accepted, there were also little offerings of food from the local women. It must have been very moving when they first approached and, with the gentle purring Buganda greetings, knelt and proffered a few eggs, mealies, sweet potatoes, or, occasionally, a scrawny chicken. It is evident that the greatest dietary deprivation was the lack of bread. It was some years before an Indian trader began importing flour, and even then, the Sisters had to study the mysteries of yeast before they had bread on their table. By the time they had learned to grow vegetables in tropical conditions, they had an austere but adequate food supply, though at missions founded later in less friendly and less fertile parts of the country, the nuns were to experience real hunger.

Apart from the severely practical details of daily food, there was a great deal to be gone through by way of acclimatisation. Much of Buganda is over 4,000 feet high, so, although it bestrides the Equator, it is not distressingly hot for Europeans. But by English standards, it is generally very warm, and the nuns' day always included long hours of physical work, much of it in full sunlight. Besides a number of minor tropical afflictions, various bites, and jiggers, they all had malaria within the first few months. Quinine, the malarial remedy of the time, was reasonably effective but also lowering and depressing. But however tired and debilitated they must have felt, there was no delay in beginning the missionary work. Fortunately, there was no isolation from the local people; it was not necessary to go out into the highways and byways. The compound of the convent was always thronged with visitors: the night watchmen came along to inspect their charges by daylight; the curious, unaware of the Rule of Enclosure, peered in at unglazed windows to see the sewing machine and the other wonders that had been brought from England; stately royal women, overcoming their natural shyness, drifted in more and more; and the children came in hundreds. So did the sick, the wounded, and the dying.

For all the stresses and the worries of the early months, the nuns were, in one sense, still on honeymoon. Bishop Hanlon had been given a sum of money to cover the necessary tropical equipment, the fares out from England, and the building of the convent. The money had lasted long enough to help with the settling-in, but, inevitably, it came to an end, and the Bishop had to tell Mother Paul that for the future, she must find the necessary finances. Before telling all the nuns, Mother Paul decided to discuss the situation with Sister Kevin, who was from the first her second in command and confidante. She asked her to walk a little way off into a banana shamba, where she sat down on an old tree stump and broke the news. Sister Kevin was offering sympathy and encouragement, when the rotten, ant-riddled stump suddenly disintegrated, and Mother Paul descended to the ground in a heap. There was a moment's silence and then peals of glorious Irish laughter, in which Mother Paul had to join. And it was in this spirit of laughter that the nuns tackled their bankruptcy. They sewed for the tiny European community, they made clothes out of bits of silk given them by generous Indian traders, they turned the native bark-cloth into African souvenirs for export to England, and, of course, they wrote to kind friends in England, Ireland, and America for help. With their Franciscan faith, and working themselves almost beyond exhaustion, and, as Sister Kevin used to claim, with God as their banker, they won through to very modest stability.

The learning of Luganda, the native language, was a high priority. The Fathers had surprised and delighted the Sisters on their arrival by finding six young girls to help them at the convent, and it was from these girls that a solid vocabulary was acquired. Mary Kingsley used to say that many African rivers had been named with a word for "I don't know" by ignorant European enquirers. One of the nuns' young helpers was reduced to tears of exasperation at being asked repeatedly to fetch some incomprehensible commodity, before Sister Kevin realised that the humble—but to the Baganda, exotic—cabbage had been so named.

But in spite of mistakes, progress by question-and-answer method was rapid, and in six months, Mother Paul reckoned that she could start a school. There was no lack of candidates for enrolment. Indeed, the daily congregation in the compound already constituted enough for several schools. There was no school furniture; the nuns themselves had only six little camp stools to sit on at any time. So, down on the good red earth the pupils squatted, and the first pothooks were scratched on it. The purpose of school was not remotely understood at the beginning. It was just a novel entertainment out of which you could opt at will. But gradually, the idea penetrated that instruction was being given in the art of making the white man's magic talking paper, and the excitement grew. It was not confined to the young girls, whom the nuns had come out principally to teach. Small babies accompanying their mothers crawled everywhere, old ladies of 70 were not excluded, and attendants arrived and placed mats for the royal widows, who enrolled eagerly. Before long, there had to be more than one shift, and although first-generation learners were far from easy to teach, to work must have been stimulating and rewarding.

Even before the school had started, Sister Kevin had begun to care for the sick at the other end of the compound. Two little tables under a mango tree, spread with such meagre medicaments as she had, and two bowls of all-too-precious water constituted her surgery and dispensary. The patients were legion, many of them with complaints far beyond Sister Kevin's skill. She dealt with fevers, oncoming blindness, septic wounds, horrid burns, dying babies, and a good deal else, much of it hideous and nauseating. In contrast to the excitement of school work, it must have been harrowing and heartbreaking. With no hospital, not even a hut for shelter and privacy, suffering patients had to be carried back to unhygienic squalor. Little Sister Kevin longed and prayed for a cool hospital in which the battle against suffering could be waged in more hopeful conditions. Her own name, Africanised to Kevina, was one day actually to mean hospital to many people. But among the harsh realities of these early poverty-stricken days, even one hospital was scarcely dreamed of. There were harsh realities, too, out in the countryside, where the overworked Sisters went when they could. There was recurrent plague, and in the first decade of the twentieth century, there were several widespread epidemics of sleeping sickness, in which many thousands of people died. The proportions of the epidemic were far beyond the scope of the little community of Sisters, but there was charitable witness to be given in comforting those who were dying in perhaps understandable but nonetheless cruel isolation from their own kind. It is a highly contagious disease.

In the early years of the Mill Hill Fathers mission, Buganda had been recovering from the horrors of the civil wars, and the people had continued to be unsettled and sometimes suspicious. But in 1900, a Buganda-British agreement produced a form of protectorate that, in fact, maintained reasonable peace for over half a century. Old Baganda, who had lived before and during the disturbed times, used to say that the greatest effect of the British presence had been the elimination of fear. By the time the Sisters arrived, the country was comparatively settled. In a very few years, the tiny Franciscan community was clearly established and respected in the vicinity of the capital. Six white strangers had become a part of the African scene; tidying it a little, even beautifying it a little by cultivating flowers, but never really impinging on its Africanness. They lived their busy, charitable lives to the reverberating African drums from the capital hill across the valley that told the story of the Kabaka's comings and goings, and other drums from his royal mother's thatched palace on another hill, and by now the drums of Nsambya Cathedral, sounding the Angelus and calling them and the local Christians to prayer.

As the financial situation eased, the buildings in the compound grew. There was a schoolhouse of sun-baked brick, always overflowing but more conducive to concentration than the open air. The little dispensary under the mango tree moved into the grateful shelter of a shed, and the medical supplies were slightly more adequate. It was all encouraging, but there was far more work than the little community could deal with at full strength, and they were seldom that. They prayed for reinforcements, but there were none in prospect when, in 1906, Bishop Hanlon asked them to open a new convent at Nagalama, 30 miles away.

For some time, successive Kabakas had jealously kept all the white missionaries in the vicinity of the capital. Then, permission to go further afield had been quickly acted on by the Fathers, and they had gained a tenuous foothold at Nagalama, on flat and unfertile land above the Nile Valley, where it flows between Lake Victoria and Lake Kyoga. A Dutch priest, Father Biermans, who was later to succeed Bishop Hanlon, was in charge of the mission. He had reported that the hard-won foothold was in danger of slipping unless he could have the help of some nuns. Two of the Fathers had died in establishing Nagalama, and Mother Paul and her Sisters felt unable to refuse their assistance.

So, Sister Kevin, with Sisters Alexis and Solano, set out in rickshaws to found the first daughter convent. They had a hard struggle. This time, there were no welcoming crowds in the compound. Instead, they were surrounded by hostile suspicion, uncomfortably evident in strange happenings during the night. Sister Kevin had to lead her nuns out into the surrounding villages, and at first they met with no success in making contact with the local people. Then, after many disheartening months, they broke through with the children, who started to follow them back to the convent. Where the children went, the mothers followed, and gallant patience had its reward when enmity started to dissolve into shy friendship. Then a little dispensary was set up, and Sister Kevin gained rapidly in reputation with the local practitioners, whose fees in sheep and goats were exorbitant. In time, a school became possible, and an active mission was firmly established.

The battle was won, but a heavy price had been paid in physical suffering. At first, there had been real hunger, unalleviated until friends had been made locally and little presents of food began to arrive. Not very high above the Nile Valley, the heat was excessive, mosquitoes abounded, and all three Sisters suffered virulent and recurrent attacks of malaria. Sister Kevin must have had a robust constitution. On one occasion, when she and Sister Alexis had malaria so badly that they had to be carried in hammocks to Nsambya to be nursed, she was thought very unlikely to last the journey. Sister Alexis was poorly for years after, and little Sister Solano, the baby of the party, perhaps never recovered from the experience. She died at Nagalama of blackwater fever in 1914. Sister Kevin was always grateful for her four years there, where she felt that she had got closer to the indigenous religion than at any other mission. Like all great missionaries, she knew that a real understanding of native religion was essential to the successful propagation of her own faith.

Mother Paul's health had been failing for some time, and in 1910, she was recalled to England, and went thence to her native America. Sister Kevin returned from Nagalama to take com-

mand at Nsambya. She became officially Mother Kevin, or
Mamma Kevina, though Africans seldom bothered with her title;
she was just Kevina or Little Kevina, and her name was rapidly
becoming a household word. Three additional nuns had arrived
in 1908, of whom one was unable to stay the course. With
Mother Paul's departure, there remained seven nuns to run two
thriving but seriously understaffed missions. The building programme had progressed splendidly. A small hospital had been
opened at Nsambya in 1907. It had been built with American and
Dutch money, and was relatively well equipped. A school with
400 pupils had the appearance, at least, of orderliness. The community exchequer amounted to 50 shillings.

Not that Mother Kevin was unduly worried about finances.
Her faith in God as her banker was to carry her through worse
financial situations, and, always a gallant gambler, she seldom
allowed lack of funds to slow down the advance of missionary
work. It was the lack of personnel which did that. The range of
effective colonial government was expanding all the time from
its early centre in Buganda to include many other peoples who
lived within the wider frontier of the Uganda Protectorate. One
after another these newly contacted peoples asked if they might
have missions, and it cannot have been easy for zealous missionaries to refuse them. But seven overworked women had to say
no. Mother Kevin wrote again and again to St. Mary's Abbey for
help, and Bishop Biermans added his desperate pleas to hers.

Their prayers were answered in 1913, when three more Sisters arrived. A new convent was possible, and Mother Kevin was
glad that it was the Bishop and not she who had to decide where it
was to be. He chose Busoga, across the Nile and to the east of
Buganda. Mother Kevin accompanied the three Sisters who were
to attempt the venture. They left in rickshaws, spent the night at
Nagalama, and crossed the Nile in dugout canoes. The Fathers
were established at Kamuli, which they reached in three days
after leaving Nsambya. It proved a very tough assignment, and
the hostility of the Basoga manifested itself more unpleasantly
and lasted far longer than hostility at Nagalama.

There were the usual pioneer conditions of greater than Franciscan poverty. The little convent building was comfortless;
though by then, *bati*, or corrugated iron, with its comparative

freedom from rats and insects, had replaced thatch for roofing. The outlook onto dusty, flat elephant-grass country was unendearing. The district was very malarial, and the Fathers and the nuns suffered continuously. And Mother Kevin had, of course, to return to her headquarters and leave the three pioneer Sisters without her courageous leadership. She visited them once a month, and this was the beginning of her long years of regular journeying about East Africa.

In her rickshaw, and later in the cabin of her lorry, she became a familiar sight along the dusty roads and bush tracks, just as her name saint, Saint Teresa of Avila, had been in her covered wagons along the dusty roads of sixteenth-century Spain. She travelled early, and at Nagalama or Kamuli, the Sisters used to find their beloved Mother Superior on the baraza, or verandah, quite unexpectedly in the morning. Just as a mother on a visit to her children away from home, she would be laden with packages, little individual presents for the Sisters, little comforts for the bare convent. There would be news and there would be laughter, and after a brief visit, she would leave them infected by her great love for mankind, and with the courage to continue the lonely struggle. They were sorely in need of courage.

In the early days of World War I, so little progress had been made that Mother Kevin nearly decided to recall them. Then, a bad outbreak of plague made it impossible to abandon the mission. Plague was followed by ghastly famine and such times of horror that in later days, the community seldom spoke of them. In the bad times, Mother Kevin almost doubled her visits, and the local people asked why "the little one with the bright eyes that see everything inside you" could not stay with them always. A recital of all her other commitments by the Sisters made her seem a great wonder to them. But save for a little nucleus round the convent, even with the miracle of Mother Kevin and the breaking down of barriers during the famine, the Basoga remained aloof. Eventually, Kamuli became a thriving Catholic parish, with fine schools and a hospital, but it took a very long time.

World War I brought its own trials. East Africa was itself a theatre of war, and there was a German frontier immediately to the south of Buganda. For a time, there were both British and

Belgian troops in or near Uganda. The convent at Nsambya was turned into a hospital for the Native Carrier Corps, the porters for the European troops. They were the lowest form of army life, not even reckoned as soldiers, but Mother Kevin gladly accepted them into her care. It was very much a Franciscan commitment. Convoys of sick men arrived all the time, many of them suffering from contagious diseases. The unskilled African nurses who now helped in the hospital deserted in terror. The majority of the nuns were away for most of the war years, helping to staff a base hospital at Kisumu. Mother Kevin and one nun carried on together, and in the end, the spectacle of the generous love that she squandered on suffering humanity proved as infectious as it always did with her nuns, and a number of her African helpers returned to her.

With the army she met, for the first time, the insulting behaviour of many Europeans towards her lowly patients. Being Mother Kevin, she met it with very articulate rage, and she bitterly regretted that she did not know all the relevant languages. Altogether, she had a difficult command. Nuns do not find it easy to be taken away from their routine lives and sent to military hopsitals. There were stresses and there was tension. But the contribution of the community to the war effort was valuable, which the government acknowledged by awarding an M.B.E. to the Mother Superior. She was always adamant that it was the community and not she who had earned it, but she accepted the fact that they had to pin the medal on somebody.

Two saints named Teresa influenced Mother Kevin's life, two saints that have been written of together as "the eagle and the dove." The first, Teresa of Avila, was her name saint, whom she admired greatly. The second, Saint Teresa of Lisieux, was her contemporary and had not yet been canonised when Mother Kevin first read her autobiography, *L'histoire d'une âme*, during the war years. The "Little Flower" of Lisieux, a humble little nun like herself, who had not lived to fulfil her missionary aspirations, completely won her devotion. She seemed to Mother Kevin to have been a "genius in the science of love," and her own spirituality deepened in the knowledge of her. She began what can only be described as a lifelong friendship with her. She talked everything over with her, and solicited her interest and her help; it was a collaboration that bore splendid fruit. The saint had to submit to an occasional scolding. When some new project was not coming along quite quickly enough for Mother Kevin's liking, she would be heard saying, "Come on now Teresa dear, you'll have to do better than that." And Mother Kevin herself had a scolding from Rome when she wanted to dedicate a new hospital to Teresa before the ancient machinery of the Vatican had creaked into officially declaring her a saint.

Mother Kevin had some of the qualities of both her saints: certainly, the force and great organising ability of the eagle; and certainly, the profound simplicity of the dove. She had her own individual qualities, too, and of these, the breadth of her forward-looking vision was the most remarkable, in that it operated within the narrow confines of conventual life in the African bush. When the war ended, she had not been in England for 16 years, yet she knew that the war had brought about almost revolutionary changes, and realised that this would, in time, result in changes and development in East Africa. She was certain that the Catholic missions must be ready to be in the vanguard of this development, especially in the field of social services. But the Catholic missions were gravely handicapped. There were not enough nuns, and such nuns as there were either did not have sufficient skill, or were not allowed to practise the professional expertise that was soon going to be necessary.

Regret has often been expressed that two Christian denominations were competing so close to each other in Buganda. The Catholics defended their intrusion into the Anglican preserve with the undoubted fact that in the beginning, the Kabaka would not have allowed them to operate anywhere else but in the vicinity of the capital and, therefore, of the Church Missionary Society. There had, in fact, been plenty of scope for both missions. The rivalry had had its unfortunate side and, especially during the civil war, its ugly side. A Quaker who came out years later to administer girls' education in Uganda expressed her conviction that the competition had been of inestimable value in education, and a considerable factor in the creation of great schools of both denominations.

In the field of medicine, the Catholic missions were not able to compete on equal terms. The Church Missionary Society had a well-established medical side and a very fine medical record. They had the professional services of lay doctors and trained nurses. The brothers Albert and Howard Cook, both doctors, had founded a hospital, remarkable by all standards, at Mengo, a hill near the capital. Lady Cook, wife of Dr. Sir Albert, had pioneered the training of African nurses at Mengo before it had been started anywhere else in Africa, and at a time when an African girl risked being disowned by her family if she went to work in a hospital. Now the government was actually going to give a small subsidy for a training school for African nurses, and only the Protestant Mission had the necessary professional personnel to avail themselves of it. The Mill Hill Mission had done gallant work: the nuns' hospitals had grown rapidly from a table under a tree to cool buildings with whitewashed wards; they were experienced in many tropical ailments; but they were amateurs. And they were disastrously handicapped in that they were not at that time allowed to qualify medically or to practise any sort of midwifery.

As a good general, Mother Kevin pondered on the reshaping of strategy that was necessary if her mission was to move with the times. In 1919, she was summoned home to St. Mary's Abbey to take part in the general chapter of the congregation. It seemed a God-given chance to consult with her superiors and other Church authorities. Bishop Biermans agreed with her wholeheartedly over her medical aspirations and over the vexing and delicate question of midwifery. With his blessing, she set off alone to Mombasa, en route for England. The railway line had not then reached Kampala, but an adequate little steamer now ran to Kisumu, and a regular weekly train went from there to Nairobi and the coast, with little inconvenience or danger. At Mombasa, where she was the guest of the White Sisters, she found that shipping was still disorganised by war, and she had difficulty in securing a passage.

Eventually, she got a berth in a ward on a hospital ship which was homeward bound via South Africa. Four weeks on her own on board ship must have been strange after years of unalleviated, hardworking community life, but she welcomed them. Throughout the rest of her life, she always used the hour-long crossings of Lake Kyoga that she made so many times in her journeyings as a chance to commune with herself. Now, rising long before the other passengers and revelling in the dawns at sea, she meditated deeply, and she made her plans for dealing with the forces of reaction. In her simplicity, she did not know how powerful these forces were.

She needed nuns and she needed nurses, but above all, she needed permission for maternity work. Both maternal and infant mortality in Uganda were exceptionally high, and there was urgent need of midwives. Furthermore, the new official interest in nursing services was becoming the exclusive preserve of the Protestants, a fact that might have worried the Vatican, even if the necessity for nurses was hard to understand at a distance. And what was immediately more frustrating to Mother Kevin was that when, as was inevitable at times, she or her Sisters were faced with the Christian necessity of helping a woman in her labour pains, officially, they must turn their backs on her. This was no way to teach the love of God through the love of your neighbor. Among Mother Kevin's many admirers was a distinguished judicial knight, who used to describe a visit he paid to her at Nsambya one morning when he found her in a state of raging Hibernian fury. She had just received a severe reprimand from the Vatican, which had heard that she and the Sisters had been disobeying the rules. Someone had been telling tales. "I tell you what Sir John," he used to report her as saying in her rage, "the Pope and all his cardinals are just a lot of blithering old bachelors." When Mother Kevin went to see the Pope, she was so overcome at being in the presence of the Vicar of Christ that she was unable to open her eyes to see what he looked like, and it is very unlikely that she really included the Holy Father in her strictures. But even if the story had some artistic additions, it gives some idea of what she was to feel on the subject for the next 17 years, before the battle was finally won.

At St. Mary's Abbey, she was promoted Vicaress of the Upper Nile diocese, which gave her some added authority. She found sympathetic listeners for her maternity projects but was always warned that her ideas were too progressive to succeed. The ban was a part of canon law, and only occasionally were dispensations given. She went on to Ireland and consulted priests who were unexpectedly sympathetic but who could give her no official encouragement. The reaction of her own family was distressing. A cousin who was a nun was outraged at the idea, and told her that the family would be shocked. It had, indeed, been shocked when, at the height of the Irish Nationalist movement, she had accepted a medal from the British Government.

Mother Kevin had, of course, far outgrown such insularity, and was too sensible of the interests of her mission to show bad manners to the power that administered the country in which it operated. But this was something far more serious. Apparently, the fact that the nuns were having the privilege of baptising lots of dying mothers and babies should satisfy their missionary aspirations. Mother Kevin, as a good daughter of the Church, would not have disputed the value of baptism; but when her relations could not understand her impassioned plea that the living Church she wanted could not be founded on dead babies, she was bewildered. It was sad for her, and spoiled the pleasure of being once again in her native land. Back in England, she was greatly encouraged by an interview with the Archbishop of Westminster, Cardinal Bourne. He could not give the necessary dispensation, but he was in complete agreement with her. He arranged for her to take a short course in obstetrics in a hospital in Alsace run by a religious group. It was only permitted on the understanding that she did not qualify officially and that she would never practise. The blithering old bachelors were not being very consistent, but the training was to prove of great value to Mother Kevin in planning and organising the hospitals of the future.

In March 1920, she had been a year in Europe, and she had to return to Uganda. None of her dreams had come true, and she was terribly disappointed. Then, at the last moment, a miracle happened. She went to pay a farewell visit at a Poor Clare Convent. When she arrived, she found that the Mother Abbess was engaged with another visitor. This was a young woman and, in fact, the Abbess's own younger sister. Mother Kevin went to the chapel to await her turn, and there the young woman was sent to summon her. The Mother Abbess had told her who Mother Kevin was, and as she introduced herself, she confessed to a great interest in missions. Mother Kevin replied by pouring out her troubles, without having any idea that she was talking to a highly qualified doctor. She was Doctor Evelyn Connolly, and there and then she volunteered her services. With this brief chance encounter, Mother Kevin had found a lay Catholic doctor for her mission, someone who could train her African nurses in midwifery. It was arranged that Dr. Connolly should come out in a year's time for a three-year period, and she did not require to be paid. The time was extended indefinitely, and some years later, she was received into the Franciscan Order as Sister Mary Assumpta.

The Uganda Government budget was still mainly devoted to law and order and to the development of commerce and communications. Just a little money was available for the social services, but their main expansion had to wait until after World War II. In the meantime, social work was left to the missions. Mother Kevin had to get official sanction for her nursing school, and there was some difficulty. The bureaucracy did not understant why Catholic girls could not be trained at a Protestant school, and there was not enough money available to subsidize a Catholic school. As usual, money did not greatly worry Mother Kevin, nor did the polite opposition. Both she and the officials knew how it would end. Mother Mary Louis quotes a senior government official's impression of her calls at the Secretariat:

She is an amazing woman. The whole department may have decided that she cannot have approval for all her private enterprises. She calls on us. She is perfectly simple, perfectly charming and perfectly inflexible! Invariably she gets what she has come for; invariably she is proved to be right. She is a wonder, a woman totally dedicated to religion, she keeps us all on our secular toes.[4]

Another official put it less gracefully but more succinctly when he expressed regret that she was not available to run the British Empire.

Mother Kevin, now in the middle of what her nuns called her "roaring forties," was brilliantly preparing her mission to take advantage of the developments that she was sure were on the way in East Africa, Already, in the 1920s, there were increasing signs of encouragement. In 1922, the succession of Pope Pius XI, known as the "Pope of the Missions,"promised more cooperation from the Holy See. In 1924, when education was still entirely missionary, a Uganda Government Department of Education was started. Private subscriptions were flowing in at a much greater rate, as the world became more Africa-conscious. At an opportune moment, £1700 came from an American donor for the nursing school, and £1700 went a long way in Uganda in the 1920s. As always, the great difficulty was lack of staff; there were still only 12 nuns. Dr. Connolly was progressing well in the training of at least a few African nurses, but African teachers of advanced level did not exist, nor seemed likely to exist for a long time.

It was while the nursing school was being built that an event happened which, apart from being very moving to Mother Kevin personally, gave some hopes of a supply of teachers for the future. There were by now some girl boarders at Nsambya, and one day they approached Mother Kevin about the possibility of their joining the order as nuns. .It was not entirely unexpected; indeed, the girls themselves were convinced that she had been avoiding them for some time by dodging away to the brick-kilns when she saw them coming. Many wise churchmen have confessed to diffidence when dealing with the question of vocation for the first time, and it is likely that she was taking her time in deciding how to react. There were great difficulties. How would African parents, accustomed to a bride-price in cattle for their daughters with which to subsidise their sons' marriages, like the idea? How could anyone know if African girls really understood the meaning of vocation? How much stamina would they have for the long years of higher education and training that would be necessary? Could they remain celibate? Mother Kevin discussed it all with the girls at great length. Material hardship was irrelevant, but she conscienctiously took them through all the other hardships of religious life.

Finally, it was the extraordinary persistence of the girls that convinced her that the experiment should be made. From that moment, of course, the matter was virtually decided. Having equipped herself thoroughly with the relevant canon law, she prepared to storm and charm her way through formidable opposition and acid criticism. The idea of African nuns seemed absurd to many people, and the cry "they're not ready for it," which reechoed so persistently in European bars and clubs in the next decades, was heard on all sides. But Bishop Biermans agreed with Mother Kevin that African development would not go on evolving at the old pace but would almost certainly erupt, and before so very long. He also knew that if she was prepared to try, she was probably right. At worst, the result would be the training of some comparatively well-educated African girls. With the Bishop's cooperation, it did not take long to get permission from her superiors and from the Holy See to accept African aspirants for the Sisterhood. Thus, Mother Kevin pioneered the Africanisation of the mission and the higher education of Catholic African women.

The congregation of the Little Sisters of Saint Francis came into being officially on May 3, 1923, when eight aspirants who had miraculously persuaded their parents to allow them to be *babikira,* or virgins, were received by the Bishop at a simple ceremony at Nsambya. Precisely three years later, 14 postulants entered their novitiate and donned the Franciscan habit. The numbers were steadily growing, and the converted shed at Nsambya that was their first convent was hopelessly inadequate. Mother Kevin's faith in her great experiment was now confirmed, and she planned the next move. With her usual eye on the future, she wanted her African Sisterhood to develop quite independently from her own congregation. She also wanted their education to be the very best possible, and to be carried much further than that of other African girls at the time. A short visit to England in 1925 had brought three more nuns, one of whom, Sister Cecilia, a musician as her name suggests, was well qualified to teach novices. So, on the educational side, Mother Kevin was not too badly off. What she needed was accommodation; preferably, quite separate from Nsambya.

On September 16, 1926, Mother Kevin and the now elderly Mother Alexis went to inspect a piece of land that the new Bishop Campling was able to offer her. It was at Nkokonjeru, in the hills 35 miles from Nsambya, and they were delighted with it. In the centre of the site there was a lightning-blasted tree, which was apparently the habitation of the *lubale,* or spirit, which had to be humoured by sacrificial offerings of white hens. There was con-

siderable evidence of this round the tree, and the name Nkokonjeru means white hen. The lubale was powerful enough to have
defeated the tentative efforts of some previous missionaries, but
Mother Kevin was quite undismayed.

Installed in a little bush hut, she had more tangible worries in
the shape of rats, snakes, scorpions, jiggers, and other insects.
The day after her arrival was the feast of the Stigmata of Saint
Francis. There was a fierce thunderstorm, and the lubale tree
was dramatically struck to the ground. She was already planning
and plotting the buildings she wanted, and already casting an eye
round for the fuel potential for her brick-kilns. Here was some
fuel ready to hand. Apprehensive crowds had been drawn to the
scene of their fallen god, and she sensed instantly that this was
the psychological moment to act. Carrying axes, hatchets, and
saws, she and old Mother Alexis approached the tree, and looking
rather like a little white hen herself, she picked up an axe and
advanced to strike the first blow. Perspiring freely and with
aching arms, she carried on while the crowd watched in fascinated expectation. Mother Alexis relieved her for a short while,
and both nuns were seen to be miraculously still alive. In time, a
few of the watchers, while informing the lubale that this was
Kevina's doing and not theirs, were shamed into helping her, and
the lubale was all but defeated. It gave a final death kick a few
nights later, when a vast fallen tree nearby, in which it was
alleged to have taken refuge, mysteriously reared itself up nearly
six feet. But Mother Kevin was in need of a great deal of fuel, and
she headed another successful attack with axes and demolished
it.

As in Europe in the Middle Ages, so, too, in tropical Africa,
most of the first buildings of any size were those of the Christian
churches. Today a splendid red-brick Roman basilica in northern
Uganda rears up in startling and inspiring contrast to its surroundings. It was designed by a 23-year-old Verona Father, the
son of a well-known Italian architect. On a headland near Bukoba
on Lake Victoria, the pretty silver spire of a Catholic church
marvellously enhances a fine sketch of lake coast. One of the
several flat-topped hills around which Kampala is built is
crowned with the twin-towered cathedral of the French Fathers,

and another by the mellow red-bricked and black-domed Anglican Cathedral. Mother Kevin was a great builder in her own
right, because she had, of course, no money for architects or
other professional help.

In the early days, the Fathers helped her with the simple
designs, but she herself became virtually a master builder,
though inevitably her buildings remained simple. She worked
long hours in the blazing sun doing everything herself, from
stoking the furnaces for the brick-kilns so that the steady flow of
bricks never faltered and delayed the brick layers, to taking the
plumb line and turning the corners. Her enthusiasm and sense of
urgency infected her workmen, and they sang improvised songs
about her as they worked:

> This Kevina is building. She is building a house for God.
> She is building it big. She is building it fine.
> She is a little woman but she works like a strong man.
> She is a great builder is this Kevina.[5]

In time, her own special group of workmen became known as the
Ba-company, and they went with her wherever she was building,
gaily crammed into the back of her lorry. She had to find wages
for them, but to have a nucleus of men whom she knew and who
knew her was economically sound. And when the exchequer was
in poor shape, they trusted her and waited patiently for their pay.

Just as the founding of the African Sisterhood was her greatest
missionary achievement, so, too, Nkokonjeru was her most complete building enterprise. She started as soon as she had decided
on the site. At 7 A.M. every morning, when the nuns had finished
their early devotions, they got ready to organise an army of
diggers, brick makers, brick layers, and carpenters. Except for
some very simple drawings of dormitories, community rooms,
refectories, classrooms, and kitchens done by the Fathers, they
were completely responsible for the operations. At the end of the
day when the workmen came to be paid, Mother Kevin was
always required to doctor their sundry ills, and her working day
was not over when the building stopped. No wonder that nuns
arriving from England commented on tired white faces.

But the work went on rapidly in spite of occasional hitches and one temporary cessation for lack of funds. An opportune cheque for £2500 from Australia got it going again. By the beginning of May 1927, Brother Giles, who was prevented by ill health from doing ordinary field work, had been appointed chaplain to the African Sisterhood, and he was comparing the first buildings to the dwellings at San Damiano which Saint Francis built for Saint Clare. Mother Kevin had set her heart on a permanent chapel of great beauty, and would not allow it to be built in a hurry. Eventually, two Fathers who were expert builders designed a lovely cruciform church to seat 300 worshippers, and almost every rose-red brick was hand selected.

Before the young community could come to their convent, there had to be some furniture. Mother Alexis was adept at soliciting material from kindly Indian and Goan traders. With irresistable charm she approached them with "Mother Kevin said she felt sure you would oblige with a few packing cases," or "We were wondering if you were going to use those old motor spirit tanks in your yard." When scrubbed clean, the latter would collect bath water. The packing cases, piled three high, were for cupboards. The fact that they bore the indelible print of firms like Johnnie Walker and John Haig was no worry. Even after Sister Euphemia from Country Wexford had decorated them with dark oak varnish stain, their origins were still apparent, and visitors used to ask Mother Kevin if she had a licence. Sister Euphemia and her varnish stain became famous. Once, she inadvertently decorated a beautiful, young District Officer in immaculate whites. He had sat down on a newly treated bench before he heard the warning shouts. But in spite of minor accidents, and a local dog who kept running off with the frying pan, one way or another the furniture was collected. By dint of desperate hard work and a lot of laughter, the unpretentious convent was ready for habitation.

At the end of May 1927, a cavalcade of lorries arrived at Nsambya, and 70 Little Sisters climbed in for the journey to Nkokonjeru. Brother Giles, the chaplain, went separately on his new motorbike, one of the first to be seen in Uganda, and a spectacular success everywhere he went. It was not, however, suitable transport for his cat, which had to ride in one of the lorries. By evening, the empty convent was thronged with laughing young black nuns. Thus, as a result of a great collaboration between God, Saint Francis, Saint Teresa of Lisieux, and Mother Kevin and her nuns, Nkokonjeru was born.

The advent of a Department of Education in 1924 had been largely due to the statesmanlike campaigning of Dr. J. H. Oldham, the secretary of the International Missionary Council. Equipped with incomparable expertise, he had organised a powerful lobby, and in a memorandum to the Colonial Office in May 1923, he had presented a policy whereby the State and the missions would collaborate in African education. To build on the already existing mission schools, the only schools at the time, had the merit of economy. More importantly, most educational experts, whether Christians or not, thought that an education tied to religion was desirable. The Colonial Office had moved rapidly to implement Dr. Oldham's policy.

In June 1923, a meeting presided over by the Under-Secretary of State and attended by a large number of colonial Governors as well as by representatives of the missionary societies, had formally accepted Oldham's recommendations. There was to be Catholic representation on an Educational Advisory Committee at the Colonial Office and on similar bodies in the colonial terrritories. The Catholics did not, however, take full advantage of the new situation until the appointment of Monsignor, later Cardinal, Hinsley as Apostolic Delegate to British tropical Africa in 1927. He had formerly been Rector of the English College in Rome, and the appointment of such an eminent Englishman was largely in the interests of establishing a good relationship with the State in educational matters. His message to the missions on his arrival was that good Catholic schools were the essential foundation for the Catholic Church in East Africa, and that they were to take precedence over ordinary evangelising work.

Mother Kevin had found the powerful ally she needed for her educational plans. Financial help would be coming from the government, and now she must somehow acquire the requisite staff. The dribbling reinforcements of two or three nuns at a time would no longer be remotely adequate, and, knowing for some time that this moment was coming, she had her plans. She applied to her superiors for permission to open a novitiate at home, especially for the Uganda missions, and her request was granted. She had only £50 towards the expenses, not even enough for a fare home; but as usual, she was not discouraged, and as usual, providence provided.

In 1928, an English woman living in Uganda invited Mother Kevin to choose a nun as companion and to come with her, expenses paid to England. They were to sail to Marseilles and make a pilgrimage to some of the great French shrines en route, so she chose a young French nun, who would thus have a chance to see her family. They visited Lourdes, Paray, and Ars, and the crowning delight was Lisieux. There, Mother Kevin added a dimension to her devoted relationship with Saint Teresa by forming a lifelong friendship with the saint's own Mother Abbess and her Carmelite nuns. Then she crossed over to England to begin her search for a house in which to start her novitiate. She had just £50 and the return half of a ticket to Uganda in her pocket. She confessed in later years that the size of her task often daunted her, but her burning faith, refreshed by her spiritual pilgrimage in France, carried her along.

She started full of hopes in Ireland, which was always sympathetic to missionary causes, but she met with no success or encouragement. Then she tried Scotland, but except for gaining the friendship of a distinguished Scottish prelate who shared her love for Saint Teresa, she found nothing. When she went on to the north of England, winter was approaching, which made house hunting a more than usually dreary occupation. In December, when she was desperately tired and depressed, she sought the hospitality of the Bar Convent in York, and there she at last found some definite news of a possible property. The nuns told her that the Duchess of Norfolk had a house that she was hoping to sell to a religious order. It was Holme Hall, near Selby, a great seventeenth-century house which had belonged to a Catholic family that had given sanctuary to French nuns, Augustinian and Franciscan, during the French Revolution. The house had its own chapel, and it was in order to preserve this as an amenity for the neighbourhood, and to keep the sanctuary lamp burning, that the Duchess had bought it. Mother Kevin went to see the Duchess, who welcomed her with open arms. She, too, was a devotee of Saint Teresa.

Amid the ice and snows of the Yorkshire winter, Mother Kevin went to inspect Holme Hall. The vast mansion was empty, neglected, and forbidding, but she knew that she had found what she was looking for, and she knelt and thanked God and her special saints in the little chapel. Six weeks later she took possession with a little band of helpers: Sister Alcantara of her own congregation, some nuns from the convent at York, and two postulants. The snow was falling, the house had no lighting or heating—in fact, no comforts at all—and the rats and mice were in full possession. There were great scrubbings and great paintings; one wing was especially spruced up for guests as a possible source of revenue; and the little party worked long hours, from candlelight to candlelight. The nuns at York sent some furniture, and in a very short time, noisy young aspirants arrived from many different places, principally Ireland, and the old house came to life again.

Then, of course, it had to be paid for. The Duchess of Norfolk well knew that Mother Kevin's acceptance of Holme Hall was a gallant gamble. She let her have it rent-free for a year, which was a tremendous help. £10,000 then had to be found for the modest purchase price and the necessary modernisation. Subscriptions were coming in well, especially from Ireland, but a lot of money was needed before the novitiate could be a going concern. Mother Kevin set off on the first of many visits to the United States. It was in the dark days of the American Depression; nonetheless, her fund-raising trip was a tour de force. She looked almost impudently young for a great founding Abbess, but the depth of her love and the breadth of her vision were radiantly evident. She made many valuable friends, among them Father, later Cardinal, Cushing, then Director of the Society for the Propagation of the Faith in Boston. She also had a happy reunion with some of her family who had settled in America and whose children were enchanted to meet their famous Aunt Tessie.

Mother Kevin returned to Yorkshire in August 1929 with her immediate financial problems solved. She found the novitiate progressing well. A supply of teaching nuns for Uganda was assured, and one of her greatest dreams was realised. The wisdom of her far-seeing policies received confirmation when Monsignor Hinsley returned to England for a visit that autumn and gave his opinion publicly that the great opportunity for the Church in East Africa was in the education of women. He also said that one of the main priorities should be the creation of an African priesthood and Sisterhood. Then the Holy Father put the seal of approval on her work by honouring her with the medal Pro Ecclesia et Pontifice. Having business to transact in connection with the novitiate, she visited Rome on her way back to Africa, and had a special audience with His Holiness. She reached Uganda in great heart. She had now brought into being two fountainheads, from which two streams of teachers, one European and the other African, would soon be flowing steadily into the schools of the future. The way ahead was clear.

A brief return to England in 1931 nearly resulted in tragedy. Like most Irish people, she loved concerts and amateur dramatics, and a performance had been arranged by the postulants at Holme Hall to celebrate her visit. The curtain was about to rise, and she was on her way downstairs, when she suddenly collapsed with blackwater fever. For many days, her life was in grave danger, but Africa had taught her how to fight serious illness. The doctor was amazed at her resilience and, incidentally, at her knowledge of the disease. Before very long, she was issuing commands for the postponed concert to be put on, and to everyone's concern and the doctor's despair, she set out on a fundraising tour shortly afterwards.

With all her worldwide travel, all her contacts with the great, and all her ambitious plans, Mother Kevin was still very much the mother of her two families in Uganda. Had the call to the mission field not come, she would probably by now have been an indulgent grandmother to a great many descendants in Dublin. As it was, she still dearly loved to be indulgent within the limits of the Franciscan Rule and resources to all those in her charge. There were some things in which she never pretended to go all the way with her beloved Saint Francis. Once, when the nuns were acting a play in which the saint throws a handful of gold coins on the fire, she burst out with, "What waste! I could never be as Franciscan as that."

Her two families seem to have occupied different compart-
ments in her mind and her affections. The growing number of
European nuns, who, for all their devotion and practised discipline, inevitably varied in their ability to face the interminable
frustrations of a difficult life, needed much from her. The sever-
est hardships of the pioneer days were no more, but with them,
some of the intimate trust and understanding had gone. The
fight for survival through sickness, hunger, and hostility had
bred strength and unity. Now, newer brooms had time to be
critical of what they found.

Mother Kevin's temper, always formidable, had full play at
times. But just as the sudden storms of Irish rain are chased away
by bright sunshine, so, too, her temper could melt to sunny
gentleness or even to radiant laughter. She frequently used to
prescribe a bit of digging for bad temper in her nuns, and no
doubt she used to prescribe it for herself as well. As a farmer's
daughter, she knew the soothing satisfaction of contact with the
good earth. But if the nature of her office made her a disciplinarian, she also gave freedom to her nuns to develop their own ideas,
and was ever watchful for an individual teaching talent that
needed free rein in order to mature.

On the lighter side, she was aware of the human need for the
anticipation of pleasure, however slight and austere. It could be
the short evening recreational hour with its relaxed chatter,
sometimes enlivened by an impromptu concert, occasionally
made memorable by Mother Kevin herself in inspired spiritual
mood. It could be one of the great feasts of the Church, when the
Solemn Mass was followed by a welcome change of menu, and
maybe some theatricals. Little unexpected treats had their value,
too. She never returned from England without a present for
everyone, the results of what she used to call a spending binge at
Selfridge's bargain basement. When a Boston family accidentally
strayed into the mission, "our little Sister from Boston" was
given the day off. And it was a French nun who was chosen for
the French tour. It was partly her natural generosity, but it was
also a deliberate cosseting—if such a word can be used in a
Franciscan context—because she knew that a bit of spoiling is
encouraging.

And there were times when the nuns had great need of encouragement, times when Mother Kevin went to them if she possibly could. Once, she rushed off to one of the mission's leper colonies when the Sisters had had to be drastically inoculated against plague then raging in the neighbourhood and adding to their cares. Strangely isolated from normal life by horrors, their insides full of injected bugs, they came to the evening recreational hour hungry for something familiar to hold on to. Mother Kevin suggested a game of cards. The interlude of family pastime worked wonders, and the Sisters could even smile at the strangeness of the circumstances for card games. The brief taste of happy normality was rounded off by Mother Kevin ordering a homely treat of hot milk and biscuits.

The success of her relationship with her other family at Nkokonjeru can be judged by the rapid increase of aspirants and postulants. She probably had to be more of a disciplinarian there than at her other convents; certainly, more patient and, perhaps, more indulgent. Egalitarianism was a foreign concept to ethnically divided and socially stratified young Africans, and on that, the Franciscan Rule demanded implicit obedience. The African rhythm is a slow one, and this had to be allowed for in what was in many ways a forcing house. If the young nuns were to develop their best, they must be given responsibility quickly, even before some of their tutors thought they were ready for it. And perhaps more than anywhere else, there had to be fun, which Mother Kevin was good at, and there was good community music. Nkokonjeru became virtually her base, and its creation and the deep affection of the young African girls who had followed her into religious life, and whom she had to discipline rigorously, was, perhaps, the greatest achievement of her life.

The years between 1932 and 1948 were years of tremendous expansion. Mother Kevin opened 15 new convents, each one complete with chapel, catechumenate, school, and hospital. The old Ford lorry, with herself in the cabin beside the driver, and the crack building troops, the Ba-company, in behind, became a familiar sight along the dusty roads of Uganda. "*We* are going to found a new convent," the company shouted to their admirers as they raced through the villages. They crossed over the Nile to the east and over Lake Kyoga to the northeast, filling in the great empty spaces of the Upper Nile Vicariate. The building operations followed the same pattern, with Mother Kevin supervising every detail. Her expertise increased all the time, as did that of her workmen. Between them they made a wonderful team.

The other expertise that Mother Kevin was acquiring was educational. First of all, she was herself a born teacher, and with all the many demands on her time, she never gave up her teaching. She also planned textbooks which were especially suitable for African children. She had no higher education herself, but she wanted it and strove for it for every African girl in her care who was suitable for it. In the teeth of opposition, she opened a training school for secondary-school teachers, and the opening of a girls' senior secondary school in 1940 was a landmark. When the first East African university, at Makerere in Uganda, began to materialise in the years after World War II, among the few girls with the requisite university entrance qualifications were a number of her Franciscan Sisters.

But higher education was only for a few. Beyond that, the goal was that every African girl in touch with a Catholic mission should be educated to the full extent of her ability, be it in sewing, washing, or cooking, without even the three R's. The founding of vocational schools proved a great success, and led to domestic science and secretarial schools. Raising the status of African women was basic to all her teaching policies, but she was insistent that education must not estrange the girls from their home background. If one of her nuns protested that it was no longer suitable for educated girls to work on the land, it made her very angry. It was an essential and perfectly dignified contribution to family life, and to a farmer's daughter, it was both understandable and desirable. Her nuns also had to be restrained from the "quicker to do it yourself" impulse, however slow their pupils. Altogether, she ran into considerable criticism over her educational policies, especially over her insistence on teaching English from the beginning. In Uganda, where upwards of a dozen languages are spoken, the chances of there ever being the requisite textbooks for advanced education in the vernacular languages were remote. As usual, she was looking ahead, and as usual, she was right.

Smart schools and university degrees generated an elite. Mother Kevin knew that this was important in strengthening the Catholic Church in East Africa, and in rescuing African women from their inferior status. She also knew that it was not in the Franciscan tradition. And so, with girls' schools forging rapidly ahead, she found time to turn aside and, like the blessed Saint Francis, embrace the lepers. In 1932, when she started the first leprosarium, it was thought that there were over 80,000 lepers in a population of 5,000,000 in Uganda. The numbers were probably higher, because the disease was held in such horror that people tried to disguise it in the early stages. She was given a site by Lake Victoria, not far from the exit of the Nile. There was a leaking grass hut in which she camped while she surveyed it, and the Ba-company was set to work immediately.

Apart from the ugly maiming and distortion, the isolation that such an infectious disease imposes for life is tragic. It affects the lepers' children as well, though they do not necessarily develop the disease. In fact, what Mother Kevin brought into being was a complete leper village, with a community life of its own. The psychological value of this to lonely outcasts is obvious, and it was the pattern of missionary leprosariums all over Africa. There was a chapel, a hospital, an infirmary, and, miracle of miracles for the children of lepers, a school. Long before the Ba-company had completed the simple buildings, the patients started to arrive. There was no accommodation for them, and Mother Kevin, who never encouraged them in self-pity, harnessed the less afflicted to build huts and make gardens, for which she was able to pay them a small wage. There were community activities such as football, music, and acting, and a great deal of occupational therapy from carpentering to food growing. They were poor but welcome little activities, and were a valuable adjunct to the medical treatment. Many of the patients were incurable, but with drugs improving all the time, there was hope for many more, especially the younger ones.

Mother Kevin received great official encouragement, and funds were available from the government and from worldwide charitable sources. Of course, she could have used ten times the amount; but such is human concern for leprosy that enough money for one leprosarium came in without too much seeking.

The Sisters volunteered for the work, so that at first, there were only white nuns, a fact that was commented on by many admiring Africans. The disease is so repulsive in the later stages that exceptional courage is needed for the care of lepers. There were no denominational barriers at Nyenga; Catholics, Protestants, Muslims, and heathens were received because they were sufferers. Like Saint Francis, Mother Kevin forbad the use of the word for leper because of its "outcast" significance. For her, they were the "patients" or the "family," and, not infrequently, the "rascals."

Nyenga was full to capacity in a very short time, and expansion there was impossible. The Bishop was able to acquire another lakeside site at Buluba, which was isolated and vast, but space and water were the basic essentials. There were, of course, initial difficulties, chief among them the local beast population— elephants, hippopotamuses, buffalo, and wild boar—which demolished the all-essential crops. The nuns and even the patients had to go out big-game scaring, and the chaplain was a crack shot and filled the mission larders with hippo steak. The game interfered with the building operations, too, but it was not very long before another and larger village community was in being. And in a fine hospital, the Sisters researched in leprosy under the guidance of a devoted Polish woman doctor, who also trained them to work in leper clinics all over the Vicariate. Mother Mary Louis quotes a sermon given by the African Bishop Kiwanuka:

Do you know how these Franciscan Sisters love us and our people? Then go, as I have done to their leper missions at Nyenga and Buluba, and watch them at work, day in and day out, in their ceaseless care of our lepers; spending themselves and being spent, by night and day looking after the sufferers, so ravaged and disfigured by disease, that even we Africans, many of us, shrink from contact with them.[6]

The establishment of Buluba, in fact, brought the first African volunteers, a group of Little Franciscans from Nkokonjeru. Saint Francis must have been delighted.

Time and again, Mother Kevin's problems were solved, or her dreams realised, by what seemed to be little miracles. Saint Teresa, of course, always knew about the problems and the dreams, and Mother Kevin called the miracles "Teresa's little roses," for Teresa of Lisieux had promised to "spend heaven" doing good on earth, and sending down showers of white roses, or blessings. In 1935, one of her most cherished dreams came true. She made a quick trip to England on business connected with the Yorkshire novitiate. She found little to worry her there, and there was a promising supply of recruits in training for her missions.

From Yorkshire she set out for Ireland to visit her family. In her carriage in the train to Liverpool was a veterinary surgeon from Dundalk in County Louth. No one was more sociable than Mother Kevin when she had the time, and they fell to chatting. He listened fascinated to the account of her work in Uganda, and then suddenly asked her why she had not got a convent in Ireland. Why, indeed? There was nothing she wanted more, and little about which she could be so eloquent. He responded quite simply by telling that he knew of just the right house for her. An estate had recently been sold near Dundalk, and the mansion house, Mount Pleasant, was threatened with demolition. He thought he could get it for her for £1200. She did not have 1200 pence, but as a train journey interlude, it was fun talking about it. After they parted, she thought no more about it. Then, when she had been in Ireland for a few days, her friend telephoned and scolded her for not hurrying to see Mount Pleasant, and told her that he had made arrangements with a Dundalk bank manager to lend her the money on his surety. It would have been letting Saint Teresa down if she had not responded, for the choicest of choice roses had fallen from heaven. Mount Pleasant was a delightful white house in a magnificent position overlooking Dundalk Bay. In no time at all, volunteers were scrubbing, decorating, and gardening. Renamed Mount Oliver, it eventually succeeded Holme Hall as the mother house of the congregation of Franciscan Sisters for Africa. Saint Teresa had done very well indeed.

In 1936, the long-awaited legislation was passed by the Holy See, and the ban on obstetrics was lifted. Over the years, Mother Kevin and another founding Abbess, Mother Mary Martin, had gone on quietly working for this legislation. When Monsignor Hinsley had arrived in East Africa, Mother Kevin had solicited his powerful aid. Convinced that she was right, he had tackled the authorities in Rome, and his influence was probably decisive. He had been a valuable friend and counsellor in many other ways, and, clearly, he admired her greatly. He left East Africa in 1937 to become the Cardinal Archbishop of Westminster. Under the grey skies of the English winter, he wrote nostalgically of the many prosperous girls' schools he had come to know, of the hospitals and the leprosariums, and of the happy peace of the Little Sisters at prayer and at work. And "a tiny woman from Ireland, with the help of a handful of self-effacing women of limitless trust in God and zeal in His cause, has wrought these splendid works." And he went on to recall his enjoyment of the concerts, of "Snow White and the Seven Dwarfs," or "Alice in Wonderland." He remembered especially a 54-year-old Mad Hatter, and he refrained so elaborately from revealing the identity of the actress in question that there is little doubt that it was the Mother Abbess herself who played the part. After all, Saint Teresa of Avila used to dance to the tambourine.

World War II did not affect the lives of the Franciscan Sisters to the same extent as did World War I. Ethiopia was the nearest war theatre, and some refugee Italian nuns were given refuge at Nkokonjeru. Battalions of the King's African Rifles went overseas to Burma. Many old pupils or friends of Mother Kevin's were in the regiment, and the Dakota planes that brought up supplies to advanced troops were named after her. There are various accounts as to how this came about: one, that the planes brought the food, is not very convincing: another, that the planes took away the sick and wounded, is rather more likely; a third, that one of her old boys suddenly spotted a resemblance between a Dakota swooping along the runway and Mother Kevin, is still more likely. However it happened, Dakotas were Mamma Kevinas to the whole regiment.

In 1941, the Franciscans expanded beyond the borders of Uganda for the first time. The Holy Ghost Fathers, who were the pioneers of missionary work in East Africa, asked for help in starting girls' schools in Kenya. The whole question of girls' education there had been complicated by the Kikuyu initiation rites, known, for want of a better term, as female circumcision. The Church of Scotland had made a brave stand in banning it for their students, with the result that they had lost most of them to what were known as independent schools. The Catholic missions had left the vexing question more or less alone, but now, in the early forties, they saw the absolute necessity of developing girls' education.

Amid criticism that it was unsuitable to go in for expansion in the middle of a world war, Mother Kevin felt she must respond to the Fathers' call for help. She had available a party of nuns who had been on the point of going to Ethiopia to take over Italian missions but who had been prevented by visa technicalities. Two schools were started under conditions very different from those of Uganda, which was a Protectorate, while Kenya was a Colony. Much of the land of the African peoples had been alienated for European occupation, and a great many Africans were in European employ. This often resulted in an attitude of suspicion, very different from the self-assured courtesy of the Baganda and some of the other Uganda peoples. It was sad to Mother Kevin, but what helped her enterprise greatly was the enthusiasm of the girls themselves to be educated.

A decade later, she was staying with her relatives in County Wicklow when she heard that the Irish missionary order, the Kiltegan Fathers, also working in Kenya, had more acute problems than the Holy Ghost Fathers. They had a prosperous boys' school at Kiminini in the Kitosh country, which had been inadequately housed in squalid grass huts. Fine new buildings had been completed, but on the evacuation of the grass huts, a large number of the local girls moved into them and demanded education. Mother Kevin could never have resisted such a call from neglected African womanhood. There and then, in County Wicklow, she promised that she would give the girls the school they wanted. With intensive building operations by the Fathers, they got it in record time, in spite of the Mau Mau troubles which were then at their height and making life in Kenya very difficult. But if one thing shone brightly during those tragic Mau Mau days, it was the courageous fortitude of many African Christians, who frequently resisted horrid pressures and even torture for their faith.

For all her successes, Mother Kevin had also had her failures, some setbacks, and many disappointments. These were her minor crosses. It was during the war that the major cross of her

life was given her to bear. Her biographer is very discreet, perhaps because others were involved. She barely suggests what
kind of trouble it was, "... the classic trial of all religious foun-
dresses. In 1942, a certain betrayal of trust on the part of some
members of her Community, caused the most poignant grief to
her sensitive nature." Whatever it was, it was so intense a grief
that her magnificent physique began to feel the strain at last. She
was 67. She had had 40 years of phenomenal activity in a tropical
climate, frequently with material hardship and grave illness, and
now came this mental distress. Her biographer does not mention
any specific disease, though there may well have been one. It was
clear that she must have a rest, and she relinquished the arduous
office of Provincial Superior General to the charming and able
Mother Alcantara, her colleague in many ventures since they had
arrived at Holme Hall together on a snowy day in 1929. With the
profound humility that underlay the dynamism of her personality, she reverted to being just an ordinary member of her own
community. In fact, she welcomed the discipline of submission,
and she went off into the wilderness for nearly ten years.

As far as most people could see, it was a happy wilderness. It
was certainly accepted without question as the will of God. She
had long had it in mind to provide some sort of retreat house
combined with a convalescent home for her nuns, for whom she
could not afford the fares for home leave. Her retirement from
the direction of the mission was a perfect opportunity for this. A
first attempt to found such a place on the Kenya-Uganda border
failed. It was thought that she was founding another mission,
and patients and pupils arrived in expectation. So, another mission it had to be. Then, the Baganda insisted on the privilege of
housing her. An attractive lakeside site was provided at Kavule,
but it was land on which, by Buganda law, hospitals and schools
could not be built. This time, her convent was built for her by
Italian prisoners of war. Then, she moved in to begin a job that
was well within her physical powers and yet gave some satisfaction to her creative ability.

The picture given by young nuns who met her for the first
time at her lakeside retreat is of a charming elderly woman, with
infinite capacity for enjoyment, sympathy, understanding, and
above all, for spiritual devotion. The impetuosity and the temper

were mellowing, and in this peaceful life, there was no need to sweep her nuns along at her own zealous speed. She loved to arrange holiday amusements for them. Her own enjoyment of the lakeside picnics made them a delight to others. She had always created lovely flower gardens round her convents, and now she collected wild flowers with her usual infectious enthusiasm. She watched birds and other animal wild life with wonderment, and revelled in the splendid sunrises over the lake.

She was, of course, a friend and comforter to those who came to her in physical or mental distress, and her devotional life was an inspiration to renewed dedication. Always a large part of her life, perhaps at Kavule it was more in evidence than anywhere else. She still adhered to her habitual practise of a devotional hour alone with the Sacrament before she roused the convent or rang the Angelus in the morning. To all appearances, she was a happy, pious old nun, enjoying her well-earned retirement. But, in fact, though few suspected it, she was not happy and at peace. Again, one can only quote her biographer, who cites something she said to one of her older Sisters:

Pray for your old mother, who needs your prayers so much, for the dear good Lord has seemingly left her to herself. Everything is darkness and dryness, and sometimes I am tempted to despair. But I cling to Him and accept His Will in all things. Poor old weak nature wants to cry out, but His Will is our peace.[7]

She was struggling with the "darkness of the soul," even as little Teresa had had to do on her quiet way to sainthood. Also, she was well into her seventies, and perhaps "poor old weak nature" was a key phrase. She once even admitted that she sometimes found it difficult to get up at 4 o'clock in the morning.

Two important anniversaries occurred in 1948. For Mother Kevin, it was the golden jubilee of her religious profession, which, by her wish, was celebrated simply, with just a Mass of thanksgiving. In the same year, the congregation of the Little Sisters of Saint Francis celebrated the 25th anniversary of its foundation, and for that, the Little Sisters petitioned for the return of Mother Kevin. And so for four years, she gave her whole attention once again to Nkokonjeru, to the congregation she had founded, the greatest achievement of her great missionary life.

In 1948, the congregation numbered more than 200. A steady stream of African Sisters went out from it to the schools, hospitals, and leprosariums of the Vicariate. And the venture, begun with forebodings by many, and with no lack of realism about its dangers by Mother Kevin herself, had proved of inestimable value. "It is difficult to exaggerate the moral and social inflence of the Little Sisters of St. Francis," wrote a Director of Education. And her biographer comments that it was something for Africans to see that their own women could rise to the same heights of unselfish dedication as the white Franciscan nuns. Mother Kevin had known that these African girls, brought up in some subservience and yet apathetic, self-indulgent, and undisciplined, had had the right motive for wanting to enter the religious life. Assured of this, she had known of the terrible difficulties they would encounter along their path to the Sisterhood. The heroic virtue required of them to stick to that path was far greater than that of the white nuns bred in the tradition of Catholicism. She taught them to meet their difficulties in the context of holiness and love. She taught them to love beauty. And she spread her teaching talent among her white nuns, who, of course, shared in the great success.

Knowing that in Mother Kevin they had a missionary genius, the Superior at St. Mary's Abbey had always given her a free hand in the management of her missions. It had, nonetheless, been irksome and frustrating to have to refer all policy to an order not primarily a missionary order. The missionary province had, in fact, far outdistanced the parent body, and its problems were very different. When Mother Kevin was in semiretirement at Kavule, the members of the missionary province petitioned the Holy See for independent status. In 1952, the petition was granted, and the province became the Franciscan Missionary Sisters for Africa. Soon after, Archbishop David Mathew, the Apostolic Delegate to British tropical Africa, announced that Mother Kevin had been appointed the first Superior General of the new order.

She was 77 years old, and she knew it could only be for a few years, but her great energy revived and allowed those years to be as productive as any in her life. A new constitution and rules had to be drawn up. Twenty convents in Uganda and four in Kenya had to be visited, which she did in the first few weeks. She had not been to England for 15 years, and she went to visit the home convents in 1953. While there, she made a brief appearance in a documentary film on her life, an experience which she maintained was much more alarming than dealing with a band of Mau Mau. She turned her attention to schools for the blind, something she had always longed to do. Several nuns, both black and white, were sent to England for special training in the work. She went to South Africa, where, under tragically different conditions, she founded two convents. Her last foundation in Africa was an interesting, racially mixed school at Nakuru in Kenya, a portent for the immediate future.

As with her whole life, it is difficult to see how all this activity was fitted into the short time available. She gave no sign of tiring, but in 1954, she asked to be relieved of her great office. She was nearly 80, and for 52 years she had lavished herself tirelessly on the African peoples, years which had seen a crescendo of revolutionary change. Colonial rule was approaching its end, and even greater changes were imminent. It was time for the order to be directed by someone younger who could shepherd it into the new Africa. She could not be dissuaded, knowing that delegation of duties was impossible for her. "When I'm in charge, I'm in charge," she said, and so her resignation had to be accepted.

At the first general chapter of the new congregation, Mother Alcantara was elected the second Superior General. Mother Kevin was once more a humble member of the order, and prepared to serve wherever she was sent. She was appointed Reverend Mother of the convent in Boston that Cardinal Cushing had given to the congregation. "Without fuss or farewells" she left Uganda, called briefly in Ireland, and flew alone from Shannon to Boston in May 1955. She loved America and America loved her, but a new job in another country at 80 must have been a great strain. She missed her "children" terribly, and her beautiful Nkokonjeru with its famous gardens, and the many other colourful campuses that she had brought into being.

But in America, the seemingly tireless little Franciscan, whom Cardinal Cushing thought the greatest missionary nun he had ever met, was still capable of making a useful impact. She lectured endlessly, she was the star turn at many a missionary conference, and she stood outside churches with a begging bowl in icy American or Canadian winter weather. She opened the floodgates of American generosity and thus continued to serve her missions splendidly. The nuns in the Boston convent knew a "gentle, tender old woman," and wondered if this could really be the indomitable fighter of whom they had heard so much. They were very impressed when it was learned that in the Queen's Birthday Honours, she had been awarded the C.B.E. in recognition of her 52 years' work in Africa. The British Ambassador came to invest her, and the Irish Ambassador and her devoted friend Cardinal Cushing and many other dignitaries were present. She was human enough to enjoy it all very much.

In the summer of 1957, she was recalled to Africa, once again at the insistence of the Little Sisters, who wanted their Mother Foundress to be with them. She started her preparations joyfully, and began to fill trunks with the many presents she was given for the missions. In October, she wrote to her "Darling children" at Nkokonjeru that she hoped to be with them in May 1958. In the meantime, she went on with her arduous life, and a doctor told her that she had a magnificent constitution. On October 16, after a busy day, she drove 25 miles to show the film of her missions. Her audience kept her late, and she returned home very tired. Next morning, her place in chapel was empty, and the nuns hoped she was resting. But in her little attic cell, they found her dead. She was lying peacefully with her rosary entwined in her fingers, and there were no signs of struggle or suffering. She had slipped away "without fuss or farewells."

It was generally felt that she must be taken to Mount Oliver, the mother house of the Franciscan Sisters for Africa, for burial. Cardinal Cushing immediately offered to pay the expenses. He presided over the Requiem Mass in Boston on October 21. After that her body was taken to the airport on the start of what was to prove a triumphant journey half way round the world. At Shannon, there were prelates, nuns, and many of her own relations, and at the Requiem Mass, celebrated by a nephew in the airport chapel, the atmosphere was that of a homecoming. The funeral procession set out across country, paused at the Cistercian

Abbey at Rosscrea, at the Franciscan Church in Dublin, and in Drogheda, where Mother Mary Martin, who had also fought the great midwifery battle, and her congregation of medical nuns stood with the townspeople in the streets to pay their respects. In the evening, she was with her own Sisterhood in Dundalk. On October 24, there was a vast congregation in the cathedral for the Requiem, which was presided over by a Nigerian Bishop, and a long procession wound its way to the interment at Mount Oliver. Apparently, Mother Kevin had come home.

But another home and another order had greater claims on her, and Mount Oliver was only a stopping place on the long road to Nkokonjeru, the place she loved best in the world. The Baganda, and above all the Little Sisters of Saint Francis, insisted that she should be returned to them. The Katikiro, or Prime Minister, wrote to the Governor to say that a subscription was being raised for the expenses, and asked him to make the necessary arrangements. The money came in freely from all creeds and races, and Mother Kevin could scarcely not have been pleased at such a moving proof of affection and esteem, though she would probably have regretted the number of live missionaries that could have been sent out to Uganda for the price of transporting her old body.

So the long journey proceeded. There were mourning dignitaries all along the route and at Dublin and London airports. On December 2, in a tropical storm, the freight plane carrying her body and a small escort of nuns landed at Entebbe. The airport is almost on the shores of the great Lake Victoria, those shores to which little Sister Kevin had been carried shoulder-high in a canoe nearly 55 years before. Despite the storm, there were crowds to meet her, and a long procession set off for Nsambya. There, the sun shone brightly, but the people wept. Nsambya had known and loved her well. Three hundred Franciscan nuns, both black and white, as well as the Acting-Governor and representatives of the whole life of Uganda, attended the Requiem at Nsambya Cathedral. The last lap of the journey was along the 35 miles of the road to Nkokonjeru that Mother Kevin had known so well. The coffin was escorted by outriders, and a mile-long procession followed. She lay that night in her lovely Nkokonjeru chapel, into which she was carried by the Ba-company. The Little

Sisters kept a night-long vigil. Next day, the altar before which she lay was resplendent with flowers and candles for the festal mass for the missionary Saint Francis Xavier. This was followed by the last of the Solemn Requiems. Then the Ba-company carried her body through her beloved gardens to the cemetery, alongside which she herself had planted a little woodland copse. Among the trees, there is a small mortuary chapel given by Cardinal Spellman and built by Italian prisoners of war. It was especially loved by Mother Kevin, and in it a vault had been prepared. Some of the grave diggers had witnessed and, indeed, helped with the demolition of the lubale tree when she had first arrived at Nkokonjeru 34 years before. For many hours, the mourners filed past the chapel, paying their last respects to a great woman who had loved them. At night, the vault was closed, and the solemn rituals were over. Later, a plaque was placed on the side of the little chapel, which gives simply the relevant dates of her life and her lifelong motto, "Propter te, Domine." ("For your sake; O Lord.")

NOTES

1. Sister Mary Louis, O.S.F., *Love Is the Answer* (London & Dublin: Fallons, 1964), p. 20.

2. Ibid., p. 29.

3. The tiny wayside chapel close to Assisi, where, in the 13th century, Saint Francis and his first disciples used to meet. It is still in existence, though now enclosed in a large basilica.

4. Sister Mary Louis, *Love,* p. 116.

5. Ibid., p. 119.

6. Ibid., p. 180.

7. Ibid., p. 209.

CONCLUSION

For much of my life, I assumed that early colonial Africa was virtually a masculine preserve. Most people, I think, will have done the same. There were the great explorers, men such as Mungo Park, David Livingstone, Henry Morton Stanley, John Hanning Speke, Savorgnan de Brazza, and many more. There were the men who went to hunt big game. The fiction I read, by Joseph Conrad, Rider Haggard, Edgar Wallace, and others, was all about men. My assumption was, of course, largely true; largely but not, in fact, quite completely true, because, as I have tried to show, from the early days of the colonial period in the mid-nineteenth century, women were not quite absent from the scene. I hope that my essays about five women, all of different nationalities—Dutch, Hungarian, English, Scottish, Irish—may do something to put the perspective right. The fact of grouping together such disparate women adds, I think, to their significance. They were the essential beginners of something that became important. They showed their white women's faces to many Africans for the first time, often with startling effect. A friend, who had been a Bishop in Uganda, told me once of his meeting with an elderly Ugandan who had been present when the first Church Missionary Society ladies had arrived at the capital. The man had shown great reluctance to speak of the event. In the end, he had admitted to going behind a banana palm and being very sick. One thinks of turning over a stone and seeing some creature on which the sun has never shone. I remember myself once terrifying a tiny African child who had never seen a European face.

The main reason for the absence of Western women in tropical Africa was the climate. West Africa was known, with good reason, as the white man's grave. Unlike in India, there were no hill stations like Simla and Ootacommund where families could escape from the most trying and dangerous season of the year. In East Africa, there are more healthy hill lands, but there was still the danger of lethal fevers, such as malaria and its attendant ills and sleeping sickness. The introduction of quinine in the second half of the nineteenth century dramatically reduced the incidence of death from malaria, but the cause of fever was not known until the turn of the century. It was traced to the night-flying anopheles mosquito, against which defensive action could be taken. Then, the discovery of efficient, anti-malarial drugs during World War II almost eliminated its dangers.

The first men who went out to administer the scarcely known continent were, therefore, rarely accompanied by their wives. When the wives started to come in appreciable numbers, the contact they made was, I think, generally courteous but seldom of much significance. Their position as the wives of the rulers was perhaps a difficult one. Homesickness made them stick together. Material differences in living standards made social intercourse awkward. And even many of those who felt that they had a "civilising mission" remained unaware of how superficial their knowledge of the people of the country was. I remember well hearing Englishwomen discussing the best way to entertain the African personnel in the district offices on Empire Day. "We always have them in the garden. We know they prefer that." The colonial situation was not easy, but I used to wonder whether they really knew. It was perhaps a pity also that the existence of their own homes and families to escape to tended to separate the best-intentioned District Officers from Africa. The walking safari and the campfire in the bush had kept them in touch with the common man. The wives did not often accompany their husbands on these peregrinations, and, therefore, especially after the advent of the motorcar, they tended increasingly to be eliminated.

Of my five pioneer women, only one, Florence Baker, was a wife. Without her, Samuel Baker would probably not have reached Lake Albert. She and Alexandrine Tinne were great and adventurous women, though apart from breaking the ground, their legacy to Africa was not enormous, The advent of women explorers was nonetheless important, and their names were long remembered by the African peoples amongst whom they travelled.

My third woman, Mary Kingsley, unveiled no geographical secrets, though she was certainly the first stranger to tred many forest paths. Her scientific work was undoubtedly useful; some rare tropical fish bear her name. But her real and incalculably valuable contribution to Africa was in her interpretation of it to the world. Her brilliant, often witty writing, blessedly free of the esoteric jargon of the anthropologist, was accessible to great numbers of people—above all, to the men who were going to work in Africa. She gave all her great intellectual ability and her blessed tolerance to trying to understand, and so made others understand. Her influence continued long after her, and is not negligible to this day.

In this, she was quite outstanding but not quite alone. Flora Lugard, the wife of Lord Lugard, who governed Nigeria in the early 1900s, had been the colonial correspondent of the London *Times,* and her book *A Tropical Dependency* interested many people in West Africa for the first time. More recently, the Oxford scholar Dame Margery Perham wrote informatively of Africa and African women. There have also been eloquent voices from South Africa, that tragic land to which I will return later.

My last two women, Mary Slessor and Mother Kevin, were both missionaries: one Protestant and one Catholic. And here we enter the realm where women's influence on the history of Africa has been tremendous. Mary Slessor herself was not an educator in the conventional sense, but a pathfinder and a reformer. But there was a steady stream of able women from many countries who founded great schools and great hospitals throughout tropical Africa. Lady Cook, the wife of one of the brothers Cook, two famous Church Missionary Society doctors, pioneered African women's nursing in Uganda. The earliest recruits had to be strongminded young women, because they were frequently disowned by their families for engaging in such pursuits.

It is also to the eternal credit of the Church Missionary Society that it founded Gayaza, the girls' school in Uganda, in 1902, a couple of years before the first boys' secondary school was founded at Budo. If there were to be educated Christian homes, there must be educated women to preside over them. A Quaker woman who had been headmistress of a famous Quaker girls' school in England went out in her retirement as a Director of Girl's Education in Uganda. She used to chuckle at the part that interdenominational rivalry had played in the rapid development of education. A fine Catholic school, St. Mary's Kisubi, was started not long after Gayaza and Budo. Sister Géneviève of Karema[1] was one of literally thousands of nuns who left home forever and gave their lives to the conversion and education of African women. Mother Kevin founded numbers of schools and hospitals far and wide in eastern Africa. Her influence on the development of Africa was incalculable, probably the greatest of my five women. For the most part, her foundations are thriving today.

I have had the pleasure of the friendship of a number of educated women from all parts of Africa. I am sure that they all generously acknowledge their debt to the women from Europe and from America who, over the years, came to help them on their way. This help, I know, continues in considerable measure in independent Africa, although, of course, now Africa is training most of its own teachers. Father Adrian Hastings, in his book *A History of African Christianity, 1950 to 1975*, says that Christians have quadrupled in number since the early days of independence in the 1950s. He says that today there are about one hundred million Christians.

I am not an anthropologist, but having travelled much in Africa, I have the impression that, though there were abuses, African women were never as unliberated as was generally assumed. Domestic power frequently played a part in politics. The Queen Mothers of Africa were formidable and influential people. Africa had to make a big leap into the twentieth century, yet there are now African women government ministers in many African states.

In the world of commerce in West Africa, women have traditionally dominated. The great market at Onitsha on the Niger River, from which trade spread for hundreds of miles into Nigeria and into French West Africa, was almost completely controlled by women. I know of a clever Nigerian girl who went to England to do a course in midwifery. She was quite outstanding, and her tutors were interested to know how she planned her future. She apparently had no intention of practising midwifery; that had only been an excuse for a spell in England. She was going back to help her mother with her market business at Onitsha. Her father had nothing to do with that, because he could not do simple arithmetic and, therefore, was of no use with the accounting. England and America proved a first meeting ground between West African and East African women. In my first contact with the latter, I met a snobbishness about the idea of being mixed up with trade. Today, I know that there are many successful East African business women.

The two social customs, polygamy and the payment in cattle exacted by the parents of a girl from the parents of a young man seeking a bride, were not abhorrent to African eyes as they were to Western eyes. We travelled once in the company of an elderly African dignitary who was rather beer-sodden and certainly far from personable. He was the official guardian of the royal tombs in an ancient African kingdom which my husband was investigating. He soon tired of my English cooking in the rest houses we stayed in, and he sent for one of his wives. An exquisite, slim girl arrived, who boiled up his bananas and made their savoury sauce to his liking, and he was happy. She, however, was bored and lonely, so she sent for one of her co-wives. Another lovely girl arrived and was greeted by the first with ecstatic affection. I think that, if asked, both these young beauties would have expressed a preference to be one of a number of wives of a rich man rather than the sole wife of a poor man, with all the digging, hoeing, grinding, and cooking for the family that monogamy entailed. As for what used to be called the bride-price, I have heard African women expressing horror at the undignified Western custom of the dowry whereby in well-to-do families, property or money was expected to accompany rather than be an exchange for the daughter.

To my eyes, the ordinary African women walking majestically along the roads, dressed with graceful flair, essentially African in its exuberant taste, seldom give the impression that they are suppressed; certainly not north of the Zambesi. The practice of carrying everything on the head is, of course, excellent for the deportment. The Kikuyu women of Kenya, being forest people in orgin, carry their loads of firewood on their backs and, therefore, do not walk so well.

But the dress sense is evident nearly everywhere. One of my most colourful recollections is of the winding road up Namirembe Hill to the headquarters of the Church Missionary Society in Uganda when it was thronged with women in their best dresses on their way to an annual service for the Mother's Union in Namirembe Cathedral. Hundreds of different printed cottons made into the deep, square-necked tunic which they wear with a full-length skirt, cleverly draped out of some yards of the same material, were fresh, elegant, and infinitely gay. In West Africa, swirling turbans frequently add to the effect, and in French West Africa, one detects a slight injection of French dressmaking or millinery expertise. I have often remarked, at diplomatic functions in London, how, in their very individual sartorial way, African women have completely stolen the show.

Very briefly, I must mention South Africa, that sunny, prosperous but tragically unhappy land, on the southern tip of the continent. The only way in which it really touches on my theme is in the realm of courage. It was feminine courage that first attracted me to write of Africa, and today I am constantly moved by tales of such courage emanating from South Africa. The close association there with the West long predated that of colonial tropical Africa, because the climate is equable. There were European women trekking along in their bullock wagons into the interior in the early nineteenth century. But here, most of the Europeans came, not just to administer or teach and return eventually to their homelands, but to settle. In this, there is a comparison with European settlement in Indian North America, but in South Africa, the blacks were too numerous to be extinguished.

Now, long after colonial Africa has become independent, over a fifth of the population of South Africa are of European origin. They alone are enfranchised, and they claim an utterly unfair share of the land and its riches. Their interest is a vested one, not only for themselves, but for their children's children. They have to close their eyes to the injustice, but in self-defense, they talk of the situation endlessly. As an Anglican Bishop said recently in a report of a tour of South Africa, people he met, basically nice people, wanted to discuss the game the whole time but, in fact, never knew the score.

This situation, in which Africans are desperately deprived and perpetually harassed by unjust laws, has called for bravery from both native and Western South African women. .It has not been found lacking. I heard an account of Mrs. Nelson Mandela after her husband had been convicted at the treason trial of 1963. She went to the end of the road outside the court to wave goodbye to him as he passed by in the prison van that was taking him on his journey to permanent exile in Robben Island. It was an almost unbearably poignant moment for the bystanders. She is still under house arrest, as are hundreds of her fellow protestors, if they are not in gaol.

Recently, a novel, *Popje*, has come from the pen of Elsie Joubert, a member of the well-known South African family of European origin. She has painted vividly, as though from the inside, the life of a large native South African family. Her heroine, Popje, struggles endlessly to help her own large family in the perpetual harassment they suffer, the perpetual threat of imprisonment over their right to be standing where they are. At one time, Popje, during one of her many pregnancies, has to undertake a considerable journey, ending in a trudge up a long, steep hill, in order to obtain a pass to enable her to stay in Cape Town for sufficient time for the baby to be born. For some reason, it is the wrong day for such passes to be issued. The tired legs have to go again the next day. In her tragic acceptance of the inevitability of her life, there is the essence of real tragedy. The novel is another fine exercise in the interpretation of Africans by a white women. One hopes the message will be widely spread. It is good to know that a number of Western women have gone willingly to prison in South Africa, because they have joined in the protest against injustice.

Having told the story of five of the first Western women to penetrate the African continent, I have tried, just very briefly, to take the story of such women on through colonial Africa, and have just touched on the Africa of today. History will give its verdict on the effect of the West on what once was known as the dark continent, a verdict that will probably change with the passage of time. I hope I have shown that there will be considerable good to balance whatever evil has come from Western women. I hope also that I have shown that they had at least a small share in the part of the historical episode that was in some sense an adventure.

NOTE

1. See Introduction, p. xv.

SELECT BIBLIOGRAPHY

Florence Baker

Baker, S. W. *The Albert Nyanza*, 2 vols. London, 1866.
_____ *Ismailia*. 2 vols. London, 1874.
Baker, Anne. *Morning Star*. London, 1972.
Hall, Richard. *Lovers on the Nile*. London, 1980.

Alexandrine Tinne

Johnston, H. H. *The Nile Quest*. London: Scholarly Press, 1903.
Gladstone, Penelope. *Travels of Alexine*. London: Transatlantic, 1971.
Nachtigal, Gustav. *Sahara and Sudan*. Translated by A. G. B. and H. J.
      Fisher. Vol. I. London, 1974.

Mary Kingsley

Gwynn, Stephen. *Life of Mary Kingsley*. London, 1933.
Kingsley, Mary H. *Travels in West Africa*. London, 1897.
_____ *West African Studies*. London, 1899.
Flint, J. E. "Mary Kingsley, a reassessment," *Journal of African History* 4, 1
      (1963), 95–104.

Mary Slessor

Livingstone, W. P. *Mary Slessor of Calabar*. London, 1915.
Christian, Carol, and Plummer, Gladys. *God and One Redhead*. London,
      1970.

Mother Kevin

Sister Mary Louis, O. F. S. *Love Is the Answer.* Dublin: Fallons Educational Supply Co., 1964.

INDEX

Akpap, mission station, 124-31, 141

Albert Nyanza, Lake, xi, 20-22, 32-34, 46

Alcantara, Mother, 172, 182, 185

Aqqad, Khartoum trading house, 12, 33, 35-36

Arochuku, oracle, 127-29, 130

Bahr el-Ghazal, River, xiv, 34, 59, 60, 63, 66

Baker, Lady Florence, xiv; marriage, 3-4, 11, 30; first journey to Upper Nile (1861-65), 4-30; discovery of Lake Albert, 20-21; Murchison (Kabarega) Falls, 23; second journey to Upper Nile (1869-73), 32-47; Ismailia, 35-36; Patiko, 36-37, 43-45; Masindi, 37-43; retirement at Sandford Orleigh, 47-49

Baker, Julian, 32, 34, 36, 40-44

Baker, Sir Samuel, xiv; travels in Hungary, 3-4; exploration of Upper Nile (1861-65), 4-30; meeting with Speke and Grant, 10-12; march to Bun-

yoro, 13-16; negotiations with Kamrasi, 17-18; march to Lake Albert, 19-20; to Murchison Falls, 21-23; back to Kamrasi's capital, 23-26; return to England, 27-30; opening of Suez Canal, 31; Governor-General, 31-32; Khartoum, 33; Tewfikiah, 34-35; Ismailia, 35-36; Patiko, 36-37, 43-45; Bunyoro and Kabarega, 37-42; summary of achievements, 45-47; retirement, 47-49

Biermans, Bishop, 155, 161, 166

Buganda, Kingdom, 15, 26, 37, 146-88

Bunyoro, Kingdom, 12, 15, 24, 26, 30, 37, 45, 46

Burton, Sir Richard, 54, 89

Calabar, 81, 83, 96-106, 111-12, 117, 123, 126, 129, 131, 140-43

Capellen, Adriana van (Aunt Addy), 55, 56, 60

Casement, Roger, 127

Church Missionary Society, 146, 160, 189, 191, 192, 194

Connolly, Dr. Evelyn (Sister
    Mary Assumpta), 164-65
Cook, Sir Albert and Lady, 161,
    191
Cross, River, xiv, 84, 105, 106,
    110, 128
Cushing, Cardinal, 172, 185-86

Debono, Andrea, 12, 15, 25, 33

Ekpo, secret society, 98, 115,
    116, 127
Eyo Honesty, King of Creek
    Town, 98, 102, 106-7, 111-12

Fan people, 85-87
Francis, Saint, of Assisi, 151,
    169, 173
Freetown, 80-81

Gaboon, 85-88
Géneviève, Sister, xv, 192
Goldie, Sir George, 84
Goldie, Hugh, 99, 107
Gondokoro, xiv, 7-9, 12, 15, 17,
    22-23, 26, 31-32, 35, 39,
    45-46, 57, 59-60
Gordon, General Charles, xi,
    45-48, 145
Grant, James Augustus, 4, 5, 11,
    16, 29, 39, 54, 57, 59

Hanlon, Bishop, 148, 150, 152,
    155
Heuglin, Theodor von, 60-66
Hinsley, Cardinal, 170, 179-80
Holme Hall, Franciscan training
    house, 171-73

Ibrahim, trader, 13-15, 24-26
Ikot Obong, mission station,
    133-34, 138

International African Associa-
    tion, xiv-xv
Ismail, Khedive of Egypt, 31
Ismailia, 35-37, 45
Ituri, forest, x, xi

Kabarega, Omukama of Bun-
    yoro, 37-43
Kamrasi, Omukama of Bunyoro,
    12, 15-18, 22-27, 37, 42
Kearney, Teresa. *See* Kevin,
    Mother
Kevin, Mother, xiv, 143; child-
    hood and calling, 146-47; early
    work in Uganda, 150-56;
    Mother Superior, 156; views
    on maternity work, 162-64;
    Little Sisters of St. Francis,
    165-67; building activities, 167-
    69, 175-76; educational work,
    170; visits United States, 172-
    73; leper colonies, 175-79;
    resignation as Superior, 182;
    retreat at Kavule, 182-84;
    Superior General of the Little
    Sisters, 184-85; retirement in
    Boston, 185; death, 186-88,
    191
Khurshid, trader, 12-13
Kingsley, George, 76-78
Kingsley, Mary, x, xiv, 6; home
    life and duties, 76-79; first
    journey to West Africa (1893),
    80-82; second journey to West
    Africa (1894-95), 82-88; books
    and opinions, 89-93; nursing
    in South Africa and death, 93,
    114-15

Lagos, 85, 137
Lavigerie, Cardinal, xiv, 145
Leopold II, King of Belgium, xiv,
    xv, 81

Livingstone, David, 4, 29, 39, 97, 120, 126, 137, 145, 189
Lugard, Sir Frederick, 140

Macdonald, Sir Claude and Lady, 81-84, 119, 120, 128
Masindi, 37, 38, 40
Maxwell, T. D., 120-21
Mill Hill Fathers (St. Joseph's Society), 147-48, 161
Moor, Sir Ralph, 128-29
Morel, E. D., 81
Mount Oliver, Franciscan training house, 179
Murchison, Sir Roderick, 23, 29
Morrison, Charles, 117-18
Mutesa, Kabaka of Buganda, 38-39, 145

Nachtigal, Gustav, 69-73
Nagalama, mission station, 155-57
Nkokonjeru, 166-70, 178, 180, 183, 186-88
Nsambya, 150-55, 169, 188

Ogowe, River, x, 85-88
Okoyong, mission station, 105-35
Ovens, Charles, 112-16, 124

Partridge, Charles, 133-39, 143
Patiko, xiv, 36-37, 43-45, 47
Paul, Mother, 148, 153, 156-57
Petherick, John, 7, 11, 59, 63, 65

Rionga, pretender to throne of Bunyoro, 15, 17, 42, 43, 45
Royal Geographical Society, 23, 29, 46, 64, 133

Slessor, Mary, xiv; meeting with Mary Kingsley, 83-84, 122-24; Dundee background, 96-98; first tour of duty, Duke's Town (1876-79), 99-100; second tour of duty, Old Town (1880-83), 101-3; third tour of duty, Creek Town and Okoyong (1886-91), 104-16; engagement to Charles Morrison, 117-18; fourth tour of duty, Okoyong and Akpap (1893-98), 119-24; Vice-Consul and District Magistrate, 120; fifth tour of duty, Akpap, Ikot Obong (1899-1907), 126-36; sixth tour of duty, Use (1908-14), 138-44, 191
Speke, John Hanning, 4-6, 11-12, 15-16, 22, 29, 39, 54, 57, 59, 63-64, 69, 189
Stanley, Henry Morton, x, xi, 6, 145-46, 189

Tewfikiah, 34-35
Tinne, Alexandrine, xiv; family background, 50-54; Nile journey planned, 54-55; Khartoum, 56-57; Gondokoro, 58-60; Bahr-el-Ghazal, 61-63; Cairo, 64-67; Saharan expedition, 68-75; in Murzuk with Nachtigal, 70-72; disaster and death, 73-74
Tinne, Henrietta (Harriet), 50
Tinne, John, 66, 71

Use, mission station, 133, 138, 140, 143

Waddell, Rev. Hope: founding of Calabar mission, 96-99; H. W. Institute, 119
White Fathers, missionary congregation, xiv, xv, 146, 148

ABOUT THE AUTHOR

Caroline Oliver is a retired member of the British Foreign Office. She is the author of *Africa in the Days of Exploration* and of articles on other African explorers.